Praise for *Forever Today*

'A compelling, poignant and exquisitely written account of a young woman reaching into the dark empty spaces of her husband's damaged brain and finding love within the limitations of his brilliant but fractured mind. It is the most dramatic description of "the abyss of non-being" since Oliver Sacks' *Awakenings*.'
**Marjorie Wallace**, founder of SANE

'This is a harrowing, haunting and heartening book – a loss-story which is also a love story. It takes us deep inside the question of what it means to be human.' **Andrew Motion**

'This is a harrowing story of a human tragedy. Harrowing yet uplifting, for it portrays the indefatigable human spirit of two people grappling with an unprecedented and shattering dilemma. A sensitive and deeply moving account, a heartrending love story – but unlike any other ever told.' **Jack Ashley** (Lord Ashley of Stoke)

'I had the privilege of filming a documentary about Deborah and Clive and like the rest of the crew I was immediately struck by the extraordinary patience and affection with which Deborah dealt with this appalling ordeal. In *Forever Today* she takes us further than ever into this remarkable experience.' **Jonathan Miller**

'Deborah Wearing's intriguing, moving account of her husband Clive's descent into the abyss of amnesia takes us close to the heart of what it means to be human . . . Above all, this is a story of human devotion in which the enigma of personal identity distils to a simple truth: we define ourselves by those we love.'
**Paul Broks**, author of *Into the Silent Land*

'Sometimes terrifying, sometimes very funny, and always deeply moving, Deborah Wearing's beautifully written testament to a love that survives all the ravages of her husband's amnesia is a book to seize the heart.'
**Lindsay Clarke**, author of Whitbread winner *The Chymical Wedding*

# FOREVER TODAY

*A Memoir of Love and Amnesia*

---

DEBORAH WEARING

## Doubleday

LONDON · TORONTO · SYDNEY · AUCKLAND · JOHANNESBURG

TRANSWORLD PUBLISHERS
61–63 Uxbridge Road, London W5 5SA
a division of The Random House Group Ltd

RANDOM HOUSE AUSTRALIA (PTY) LTD
20 Alfred Street, Milsons Point, Sydney,
New South Wales 2061, Australia

RANDOM HOUSE NEW ZEALAND LTD
18 Poland Road, Glenfield, Auckland 10, New Zealand

RANDOM HOUSE SOUTH AFRICA (PTY) LTD
Endulini, 5a Jubilee Road, Parktown 2193, South Africa

Published 2005 by Doubleday
a division of Transworld Publishers

A catalogue record for this book is available from the British Library.
ISBNs 0385 606265 (cased)
0385 607091 (tpb)

The author and publishers are grateful to the following for permission to reproduce copyright material:
'My Very Good Friend the Milkman' Words and Music by Johnny Burke and Harold Spina
© 1935 Chappell & Co. Copyright Renewed. All Rights Reserved. Reproduced by permission of
Campbell Connelly & Co Ltd under licence from Chappell & Co for World Rights excluding USA.
'Java Jive' Words by Milton Drake, Music by Ben Oakland © 1940 Advanced Music Corp, USA.
Chappell Music Ltd, London W6 8BS. Lyrics reproduced by permission of IMP Ltd. All Rights Reserved.
'Natural Causes' by Andrew Motion, reprinted with the permission of PFD on behalf of Andrew Motion.

Typeset in 12/16pt Granjon by
Kestrel Data, Exeter, Devon.

Printed in Great Britain by
Clays Ltd, St Ives plc.

1 3 5 7 9 10 8 6 4 2

Papers used by Transworld Publishers are natural, recyclable products made
from wood grown in sustainable forests. The manufacturing processes conform to the
environmental regulations of the country of origin.

To my Clive

# CONTENTS

# ACKNOWLEDGEMENTS

I am grateful to my very kind and patient editor, Marianne Velmans, midwife through labour and delivery, also to copy-editor extraordinaire Deborah Adams, and all the team at Doubleday. My grateful thanks to Camilla Hornby at Curtis Brown for her good sense and encouragement. My deep appreciation to Dr Barbara Wilson and to all the clinicians and families who have been colleagues, friends and helpers over the years, and especially heartfelt thanks to all those who have cared for Clive with such devotion. I have not named many of his carers in the book, and I have changed names, details and places of others too to protect their privacy. Clive calls his carers 'angels'. They are exceptional people and have been enormously kind to both of us for many years. We can never thank them enough.

Thanks to Lindsay and Pheobe Clarke for teaching me about sentences and nagging me to write. And heartfelt thanks to friends and family for their love and support, seeing me through, and to my teachers – in particular, to Amanda and Nora Buckett, Lynda Maclean, Moira Hutchinson, Humph Baker and family,

Rosie Smith, Sarah and Massimo Andreoli and family, Jen Waterton, Russ and Andrea Read and family, Jane and Charlie Ahern, John and Mary Angliss, Tony and Margaret Brown, and Pam and Michael Norman and family.

I am deeply thankful to my loving parents who have sustained me throughout. And of course to Clive, who has always supported me in everything, and to his children, Anthony, Alison and Edmund. Above all, thanks to the grace of God that brought us both through this experience, and enabled this book to be written.

# PROLOGUE

CLIVE HAD NO IDEA THAT TUESDAY 26 MARCH 1985 WOULD BE HIS LAST day of conscious thought. We weren't ready. Did he feel his brain disappearing that night? Why didn't he wake me? By morning he could not answer a simple question or remember my name. The doctor said it was flu and lack of sleep causing the confusion. He tucked him up with a temperature of 104° and a bottle of sleeping pills.

'No need to stay home,' he said to me. 'These'll knock him out for eight hours. Go to work.'

I went to work. When I came home that night the bed was empty. His empty pyjamas were collapsed in the middle of the bare sheet. I screamed his name. Running the length of the flat, I already knew something bad had happened. I knew it in my screaming soul before I knew it in my head.

'I'm never ill,' Clive used to say. And he never was. Then all of a sudden he was. But instead of a normal illness the doctors stand some chance of recognizing, this one is rare, sneaky. Nobody knew what was wrong with him. At the hospital, they thought he was a goner. Only they didn't put it like that. They told me what they thought he might have, and said it had a high mortality rate. I didn't know if that meant probably live or probably die and I didn't like to ask. Eventually I understood that they didn't expect him to last more than a few days because of signs they'd seen on a brain scan they did not show me that evening. Then they said, go home. We were standing in the doorway to the ward and I could see the shape of my husband under a white blanket behind them. He and I had been inseparable since first meeting and now, this night when he might be going to die, I am told, go home and don't come back until three o'clock tomorrow – visiting hours. What were they thinking of?

A sudden virus had caused holes in Clive's brain; memories fell out. But nothing could touch what was in his heart. He could not remember a single thing that had ever happened to him, but he remembered me and knew that he loved me.

# PART I

THE MAN WHO FELL OUT OF TIME

# 1

## GETTING ILL

IT'S HARD TO PINPOINT EXACTLY WHEN EXHAUSTION TURNED INTO the first stirrings of the illness. Sifting through the weeks and months before, I cannot know for sure. Maybe it was in the supermarket on our last Friday night shop. He looked black that March evening, hulked over the trolley in his overcoat. It was as if his feet were not quite taking his weight. There were broken pieces deep inside us that would sometimes catch and hurt or make a bad grinding noise. On this occasion, Clive seemed to be in a darkness we had not experienced before. We were by a chill cabinet. I had a tray of kidneys in my hand.

'You all right?' I asked.

'Yes,' he said, but he didn't look at me.

'What, love? Tell me, what is it?'

'Nothing,' he said, leaning lower over the trolley bar so that it moved off, wheels spinning.

We proceeded up the aisle towards canned goods. I sensed danger, but nothing you could put your finger on. My instinct was to stock up on comestibles.

*

That Sunday, 10 March 1985, I proposed fresh air, a walk after lunch. Clive did not want to go.

'You'll feel better,' I said.

'I doubt it,' he said.

But I could not let the storm brew any blacker. We had to get outside, to move, to breathe.

'Look,' I said, 'let's drive to Hampstead Heath. If you don't perk up, we'll come straight home.'

He was too poorly to argue.

We parked in a red sandy car park full of potholes.

'It's about to rain,' said Clive.

'Not yet,' I said.

My optimism was at odds with the gathering gloom above our heads.

'Come on, love,' I said, 'let's just walk to Jack Straw's Castle and back, stretch our legs.'

The heath at this north edge made a kind of low mound. I thought we could at least duck into the pub if the rain started. We held on to each other as we always did but the rough terrain was throwing us somehow out of step. Clive stomped, kicking up tufts. He said little. It was as if we had to press against invisible forces to cover any ground at all.

We had reached the middle of this expanse of stubbled green when a low rumble filled the sky. We stopped. A double crack split the air above our heads and a cold rain was upon us. We turned, heads bowed. Thunder rolled across the sky. The noise was everywhere, like a fury held in too long, unleashed. The sky pelted us with bullets of ice, stinging our faces. We ran, arms over our heads, all the way back to the muddy car park where the potholes had become puddles bubbling and splashing high into the air where the hail struck. I fumbled with the keys and we got into our car, slamming the doors. It was shelter, but it didn't feel safe. A curtain of white rain surrounded us and sheet lightning lit up the heath. We sat puffing and steaming up windows. The hail drummed so hard on the roof, I expected dents. Stones bounced high off the bonnet and off the ground. It was a good five minutes before we could see to drive home. The streets were awash with fast-running streams. Waters swelled around clogged drains and our wheels sent up a wave to left and right. It was raining like it would never stop.

The rain had washed our windows clean. I fetched the ironing. It towered above my head as I walked. I must have looked like a stack of laundry on legs. Clive sighed.

'So much?' he said. 'We mustn't let it get this bad.'

'We've not been here,' I said. 'Mind if I switch on the telly?'

'Has the lightning stopped?'

I watched the window for a moment. It was dark outside like twilight, though still only three.

'Uh . . . think so.'

'I can't cope with a film or anything with plot,' he said. 'My head aches.'

I fetched the aspirin and put the sport on low. At some point, Clive left the room and then came back.

The iron bubbled and spat, burning the backs of my hands. Another bubbling sound. I looked behind me. Clive was perched awkwardly on top of the laundry, mouth open, eyes shut, head back. His feet barely touched the ground. He lay at an angle as if he'd fallen from a height.

'Darling!' I called out.

He opened his eyes and looked across at me.

'Why are you there?' I asked.

'I don't know,' he said. 'I must have been asleep.'

'Go to bed properly,' I said.

I took his hand and led him into the bedroom. He seemed lost and sleepy so I undid his buttons and found pyjamas. He was shivering.

'I'll make you a hot-water bottle,' I said.

In the kitchen I had the tap running to fill the kettle but there was a noise from the bedroom. I turned off the tap. A terrible kind of moan. I dropped the kettle in the sink and ran the length of the corridor. I thought heart attack.

'What's the matter?' I called out as I ran. My voice was on the way to a scream. 'What is it? What's wrong?'

His teeth were chattering. He did not look at me but lay with eyes half closed beneath the trembling bedclothes.

'It's OK,' he said. 'I think I've got a chill.'

'Why did you make that noise?' I asked.

'It's only m-m-my teeth chattering,' he said through a new wave. 'Bb bw I'm mb fr-fr-freezing.' He sucked in breath through his trembling jaw.

Clive's pale face floated on the dark-brown bedlinen against a dark-brown carpet. I took his temperature. It was above normal.

'I'm calling the doctor.'

'No need,' he said. 'I'm probably fighting something off.'

He was the husband. I was used to taking his word for it.

I believe that shuddering was the first slight jar to Clive's brain, perhaps a momentary seizure.

*

Our cousin Lawrence felt only a slight jar one night on a voyage to America. He went on deck and spoke with people playing cards. They'd felt it too but went on shuffling. Our cousin never saw them again. They were on the *Titanic*. Lawrence got out alive in a half-full lifeboat as so many women refused to leave their husbands, preferring to drown with them than to survive widowed. 'In some cases,' said our cousin, 'they were torn from their husbands and pushed into the boats, but in many instances they were allowed to remain, since there was no one to insist.'

Clive stayed home from the office on the Monday. 'I'm just a bit under the weather,' he said. He met his friend John for lunch at a Turkish restaurant but had no appetite. They put his kebab in a box. I found it in the fridge a week later. John's mother had just died and he was bereft. He still lived in his parents' house though he'd turned forty.

'When two people are very close,' Clive had said to him, 'like you and your ma, you are always together even when you're apart. That's how it is with me and Deborah.'

The last thing Clive had said of his friend's mother as they parted that afternoon was, 'I'll never forget her.'

On the evening of Sunday 17 March Clive had a headache and he slept heavily that night. He took the Monday and Tuesday off work because of the headache. On the Monday his temperature was a little high and he was drowsy but his temperature returned to normal the next day. For the rest of the week Clive attended a conference in St Albans. He came home each night bubbling with excitement. He was among friends, talented historians, doing what he loved to do. They were considering the music, history and liturgy associated with St Alban and his shrine. The Europa

Singers, his amateur choir that we ran together, had started rehearsing the *Missa Santa Albanis* by Fayrfax. I was in the kitchen when Clive came home early from the conference that Friday afternoon flushed, tired and with a headache. He called his secretary at the BBC, where he worked as an early music producer for Radio 3, to say that he would not be returning to the office that day.

The next morning, Saturday 23 March, I was on press cuttings duty in my office, the PR department at John Lewis. Afterwards I went on to try to sell my violin. We were hard up and there was a tax bill hanging over us. The shop didn't want to pay much so I put it back in the case, reprieved. I had carried it under my arm most of my life and had often forgotten it on trains. The guard used to find my violin case on the overhead luggage rack at the end of the line and put it on the next train back home to Teddington. Everyone knew it was mine, I forgot it so often. Though I never played awfully well, I was always happy to be reunited with the instrument and now once again I was glad I hadn't needed to sell it this day. When I got up the stairs, violin in one hand and briefcase in the other, Clive's son Anthony held the door open for me. Clive was on his knees in the hall, bowed over piles of books.

'My goodness!' I said, lifting bags in the air. I edged around the books to the bedroom door where I could put things down. 'What're you doing?'

'We're sorting them into alphabetical order,' said Anthony.

'Hello, love.' I bent over Clive and kissed his cheek.

'Mm, hello. Where've you been?'

'Didn't you get my message?' I took off my coat and threw it on to the bed.

'When we got back the answerphone said "error". There wasn't any message.'

'I thought it made a funny noise. I was trying to sell my fiddle. I've been to Guivier's.'

I turned to greet my stepson. At twenty-two, he was only five years younger than I was and I had to stand on tiptoe to kiss him.

'We're going to watch the match,' he said. 'Dad, it's nearly kick-off.'

Quickly I set up my stand in the bedroom, rosined the bow and tuned up. In the next room the crowd was calling 'CI-TY, CI-TY, CI-TY,' and my boys talked eagerly. They didn't see each other nearly often enough. The violin had a good rich tone. I started to play earthy notes on the low strings. I swooped around, dipping my knees, playing as if the violin were me speaking, laughing. I wished I were a better player, to play the music I loved the way I wanted it to sound – Bartók, strong and bright on open strings, Stravinsky's *Soldier's Tale*. '*Walking down the road one day – daa, di di di di di dee – A soldier had a tune to play – diddle diddle diddle diddle diddle . . . di!*' I stumbled over the double stopping, guessing at the notes without any music, pressing my fingers where I thought the sounds were. The soldier sets out with the jaunty walk of a young man, a violin about his person; the devil meets him on the road and promises him everything if he'll sell his violin, symbol of his soul. He sells, and is consigned to hell. He thought he could resist temptation, get back on the road, but he's lost. The same cock-a-hoop tune repeats over and over through the piece as the soldier walks blindly on towards his own destruction, and strikes up one last time after the soldier's demise as the devil waits on the same road to catch the next sucker.

*

I could hear Clive calling out to me from under the music. I went into the front room, fiddle in hand.

'I'm sorry, darling,' he said. 'Do you mind not playing? It's my head, it's bad again.'

'Sweetheart!' I said. 'My poor love – another headache?' I bent over the back of the sofa to kiss him gently on the temple.

'Or the same one . . .'

'What can I get you? Have you taken any aspirin?'

He looked at his watch. 'It'll be four hours at a quarter to five.'

'Why don't you go to bed? Tell him, Anthony!'

'She's right, Dad. Have a lie-down.'

'No.' He leaned back and looked into his son's face. 'I want to make the most of you here!' A football roar came from the television and both of them turned to watch, faces entranced.

'Hold it . . . Hold it . . . Now pass! *Move! OHHH!*' The boys groaned and the crowd groaned with them.

'Tss! They left him totally exposed! What a *waste*!' said Clive. 'No point running like a madman if there's no one with you, no back-up!'

'You look flushed, love.' I put my hand on Clive's forehead. 'Shall I take your temperature?'

'I'm all right,' he said, his eyes on the action replay, one arm outstretched to the heroic runner, sighing at his slow-motion fall. 'I'll live!'

Clive had had so many headaches that past year, from working hard and being exhausted, that the aspirin bottle stayed out on the bedside table instead of in the bathroom cabinet. There was nothing unusual about his head aching, although he did perhaps seem under the weather, as though he might still be fighting something off.

\*

The next morning was Sunday 24 March 1985. We woke late. Anthony was sleeping in the back room. We were expecting his sister Alison to arrive, plus some friends for lunch. We lay in the last of sleep, wrapped up as one under the bedclothes. Clive was the first to move, while I lay lazy and warm and watched him get out of bed through half-closed eyes. He staggered forward a couple of steps, his head falling into his hands.

'*Aaach!*' he gasped.

I leaped up and was beside him, my arm around his shoulders.

'My *head*!' he said. 'It's like something hit me with a hammer.'

'Where?' I said. 'Where does it hurt?'

'All over . . . awful . . .' He stood bowed over, naked, his skin bluey-white.

'You're coming back to bed,' I said.

He let me lead him slowly back and help him in. I pulled the duvet close around him.

'Why is it so bad?' I said.

'I don't know,' he said.

'Shall I call the doctor?'

'No, it'll pass.'

'Well, I'll call Peter and Christina and put them off.'

'No, don't,' he objected.

'Well, you can't see them in this state.'

There was a pause while he registered the truth of it.

'. . . I s'pose not,' he said.

I stuck a thermometer under his tongue and phoned our lunch guests. His temperature was 101°.

\*

Later Alison arrived and sat with her brother in the front room. In the afternoon Clive was vomiting, feverish. We wanted to call a doctor. Clive said not to.

'They'll only say it's a virus,' he said. 'Nothing they can do.'

I awoke the next morning, Monday, to find the headache had kept Clive awake all night. The bed was drenched with sweat and his pyjamas were sopping. I turned the mattress. The grey line in the thermometer crept past 101° and towards 102°. Clive was still feverish, still vomiting. He let me ring the surgery. I asked for a home visit. At lunchtime I slipped home from work in a black cab. The doctor had not been but had telephoned, telling Clive she thought it was flu.

'How's your head?' I asked.

'Ghastly,' he said.

'What sort of pain is it?'

'Like a band all round. Last night it was the sides more, now it's moved behind my eyes, the top, here . . .' He put his hands around his temples and at the back.

'Is it thumping?'

'Not exactly, it's constant, terrible.'

I rang the surgery again and repeated my request for a home visit before I went back to work. It was the intensity of the headache that worried me. In the afternoon a doctor came and prescribed something for the vomiting, and a painkiller for the headache. Clive was still sweating a lot. He ate nothing all day and took hardly any fluid.

On Tuesday morning, 26 March, I woke to find the headache had kept Clive awake a second night. The pills obviously weren't working. His temperature was 102°. I had to cajole him to drink the occasional sip of water. He was still vomiting but the sweating had stopped.

'You'll get dehydrated,' I told him. 'Shall I ring the doctor again?'

'No, give the pills time to take effect.'

At lunchtime I bolted home. He was much the same. I rang the surgery. Late afternoon I phoned from the office. He said the doctor had rung him. 'Real flu can be quite bad; there's nothing they can do.'

'Phone if you need me,' I said.

'All right,' he said in a hollowed-out voice. 'I . . . I . . .' He seemed to be straining for some thought that was vanishing. 'I can't remember your number.'

How odd, I thought. 'Don't worry, love. Write it down. Have you got a pen?' I could hear him fumbling for the pad.

'Ah yes,' he said when I told him. 'I forgot it for a moment.'

I felt alarm in my stomach. 'I'm coming home now,' I said.

'OK,' he said.

I told my boss I needed to go, ran downstairs, jumping the last two steps, and out of the building. I flagged down a taxi in Wimpole Street.

Back home, Clive looked washed out. I couldn't understand why he was not sweating despite his temperature hovering at 101°. The pills had allayed the vomiting but he still felt nauseous.

He sat on the sofa that evening in his white towelling dressing gown and watched a little TV. That was a good sign. He asked me to fix the blinds, which were not evenly drawn. Clive never could bear them crooked.

We discussed Thursday's choir rehearsal and made plans for someone else to conduct it.

'You better phone, er . . . er . . .' Clive's face clouded over. 'I can't remember her name.'

'Janet,' I said.

'Janet, yes, of course . . . How peculiar,' he said.

'Do you want to go back to bed, love? You've been two nights without sleep. It's no wonder you're not with it. Do you think you could sleep now?'

'I don't know, maybe.'

I helped him back to bed and caught sight of the pad where Clive had written my office phone number. Next to it he had written my whole name, Deborah Wearing, and the words 'in the office'. On the yellow cover was printed *Devon and Cornwall – Reporters' Notebook*.

'When you're better,' I said, 'we'll go to Cornwall.' Cornwall was where his family had gone every summer when he was a kid. We had always said we would go there but had never made time. In six years we'd had only one holiday, in Spain, five days in France and a few long weekends. Other than that, Clive typically worked seven days a week.

'You need to slow down, take a holiday,' I said.

'Yes,' he said.

'You and me in Cornwall.'

'Yes,' he said. His eyes were shut. I kissed him on his hot forehead and tiptoed out.

I woke on Wednesday morning at a little before 6.30 a.m. and turned to see how Clive was.

'Darling?'

'Yes . . .' he said in a faraway voice through half-closed eyes.

'Did you sleep?'

He lay there breathing.

'Darling?'

'Yes?'

'How are you? Did you sleep?'

'No, I didn't,' he said.

'Did you sleep at all, love?'

He breathed some more, and in that pause I grew afraid.

'No, not at all,' he said.

The pain in his head had kept him awake now for three days and nights.

'How's your head?' I asked.

'Terrible,' he said. 'Sleep . . .' he said. 'I must have sleep . . . I want to go . . .'

'To the loo?' I asked.

'Yes,' he said.

I put him into his dressing gown and led him to the bathroom.

'Is this it?' he asked.

What did he mean?

'Do you want to go, love?'

He had a short pee, nothing much, and grinned at himself in the mirror.

I picked up the thermometer from by the bed.

'Er, er, darling . . .'

'Yes, my love?'

He looked bewildered.

'I can't . . . think of your name,' he said, really troubled.

'Deborah.'

'Deborah . . . oh yes.' He sighed.

'Don't worry, love. Now, let me take your temperature and I'll ring the doctor.'

I slipped the thermometer under his tongue and laid my hand on his cheek a moment. He shut his eyes and nuzzled my hand.

I dialled the number for out-of-hours calls and told the man who answered that Clive seemed confused, perhaps delirious. I took the thermometer out and read it. It had risen.

'It's 103°,' I said. 'I think we need a doctor right away.'

We waited an hour, two. At half past eight a jovial male doctor arrived. I repeated the story from the first symptoms, the shivering after our walk, his feeling unwell, the headache, the fever, vomiting, and now apparently delirium – Clive seemed to understand less and less by the hour.

The doctor took his temperature: it had risen already to 104°. He got Clive to sit up and lifted his pyjama jacket, put a stethoscope to his back. It was green and sunny outside the window. The irregular rhythms of tennis balls reached us from the recreation ground below. The reassuring voice of the doctor said ordinary things. It looked like a pleasant morning in our beautifully decorated flat with fresh polycotton sheets and books in alphabetical order. But Clive and I were in some other kind of morning. I seemed to see the room through a thickness.

'Say ninety-nine,' said the doctor.

There was silence. Clive wore a kind of half-smile of embarrassment as though he knew something had been asked of him but could not respond.

'Say ninety-nine,' the doctor repeated.

'. . . Yes . . .' said Clive.

Overnight my husband had become like an infant and the doctor did not seem worried.

'Cough! Would you cough please, Mr Wearing?'

Clive looked puzzled, then quietly cleared his throat.

I had an overwhelming urge to laugh or scream. I sat on my hands, pressing my fingers into a loose nail at the edge of the seat to try to get a grip. Without my noticing it, somewhere in the last hours the world had become surreal. Clive was always the one in authority. He knew about everything. And yet here he was, not responding, not responding. The doctor remained pleasant, flat, as if there was nothing to worry about.

'What do you do for a living, Mr Wearing?' asked the doctor.

I already knew Clive would not be able to respond. He was staring vacantly ahead, the doctor behind him still listening through his stethoscope.

'BBC music producer,' I said. 'And conductor.'

'I suppose that must be a, um, a high-powered sort of a job?' He was trying to work out if Clive was intelligent, capable of saying 'Ninety-nine' and coughing when asked to do so by a doctor.

'Yes, very,' I said.

He placed the stethoscope at different points on Clive's back. Why wasn't he listening to the roar in his head?

'He must have a lot of expertise?' The doctor was, I supposed, looking for confirmation that this was not Clive's normal behaviour.

'He's a Cambridge graduate,' I said, assuming that would make the point, 'extremely articulate.'

'I see.' He turned to Clive and spoke in a loud slow voice. 'Mr Wearing, do you have a headache now?'

'I . . . don't know,' said Clive.

'He said it was very bad this morning. He's been saying that since Sunday morning. It's the headache that's kept him constantly awake three days and nights.'

'Oh,' said the doctor, 'we think we've been awake all night, when actually we've slept on and off.'

'No, I really believe he hasn't slept. He's been awake and in pain every time I woke. But he's been confused since I woke this morning.'

'Sleep! I must have sleep!' gasped Clive, rallying, knowing he was expected to say something. His face was stricken, haggard.

'That's all right, Mr Wearing,' said the doctor. 'We'll soon have you fast asleep.' He went to his bag and rummaged, took out a bottle.

'It is the lack of sleep,' the doctor said to me, 'that's causing your husband's confusion.' Then, turning to Clive, 'Here you are, Mr Wearing. Take two of these now and you'll feel a lot better when you wake up.'

I went off to the kitchen to get some water. Clive took the tablets and lay back down on his pillow, gaunt, white, with deep dark circles around his eyes. I looked at the bottle: Temazepam 10.

'He'll be asleep in no time,' said the doctor.

'Should I stay with him?'

'Maybe just till he's gone off. But these'll knock him out for eight hours – yes, go to work.'

The doctor picked up the bottle.

'Mr Wearing!' he said, again speaking in a loud slow voice. Clive opened his eyes. 'If you wake up, you can take another two of these.' He held the bottle towards Clive's face. 'They'll help you sleep. All right?'

'Yes,' said Clive. I thought it odd to entrust Clive with pills when he was clearly not registering information but I had to assume I could trust the professional judgement of a doctor. I thanked him for coming to our home and showed him out.

'You'll feel better when you've had a sleep,' I said to Clive. 'I'll stay with you until you drop off; then I'll go to work, but I'll be back lunchtime. All right, love?'

I wrote the doctor's name and phone number in large letters on the notepad by the bed, and told Clive to ring me or ring him if he felt bad.

'OK,' he said. I left for work around ten.

At two, I returned. Clive woke up. He said he had just taken two more pills. I counted the number of pills left in the bottle to make sure and saw that he was right. I made him sip some water; he could not eat.

'A little drop of chicken consommé?' I had bought half a dozen tins the previous night.

'I can't . . .' he said.

'Do you still have a headache?' I asked.

He hesitated. 'I . . . don't know,' he said and settled back to sleep.

I was due to give a talk to a roomful of economics students and so left again after half an hour.

As I stood enthusing about industrial democracy, in the ordinary groove of my life, the familiar words emptied out. This world I knew seemed thin, just a flimsy film that might break up. I kept seeing Clive propped up in bed with his dark-circled eyes and the doctor saying, 'Say ninety-nine,' and Clive saying nothing and then, 'Yes.'

Back at my desk, the usual media telephoned with the usual midweek queries and requests. I checked the sales figures. My colleagues asked, how was Clive. I told them about his temperature, about the sleeping pills, about the doctor saying he'd be better after a sleep. I told them he didn't know my name that morning. Hearing myself, I wondered why I wasn't at home. But the doctor had said go to work.

\*

Later on, I let myself into the flat and called out to Clive. There was no answer. Perhaps he was sleeping. I tiptoed into the bedroom, expecting to see him snuggled in and fast asleep.

What I saw terrified me. There were Clive's pyjamas collapsed in the middle of an empty bed. I ran down the passage to the kitchen and his name tore from my mouth. *'CLIVE! CLIVE!'* The place where the shouting came from knew more than my brain. *'WHERE – ARE – YOU?'* *Oh my God oh my God oh my God.* He wasn't in the kitchen or the back room or the bathroom. He wasn't in the living room. I looked all round and behind the sofa and went back to the bedroom to look on the floor on the far side of the bed. He wasn't anywhere.

I ran out on to the landing and rattattatted next door. Our elderly neighbour, Miss Harris, had heard my cry. She had seen nothing. Miss Harris offered to go outside to see if the car was still there while I checked his clothes. She had her keys on a string round her neck and pulled her door to, hurrying down the stairs. Clive's wallet was missing, and his pinstripe suit.

I phoned the doctor to ask, had he taken him to hospital?

'No,' he said, puzzled, friendly.

'Did he call you?' I couldn't understand it.

'No – er . . . just a moment.' I could hear muffled talking, his hand must have been over the receiver. 'No, he hasn't called.'

The doctor seemed mildly surprised at my call. I said I would ring the police and asked would he stand by to come when Clive was found. He said he would. I sank down on the hall floor among the phone books.

The police were slow to cotton on.

'Have you had a row?' asked a woman with a switchboard voice before putting me through to someone else. Each new person who came on the line asked the same question.

'He's very sick, confused.'

'Have you had a row?'

'No! He has a fever, a temperature of 104°, he's delirious.'

'So you haven't had a row?'

'Row? He could hardly speak this morning! He's been ill with a fever since Sunday. He might collapse, he could fall on to a Tube line, walk in front of traffic. He can hardly stand.'

'I see. When did you last see him?'

'Lunchtime, two thirty.'

'Well, that's not long. See if he comes back tonight. If he's still missing in the morning . . .'

'No! Please! Listen!' I felt as if I were in one of those dreams where you speak but no words come out of your mouth. 'The doctor gave him sleeping pills . . .' The word 'doctor' seemed to register as nothing else I had said did. They asked the doctor's name and surgery address and only then did they begin to respond as though they believed me.

'If I were you, I'd ring round the hospitals,' the voice suggested. 'See if he's been admitted, then call us back if you don't find him.'

Finally, a plan of action. First I rang BBC security in case he had tried to go to work. I imagined him automatically heading for the office.

'He's five foot eight,' I said, 'thick dark hair, black overcoat . . .' How would they ever know him from that? Clive's colleagues told me afterwards that the guards had been up and down Clive's corridor checking each room.

I looked up hospitals in the Yellow Pages and rang each one. They put me through to admissions. No one had anyone of that name. Did he know his own name? I wondered. Would he be able to say it?

I called the police back and a new voice answered. I ran through it again.

'Have you had a row?' said the voice. I lost my rag.

A man and woman in uniform arrived at our flat. They came in slowly, took their caps off slowly and made themselves comfortable on our new white suite in our new white living room. They asked laborious questions that seemed to have no bearing on the situation and wrote down the answers in longhand in black notepads. They seemed to keep going over the same ground while all the time Clive could be moving further away. They asked for a photograph. I'd looked for one before they showed up. Apart from his professional portraits, which were out of date, and snapshots where he was tiny against buildings, and wedding photos, stuck fast in an album, all I could find was one taken on holiday in Paris, the only decent headshot to hand. We were sitting in a café in the Jardins du Luxembourg, horsing around. He was pulling a French face, pretending to be an existentialist. I started to explain about the face, and petered out.

'That's him, anyway,' I said. 'It's a good likeness.' Meanwhile my imagination reviewed the possible scenarios. I saw Clive on main roads, on the edge of the platform at Maida Vale Tube. He could be just on the corner and I wouldn't know. Why did I have to stay inside? I wanted to be out looking.

They told me to stay at home in case he came back. I called a friend, a soprano from our choir, and asked her to come and wait with me. I sat on a gate-leg table in the kitchen, kicking the flap. We went over the events of the last few days, what the doctors had said, the symptoms, how Clive wouldn't have gone far. We did not talk about how we expected the police to find him. She talked when I couldn't.

The phone rang. I had been waiting for it, but when it came it shocked me. I reached the phone table in a few bounds.

'*Hello?*'

I did not understand who was speaking to me at first. It was BBC security to say they had conducted a search and found no trace of Clive, but would keep a lookout. They had alerted people. It was nice of them to search, kind to call back. I thanked them.

We sat in the kitchen a while longer. The phone rang again. It was West Hampstead police. A man asked, was I Mrs Wearing?

'Yes, yes,' I said.

'It's about a Mr Clive Wearing.'

'You've got him?' I said.

'I believe so.'

'Thank God!' I said. 'Is he OK?'

'He's fine,' he said, 'although quite confused.'

A taxi driver had brought him to the police station. Clive had hailed the cab to go home but could not remember his address. Fortunately the cab driver was a good person and brought Clive to safety. And fortunately Clive had his wallet with him so the police were able to trace his address and phone number by his Barclaycard. Thank God. West Hampstead station hadn't been alerted to the fact that he was missing although I think it was the station nearest where we lived. It was the Harrow Road police who were looking for him. West Hampstead said they'd tell them to call off the search.

'I'll come straight away,' I said. 'Keep an eye on him. Don't let him wander off.'

'We'll put him in an interview room.'

'He's very sick. I'll call the doctor to meet us back home.'

My friend drove me to the police station. I was glad she knew where it was. At the counter, a number of policemen looked up and chuckled when they heard whom we had come to collect. One unlocked the interview room. There was Clive dressed in his overcoat and suit, open-necked shirt, unshaven, a copy of *The Times* in his lap. He never went anywhere without it. This was Saturday's copy he'd picked up from the chair in the bedroom. When he saw me he stood up, beaming from ear to ear, arms open to embrace me. We hugged exuberantly. I was nearly crying. The policemen bade us cheery goodbyes.

Our friend pulled in at the entrance to our building. We got out of the car but Clive went to walk right by the gate. I stopped him, turned him to face our front door.

'Oh . . . is this where we live?' he asked.

'Don't you recognize it?' I asked.

'Not at all,' he said.

He did not recognize the flat either but was pleased to be home with me. I rang the doctor and put Clive to bed like a little child. He could tell me nothing about where he had been or when he went out.

'I don't remember,' he said. His temperature was still 104°. He managed to drink a mug of tea and fell fast asleep. An odd kind of flu this, and Clive's sleep had not made his confusion any better.

Our GP arrived, the same one who'd seen him in the morning. He put his head into the bedroom but stayed standing at the bedroom door. I stood next to him, both of us looking across the room at Clive breathing.

'He's sleeping like a baby,' whispered the doctor, and quietly withdrew into the hallway.

'Don't you need to examine him?' I asked.

'Oh no, I won't disturb him. Let's leave him to sleep. It'll do him good.'

We offered the doctor coffee; he accepted and settled into one of our comfy armchairs. My friend put the kettle on and we discussed the odd progress of this illness. The doctor's diagnosis seemed to have changed since the morning. Clive had, he told us, a particularly nasty kind of flu virus sweeping North London that week and characterized by a very bad headache. The Royal Free had so far seen eleven cases of suspected meningitis. It was flu – but with a cerebral irritation, 'a menengism', said the doctor. That explained it, we thought.

Clive would be poorly, he warned, for some time, off work for up to four or five weeks. The doctor advised me to take a couple of days off work to nurse him over the worst of it. He encouraged me to ring if I was worried.

When he'd gone, I rang my boss to say I wouldn't be in to work for the rest of the week. His wife worked in a hospital and called me back.

'Write down everything you can remember,' she said, 'in case you need it later. If his temperature goes up to 105°, call an ambulance. Write down his fluid intake, his urine output, his temperature. Write down the whole case history, everything you can remember since the beginning, with dates.'

I did as she advised. I still have those pages nineteen years later. The paper looks fresh but my handwriting was larger and rounder then than now.

\*

That night I lay listening to Clive, looking at his profile. He lay facing the ceiling. He continued to be restless and disorientated, not quite coherent. But he did sleep. By about 4 a.m. his breathing seemed quicker, shallow. I called the GP. This time the lady doctor came who had seen him on Monday. She examined him.

'It's not meningitis,' she said. 'See, no stiff neck. And it's not pneumonia, not a tumour.'

I felt reassured. She was pleasant and gentle, with red hair. She said she did not mind being called out in the night. She said I'd done the right thing.

The next day, Thursday 28 March, things looked better. Clive's temperature was down to 100°. The lady doctor returned at 8.30 a.m. and seemed content with his progress.

Clive slept heavily nearly all the time. When he awoke he remained disorientated, wandering, quiet, and he asked repeatedly what time was it, what day was it. The lady GP rang at lunchtime. She said that she and the male doctor were satisfied that Clive's illness was probably no more than this flu virus but asked, did I want him taken to hospital.

'What do you think?' I said.

She repeated the same sentence as though it were written down and asked again, did I want him taken to hospital. I imagined him sitting uncomfortably for many hours waiting to be seen, getting chilled, further disorientated. Would he not be better off tucked up in bed to catch up on so much lost sleep and fight off the flu, as he was now?

He was asleep, his temperature was right down, he was drinking properly, passing water. Could a hospital visit cause a setback? I wondered.

'What do *you* think?' I asked her again. She was the professional. 'If you want another opinion,' I said, 'I'll take him in.' There was a pause. 'Do *you* think he should go to hospital?'

'Dr—— and I are of the opinion that it is flu, but it's up to you,' she said.

'I leave it to you,' I said. I asked her about the possible detrimental effects of sitting for hours in Casualty.

'It's up to you,' she repeated.

'It's up to *you*,' I said. How could I know what was best? I had almost no experience of illness. I had read in Victorian novels about fevers breaking and then the person being all right. We were musicians, healthy people. Besides, it looked as though Clive had turned a corner.

Perhaps he had, but it was in the wrong direction.

That afternoon and evening I telephoned everyone we knew who was a doctor or nurse or had any kind of medical expertise. They seemed to feel it was right to nurse Clive at home, as long as he kept drinking and resting and his temperature was down. No one suggested any further action. Clive was, they said, in the best place. If his temperature went up again, I could always get him to hospital. But we had read of twelve-hour waits on trolleys in Accident & Emergency. Hospital could be risky. The doctors did not make a return visit that day. Clive's temperature fluctuated between 99.6° and 102° towards evening. His liquid intake that day was 1 pint 11 oz. He urinated twice.

Thursday night I slept. Whenever I woke, Clive was asleep.

The next morning, Friday, I took Clive to the bathroom at six thirty.

'Which one?' he asked, clearly not knowing which piece of white furniture was the lavatory. I showed him and then ran to the phone, called the out-of-hours number and insisted they send a doctor fast. All that sleep, and his delirium was worse.

'Please come now,' I almost shouted, and then ran back to Clive.

I got him back to bed; he was sinking. Nobody rang the doorbell, nobody came. The doctors' surgery was only just down our street but perhaps they lived further away. He stopped responding. I picked up his arm, then the other. They were floppy and his eyes were closed. I phoned the doctors' emergency number again.

'His arms are floppy . . .'

'Floppy?' The man sounded concerned.

'I think,' I said, 'he's going unconscious. Will you please get someone here right now. This is an emergency!'

I knelt beside my husband.

'Stay with me, darling!' Rubbing his hands. 'Wake up!' Speaking to him. 'I love you . . .'

I felt as though I had been pushed underwater and were being held down just inches from life, unable to get a foothold. A radio was playing somewhere in the building. Other people were going to work. What was happening?

The doctor arrived at a quarter to eight. It seemed an age since my call at six thirty. He took one look at Clive and dialled 999. He announced his name and asked for an ambulance to come to our address. Then he left us. I held the front door open and watched him down the stairs. At the landing he paused and said, not looking at me, 'This is the strangest case I've ever seen.'

\*

It was a quarter to nine, another hour, before the ambulance arrived. I had thought 999 calls were answered in minutes, like in the movies. Clive's eyes were open and he was able to sit in a wheelchair. A woman strapped him in with red tapes crisscrossing his body. His face was pale, drawn, gaunt, sweating, his eyes open but dark and fixed. He did not speak but there was again a polite half-smile on his face. I believe he was trying to co-operate. A rushing noise seemed to be coming from inside his head or maybe from around him.

'How long has he been like this?' asked the paramedic.

'He's not been able to communicate properly since Wednesday morning,' I said.

'What the . . . ?'

'The doctors kept visiting, but they thought it was flu,' I said. 'Bad flu.'

The woman shook her head and muttered. On the surface I was answering questions, recounting events and symptoms, offering the case notes I had prepared, dealing with known fact, dissociated. Inside I felt numb with each new unanswerable question, the silence, slow-moving time.

We arrived at St Mary's Hospital, Paddington, at 9 a.m. on Friday 29 March. I ran after the wheelchair through smudged rubber doors to Casualty. They flapped shut behind us, sealing us in like a one-way valve.

# 2

## THE TIME BEFORE

WE MET THROUGH MUSIC. IT WAS SEPTEMBER '78. I HAD GRADUATED from Durham and had come to work for the John Lewis group in London. Joining the choir was more or less a condition of my employment. They needed sopranos and my boss was chair of the Music Society. We talked a lot about music at the job interview. There was a theatre hidden behind the toy department and the company brought in experts to teach us. It was remarkable – shopworkers performing with conductors, designers and producers from the best opera houses in London. Once I'd dispensed with the business of calculating hairdressing commission and maintenance men's overtime, I could enjoy a rehearsal or take a course in stage management without leaving the premises.

In the choir, we were a group of unauditioned office workers and shop assistants, most of whom had been standing all day and were willing to stand a couple more hours to sing. We rehearsed in a comfortable wood-panelled room with potted palms and a Bechstein grand. On my first day, I chose a seat on the end of a row and waited. At exactly six thirty the conductor came in, dark, with intelligent eyes, a little shorter than the female stage manager beside him. He had a rich, laughing voice and talked with his hands. I looked away and then glanced up as he swept past. His face was lowered, listening, lit up. He could have been a Nouvelle Vague actor with his white mac and black polo neck. His entry into the room had a strange effect, as if his arrival had set something in motion out of the limping blank of ordinary life. The choir was alert, the music about to begin.

'We'll take it from the top,' said Clive, 'see how far we get.' Crisp copies of Britten's *Ceremony of Carols* were in our hands. 'Make sure you've got a pencil handy.' His piercing lake-blue eyes scanned each face until he had everyone's full attention. Then he silently indicated the pulse he was going to beat.

'*And . . . !*'

My lungs expanded with his; we drew breath as one. The entry was ragged, hesitant. He stopped.

'Let's get it right . . . Graham?' He looked to the pianist to play the first note for each section of the choir and people hummed their own to hang on to it, get it pitched right in their voices. My heart sank a bit. I wondered how tedious this might be if the choir had to try this hard for each entry. But the man in front of us commanded our attention, and seemed to expand as if he had all the music inside of him waiting to burst forth.

'Enunciate!' he said. 'Let me hear those words. Explode your consonants, long vowels, just a moderate tempo. Ta da da daaa, ta da da daaa . . .' He hummed all of the notes again. '*Two three, and . . . !*'

The voices were feeling their way but Clive conducted us as though we were good. He sang all of the parts and, when voices stumbled, he supplied our notes like footholds. He conducted with everything held under for economy of movement, precision. And he was gentle with us. I had the impression he had an ideal performance playing inside of him, and we just needed to follow him closely enough to catch its drift. Most of the choir were not fluent sightreaders, which left Clive singing all the entries. He was incredibly patient and stopped at each section to unravel the notes until each line held its own. But sometimes the music was too important to stop, and the choir forgot to be afraid and sang. I was aware of his hands drawing our voices, his lake-blue eyes and the piano. *'This little babe / So few days old / Is come to rifle / Satan's fold,'* rang out over Oxford Street in feverish canon.

It had been a few months since university. In Durham I did as I pleased. I floated in punts upriver between banks of wild garlic, whispering Baudelaire and dragging my hands in the water. I made daisy chains on the green. I wandered through shafts of dusty sunlight in the cathedral to the crypt coffee bar where harmony and counterpoint tutorials took place, known as H&C. Here, over scones with cream and jam, the tutor considered our exercises, small slices of string quartet in the style of Haydn or Mozart or a burst of scoring trying to be Bach chorale. I occasionally got As or A minuses but most of the time I was too interested in trying to figure out what life was about and where my place was in it to do too much serious studying.

The job came as something of a shock. Music had been at the centre of my life all my life and now my ears were filled with typewriters and telephone bells. But I didn't stop to muse on the rhythms, there were contracts and letters to type and I had to get them right and finish quickly. Treading the silent lino from credit management to lost property on the way in to the office, I could still cherish freedom, the possibility of a reprieve – a fire alarm, for example, or news that I was required elsewhere. But rounding the corner I faced the frosted glass panels that enclosed my day. The creak of the counter lifting as I passed through to the other side meant I belonged to them.

My boss had a long title involving words in brackets. She had me read the manual, memorizing policy and procedures on maternity leave, death in service, appraisal reporting and upholding the constitution in any circumstance, then she'd test me to make sure I had taken it in. Sometimes she would come off the phone grim-faced and utter the word, 'Disciplinary!' A hush would fall upon the office as she gathered lever-arch files, powdered her nose and snapped shut her handbag in readiness. We watched her stately gait down the length of the office and held our breath as she edged through the lifted counter. We might never know what the employee had done, but we knew the range of malfeasance for which a person could be summarily terminated – from smoking in the loo to helping yourself to the goods, even those destined for the dustbin. Another crime was falling in love with someone you worked with, particularly if they were not free to love you back. I don't remember reading of this in the rules but it did not need to be written. When love happened between two people in the same department, one of them, traditionally the more junior, would be transferred to another branch.

After rehearsal in the second week, Clive joined the choir in the social club. He sat down across from me and we talked music, his hands inscribing the air as he drew deep on his cigarettes, making the ends glow red.

'The most important things cannot be spoken,' he said, stubbing out a butt in a white china ashtray. 'That's why there's music.'

'Yes!' I agreed. 'For the unsayable.'

'Words deal with surfaces,' he said, 'the physical. Music carries us into the eternal, the realm of spirit.' We got into a discussion of the stock characters of *commedia dell'arte* and African theatre and everyone around us left.

I wondered if the staff manual said anything about love between a conductor from the outside and a trainee and, if love happened, would they banish me to a placement on a far shore with no chorus?

'I'm going to have to call time,' said the club manager, Miss Burden, rattling keys. The place was empty but for us. She shooed us out of the door and locked it. I took the 500 bus to Victoria en route to the YWCA in Pimlico, where I was living. At the station I stopped to call my mother.

'I met the conductor,' I said. 'We talked.'

I walked back to Warwick Square; my parents had lived there in a flat above the bank after they were married. At the Y around the corner I paid £9 a week for a top bunk in a room for six. My bed swayed like a ship at sea around three in the morning when a French girl got into the lower deck after her night shift waitressing. They said she ate bulbs of garlic like they were apples but I never saw her. The women of the Y, ladies of slender means, hung their washing in the boiler room, shared secrets around the kitchen table, and stirred the cooking of their homelands. I must have said something about Clive, for one of them, an Australian, came with me to see him conduct in a church in Marylebone – a Monteverdi Vespers by candlelight. Though it was murky and though I made sure to sit right at the back, I left before Clive turned round to bow so that there could be no chance of his seeing me. For after that one evening chatting in the social club, I found myself unable to look at him. This made following the beat during rehearsals tricky – I held the music so high that all I saw of him was the movement of his hands beyond the edge of the page.

I liked living in Pimlico; it afforded many views of the tower of Westminster Cathedral, where I knew Clive sang every afternoon from three until six fifteen, his bread-and-butter job. I saw that red-brick tower everywhere. I saw it from the company roof garden at lunchtime, and from the 500 bus coming down Park Lane at night. The little tower became for me like an emblem of the man because I knew he would be in that very place, would look up and see the same red-brick confection, every day except Tuesdays, and I saw him for myself on Tuesdays.

As rehearsals for the Christmas concert progressed I continued to avoid Clive and lost my appetite. The girls at the Y tempted me with translucent rice noodles and carrot cake. I went round singing the Britten, preparing for the concert as though it were a solo recital at Carnegie Hall. I accompanied myself on an imaginary keyboard on the bus seat or on the desk at work. I seemed to hear the sublime performance that Clive had conceived. I knew what he wanted. I practised in the park and in the shower. I sang in the boiler room at lunchtime, and when no one was in my dorm at night I sang the lullaby *'Balula low baluu lula low balula lula luu laa laa low . . .'* The choir was slow but Clive pushed us to something beyond ourselves. My whole week led to Tuesday evenings. My main place in life was the back row of sopranos in Clive's choir.

*

With not long to go before the concert, I lost my voice. Too much singing, not enough sustenance. I missed a rehearsal. Without my lead the sopranos went quiet. Clive asked who was missing and it was then, by my empty chair and the faltering soprano line, that he remembered me. He'd not seen much of me lately, hidden behind the music. At dress rehearsal the following week he read out a list of notices and at the end asked would I stay behind. I assumed he wanted me to turn pages for the pianist or some such concert duty. But, in the same public voice he had used in rehearsal, he invited me to join him that Saturday to hear an opera. He was scouting for a children's choir to perform in an opera he was doing at Covent Garden and said he would value another pair of ears. In my rehearsal voice I managed to say yes please. I raced out into the street, climbed up to the top deck of the bus for the cathedral tower, and then ran from Victoria through white stucco streets, as if the great pillared porches were already wedding-cake decorations and I the bride in miniature. Back at the Y I sped up to the top floor and up to my bunk, then wandered down to the basement kitchen and opened the fridge door a few times until someone asked me how rehearsal went. They asked about Clive and I realized I knew little beyond the sparse career details I'd read in a concert programme and the social club gossip – only that he'd once been married and wasn't now, and even that didn't turn out to be true in legal terms. How was it I felt so much when I knew so little? It was as though something in me recognized him. I knew him. I don't know how, but I knew him.

That first opera went in a kind of blur. I remember pizza afterwards and walking through a lit bus shelter, the bus, Clive's arm around my shoulders, a brief goodbye. A few days later I picked up the phone at work and his voice in my ear made the office suddenly a much bigger place. Saturday, he said. Saturday.

Clive picked me up at the Y after singing matins at the cathedral. The receptionist, an elderly Polish lady, peered at him through a crack in the hatch while someone went to fetch me. She did not approve of male callers other than brothers. And Clive, at forty, was no boy. I waved a cheery goodbye to her and the hatch clicked shut. We walked to the Tube, changed at Oxford Circus and took the old Bakerloo northbound to Swiss Cottage. The opera was somewhere in Clive's neighbourhood that afternoon and he was going to cook me lunch. It was strange walking side by side from the Tube station towards his flat in Goldhurst Terrace. I tried to match his wider stride but that felt like playing giant's hopscotch. I tried three to his two but that came out mincing and he gave me a curious sidelong glance. So I had to walk normally even though it made an uneven cross-rhythm with his steps.

The place was filled with books and papers, cardboard boxes piled high. Clive carved from a joint of cold lamb and there were boiled potatoes, frozen peas and a jar of mint jelly. We ate side by side on his sofa. Rubber slats under the foam cushions were sliding out of place, which gave a sensation of falling. Clive bent over his plate and ate quickly. He looked like someone who usually ate alone and in a hurry. He told me about his children with their mother in Surrey, two boys and a girl, all at boarding schools.

The opera that afternoon was something by Michael Nyman. Clive waved to him and introduced me as 'my friend Deborah'. So, I was his friend. Everyone had always called me Debbie but Clive called me Deborah from the first. 'You're a Deborah,' he said.

We liked the choir, the Finchley Children's Music Group, and Clive duly invited them to sing *Thérèse* the following year at Covent Garden. He was going to see the composer later on and asked me to come and add my feedback. John Tavener lived out at Wembley Park and we stopped at a Greek restaurant on the way. I was still barely able to eat so my *kleftikos* was taken away almost untouched.

On Tavener's piano was a wedding picture, the groom and his Greek bride with Clive looking out from between their shoulders, laughing.

Clive took away their old TV set as they'd just got colour. He asked would I help get it home and tune it in. We tried all the channels and every so often I said something about leaving but I didn't want to go and Clive seemed glad enough to have me there. In no time at all, the last programme fizzled out and the National Anthem played and the white dot gave way to a snowy grey buzz. Clive switched off the set and it was night. We sat on. At some point he spoke into the darkness.

'It'll be a battle for us,' he said. I wasn't sure what he meant.

Not long afterwards we spoke of a life together. A parade of dilatory boyfriends followed by marriage to someone sensible was never my style. I wanted Bartók and Beethoven late quartets and the *Háry János* Suite by Kodály. I wanted Takemitsu on a fine grand piano in a great stone hall. I desperately wanted Stravinsky, *Les Noces, Les Noces*, a mass of Russian nuptials with giant chords that free your soul. And I wanted mad happy like Petrushka, dancing a clogdance with Clive and *commedia dell'arte* and fest-i-val.

\*

I remember that whole season as sunny although it must have been cold because it was winter. Clive's first Christmas gift to me was a fleece coat-lining to keep me warm. I gave him a bracken plant like the ones I used to hide under as a child in the park.

Our first musical event after we got together was a nineteenth-century operetta called *Zar und Zimmermann*, a jolly affair that ran for four nights in the theatre behind the toy department at work. I had a small part as the Dutch bride. Shopworkers spent their free time sewing costumes, building sets, working under the inspired direction of a young designer from the Coliseum. Figures from the music world traipsed in and sat among our colleagues and families. Dame Eva Turner was there in a fur coat. We read about ourselves on the review pages of national papers. Clive, as chorus master, got to conduct only one out of four performances. The chief conductor arrived at dress rehearsal with an entirely different perception of the work. He took it much more slowly and his rendition ran a good twenty minutes longer than Clive's. The slower pace meant singers had to breathe in the middle of sentences. Clive would not budge on tempo, so there were effectively two versions.

I enjoyed entering into Clive's life, helping him with his work, living with him in Goldhurst Terrace. The hardest thing was his past. There was so much of it. Forty years without me and only weeks, months, a year with me. I'd never catch up. And there was all the personal archaeology of other women who had come and gone, in what was now our bed, over the eight years since he had left his wife, or the three years after a flame-haired Irish singer called Susan had left him. The handwriting of the former women was all over everything. Susan's script was especially prevalent – a large italic in odd-colour biros, green, purple. My handwriting in the address book was still in the minority. In the wardrobes were plastic bags containing a half-made skirt and swatches for patchwork quilting in a mix of psychedelia, plain and country sprigs. Kiosk photographs fell out of the bottoms of vases and pencil-holders. One desk drawer reeked of Elizabeth Arden Blue Grass, and each time I went for a paper clip or elastic band a bloom of it rose up and hit me again. I regularly encountered a comb, hair accoutrements, plastic beads, lipstick, powder compact and a series of telephone pads with notes in Susan's bold italic, saying things like 'Chops in the fridge. I love you', or 'Gone for ciggies. Back soon. Me xxx.' Sprinkled on the pages were messages to her from Clive using the words he now used to me: 'Darling, see you after rehearsal. I love you. C xxx.' I studied the pages, wondering that he could say these same things to another woman and it not last; I wanted vocabulary of my own, a different language maybe. To see 'I love you' in his deeply familiar hand-writing but addressed to another woman shifted the world slightly off its axis. If Clive was mine for ever, how come he wasn't mine then too? I studied the photos of Susan and wondered what my hair would look like red. She was at Clive's sister's wedding, standing in the front row next to Clive's uncle. He was my uncle now. What would we do with the photos? And somewhere out there in another world she would be carrying on her life in a different set of circumstances, no doubt with photos of her own and Clive in them, standing next to her relatives. How many people in how many other houses would have photos of Clive smiling back at them, Clive holding their hands? I felt in the middle of some tangled ball of string that needed to be cut off me, cut right off from all over me and burned.

The worst thing was letters from Clive on small sheets of blue notepaper – unfinished, unposted. They pleaded with a woman not to go. Just months before I met him, he writes of 'the suicide which is my daily thought'.

I spent evenings alone with such documents. Untried emotions grew and swilled about in me – jealousy, passions I could not yet put a name to, and a sense of the overwhelming power and danger of love.

The extremes threw me up against big questions. It was staggering that this man I was grafted on to had lived nearly twice as long as I had lived without me. I wanted him to fill the gaps. It delighted me to find our paths had crossed twice on the South Bank – once for a concert of eight pianos led by Radu Lupu and again for Rameau's *Les Boréades*. He could easily have tripped over my floor-length trailing purple Laura Ashley on the stairs. A number of people did.

One evening, tidying his sock drawer, I came across letters from Susan beneath the lining paper. They were about why she was leaving. 'I want children,' she wrote with a Greek 'e'; 'but at 29 with 30 looming . . .' And she wrote, 'I love you.' What did it mean, his keeping them hidden?

I waited with the light off, got bored, wanted to read, but switching on the light would have dissolved my purpose. The letters lay on the table. After an hour or so, I heard the Rover draw in a little way off. I started towards the light, to avoid this, but stopped myself. I loved the sound of his shoes on the stairs. The door opened. He called to me and switched on the light. My appearance from out of the dark startled him.

'Love! What's happened?'

I felt bad, scaring him.

'Those.'

He saw what they were from across the room.

'Can we throw them away?' I asked. The sudden glare was too much; I wanted to be back in the dark.

Clive shrugged off his coat.

'They're only old letters.'

'You don't need them.'

'They're my past.'

A slow-moving car outside sent its headlights splashing across the window.

'You're here now,' he said. 'It's you and me.'

'Me and you, and umpteen scrips and scraps wherever you look.'

'There's no need to be upset.'

'Please get rid of them.'

'They're all I've got left.' His voice slithered out black and dangerous.

'Of what?' I asked.

He didn't answer.

'And if Susan came back tomorrow, if she were out there on the front step with her bags saying, sorry, she'd made a mistake, what would you do?'

He stepped in towards me, trying to make me look him in the eye. 'She's not coming back.'

'That's not what I'm asking.'

The room was unsteady. I wanted that to be enough. It nearly was. Our eyes slid off each other. His wide spatulate fingers laced into my narrow ones. I seemed to smell Elizabeth Arden and pulled away.

Then his eyelashes wet on my neck, and his strong arms squeezing me to him, his breath coming in small sobs, mine almost stopped.

'I'm sorry, love,' he said.

It was enough. Time started up again. We moved on to supper and spaghetti Bolognese to heat on the hob. Outside, from among the dustbins, I watched him framed in the yellow-lit kitchen as he reached into a cupboard. The night air made me shiver but I wanted to stay out under the dark. Small fragments of torn purple italic moved with the breeze, words blurring among tea leaves, the open dustbins bathed in a rinse of limpid ochre lamplight. That night I lay down on my side of the bed, he on his, back to back, chilly, but in a minute we had rolled in, warm, sleepy, and all all right.

I think most of Clive's girlfriends had sung at one time or another in his amateur Renaissance chamber choir, the Europa Singers. He had me sing solos, especially echoes, the distant voice offstage. You could say echoes were my forte – well, I'd sing *forte*, but I was often so far off, the echo was *piano* by the time it reached the concert hall.

Finding the right spot to sing from was acoustic hide and seek.

'Try in there!' Clive would gesticulate towards some side room and walk backwards, to gauge the sound from various points in the auditorium over the sound of the choir.

'Bit further, love!' he'd call out.

I'd retreat, echo again.

'Can you go any further? . . . Where is she?'

I'd have secreted myself in some nook, and he'd be far back in the auditorium where the choir couldn't see him over their music and they wouldn't notice when he stopped conducting. Some were oblivious, or else enjoying themselves, and kept singing even when he ran towards them down the aisle shouting and waving as though he were trying to flag down an aeroplane.

Once I fetched up in a church kitchen next to a gaseous cooker.

I must have been scarcely audible. The rest of them sounded miles off.

'Perfect!' he shouted. 'Stay there!'

So it was I spent half a concert hiding in the kitchen. I almost forgot why I'd come, reading the Mothers' Union newsletter, an update on bric-a-brac sales, mission-giving, and the flower rota. The choir hallelujahed and I responded in kind. But I could have been knitting for the tribespeople of Malawi. No one would have known.

The Europa Singers might not be professional but Clive's idea of the music was the same, whoever was standing in front of him. It was always nerve-racking coming up to a concert but, when we forgot everything and concentrated only on Clive, we sang beyond ourselves. When he lowered his hands at the end of a concert and crinkled his approval at us, there was no feeling like it. Applause was secondary. We had pleased Clive. That was the main thing.

Around concert time I'd get so stressed I'd start to lose my voice, busk through the dress rehearsal. At the performance I'd sing, but I didn't know where it came from. Not from me, I think. I got through one tour on frequent small shots of hot Cointreau with sugar. Near the end, moments before we were due on stage, I thought I'd lost it altogether. 'I can't sing! I can't speak!' I mouthed at Clive in the dark of the wings.

'Yes, you can!' He smiled at me with great tenderness. He squared me up where I'd collapsed my ribcage, and told me, 'Breathe.' I drew confidence from his looking confident in me. 'Go on!' he said. The next minute I was walking out on to the stage. I love that moment before a performance when you meet the audience for the first time. In this ancient horseshoe theatre in Arezzo, city of Piero della Francesca, we stood flooded with hot white light, a haze over the auditorium radiating coronas, glistening circles of light in every colour. Sudden applause, and the front of the stage turned gold; through spangles of light on my eyelashes I saw Clive run to the rostrum. His face tilted to greet every part of the theatre. He bowed, his dark hair falling forwards, flipping back, and turned, gleaming. He looked at us until he knew we were with him. Then his arms rose . . . '*Splendoribus . . . magnificat . . . glorificamus . . . luceat . . . vivificamus . . . sanctus . . .*' Our voices made waves, changed space, left peace, then we stood, breathing, glinting in the silence.

Clive's professional group was the London Lassus Ensemble (LLE), which he had founded in 1974. They specialized in the music of the sixteenth-century Flemish composer Orlandus Lassus (Rolande de Lassus, Orlando di Lasso – there are a dozen or so versions of his name), but though mostly Renaissance, their repertoire could stretch from medieval to Baroque. They performed mostly at the South Bank Centre or on BBC Radio 3, but sometimes went further afield. There's a photo of the ensemble in seventeenth-century garb in a Venetian palace, the Ca' Pesaro. Princess Margaret in a ballgown is leaning across a table to present Clive with a rose. He looks like a king in his long curly wig and shiny brocade.

Clive worked from when he got up in the morning until he went to bed at night. He worked weekends and when other people were on holiday. Christmas and Easter he never stopped. If he had a few minutes' lull, he did the *Times* or *Observer* crosswords.

At night, if we were home, I'd serve dinner on an adjustable table in front of the television. A forkful of spaghetti in one hand, a pen in the other, Clive could eat, read a microfilm on his portable reader, transcribe a manuscript, watch football and talk to me about my day at the office all at once. The meal over, we'd have coffee and Clive would pat his pockets for his packet of Silk Cut king size and light up.

'Mind if I have a puff?' he'd say if I was still eating. No argument I might pose about singers and cigarettes not going together ever cut any ice. He smoked around fifteen a day. A lot of singers smoked then.

Many evenings we were out at rehearsals, concerts or recording sessions and it would be eleven or midnight when I started supper. I'd bang frozen veg on the counter, peas snookering out over the kitchen floor. Clive sometimes played patience to wind down before bed. His family used to play cards in the air-raid shelter to keep the kids from being frightened. It helped Clive relax after the high of a night's music. I'd doze off to the slap of cards on Formica.

Lassus had been close to his patron, Duke Wilhelm of Bavaria. Like the family dog, he reflected the mood of the Court. His music was jubilant and full of hope when the Duke got married, and melancholy when the Duke was miserable.

Clive used the Duke's 1568 marriage to Renata of Lorraine for three programmes going out on the day Prince Charles married Diana in 1981. It was BBC Radio 3's special contribution to the celebrations. Afterwards the music and text were bound in leather and sent to the palace as a wedding gift from the channel. Clive made a musical reconstruction of the sixteenth-century Bavarian wedding ceremony and feast.

The day of the royal wedding was a public holiday. We watched it on TV, and turned down the sound when the 1568 royal wedding came on the radio. The camera panned along the crowd, talking to tourists. They wondered in different accents what Diana, still known as 'Lady Di', would be wearing. Renata's dress had been heavy with pearls. Diana's dress filled her carriage. I wanted a wedding dress. I wanted to be called Mrs Wearing. I rehearsed my married name *sotto voce*. The Bavarians had celebrated for a week with banquets and jousting and specially commissioned music. The BBC celebrated morning, afternoon and night. Lassus had excelled himself. Charles and Diana said, I do. I wanted to say I did too. I cried when they kissed on the balcony. Wilhelm and Renata ate baked swan brought in high above their heads on silver platters. I roasted a chicken. When it was all over we went to bed with the sounds and images of weddings past and present in action replay. Dressmakers worked overnight to reproduce Diana's gown for when the shops opened next day. They needn't have lost sleep on my account. Marriage was still a way off. We had an international festival to organize for Lassus' 450th birthday the following year, and that ate up the savings intended for putting down a deposit on a flat.

Clive held a strong conviction that marriage involved furnishing your bride with owner-occupier premises, and would not wed until he could put that kind of roof over my head. I told him I would rather live in a cardboard box with him than anywhere without him. I meant it. Trouble was, so did he.

I'd met and fallen in love with Clive when I was twenty-one and he was forty. I thought about how I might have to spend my old age alone if he died first, calculated how old he'd be when our children reached adulthood if we had them this year, next. He'd be a pensioner when they were at university. 'Poor people have babies in Biafra,' I said.

I didn't like the flimsy alternatives to being called 'wife'. 'Girl-friend' sounded temporary, 'partner' tax-related. Why stick at 'fiancée'? Why not 'wife'? Clive's uncle Geoffrey suggested POSSLQ (person of opposite sex sharing living quarters) and he called me 'niece'.

'Ï lo-vé yo-uu,' Clive would say, pronouncing every syllable like in Old English.

'Ï lo-vé yo-uu,' I'd say.

'I love you totally,' he'd say. 'Honey chil', honey lamb . . .'

But I wanted to know I was different, that he loved me more, loved me most, that it was for keeps.

Pending a wedding, we had a kind of honeymoon weekend in Paris to be going on with. The paths of the Tuileries fanned out around us as we planned our future. In the Latin Quarter we ate couscous and went to the little Ionesco theatre's play of the day, *La Cantatrice Chauve* (*The Bald Primadonna*). I wore a gamine haircut and striped T-shirt and we photographed each other in the Jardins du Luxembourg pulling French faces, Clive speaking the script from the Cointreau ad. 'Bitterr herbs . . .' he kept saying, because I liked the French sound. 'Bi-terre . . . 'errbes . . .' That was the photo I gave the police when Clive went missing.

Clive smoked Gitanes and I tried to smoke them too. The smoke dissipating made us think of time constantly dissolving. There is a scene in Sartre's *La Nausée* where the character grabs a door handle and, in that moment, forgets where he's stepping out from or through to, the door handle dead in his hand, an indeterminate threshold between past and future.

I tried oysters, letting each one slip raw and whole down my throat. It was like eating the sea. Later, on the hotel bed, I lay mute, nausea coming in waves, a television sending raucous laughter from the room below. Clive got me to the bathroom, nursed me.

'What kind of hair would our babies have?' I asked, as we

lay waiting for it to be morning. 'Curly like me . . . dark like you . . . ?'

'Oh, like you, like you, I hope,' said Clive.

But when I opened my eyes I could see he was talking indefinite future. He was looking out between the shutters at pigeons roosting on a grey slate roof.

'Try to get some shut-eye,' he said.

I wondered if pigeons sleep with one eye open so they can see the future coming.

Clive was always racing against the clock. He talked fast, to try to keep up with his thoughts perhaps, or because he had no time to lose. At school, he'd been trained on Gilbert and Sullivan, and could enunciate clearly faster than most people could take in what he was singing or saying.

We lived immersed in Renaissance Europe. I think we were more familiar with life in 1580s Mantua and Ferrara, where the creative arts were central to life, than we were in 1980s London, where anyone performing outside a narrow popular range had to fight for every concert.

What we couldn't have done with a bit of Renaissance patronage. In sixteenth-century Ferrara, the best female singers, 'The Three Ladies', were so prized, the dukes would exclude courtiers from their recitals, and allow only choice guests to attend. The ladies were even taken to the palace tower to perform, for greater privacy. 'Musica riservata,' they called it. It was that kind of special music, that should have been kept for best, that Clive and the Lassus Ensemble made. No one had heard of it before, but when they heard it audiences clapped a lot. Sometimes they cried.

Maybe it was because Clive searched sources for the original impulse of the music that his performances had such impact. He recreated that impulse in himself by coming very close to the composer and the circumstances in which a piece was written. This was no mere academic reconstruction. He was interested in every detail, including the acoustics of the original buildings in which the music was performed. Clive took hundreds of snap-shots of palaces, cathedrals, paintings and artefacts of the time, many a shade of underwater green or ochre. Photo albums were full of blurry shapes on grainy backgrounds, camera flash on glass cases. To anyone else the photos were unintelligible. Only Clive knew that a grey blodge represented a fine crystal chalice studded with sapphires, or that dark patches on a wall were fragments from a fresco. We had taken umpteen shots of a miniature wooden model of sixteenth-century Munich. The pictures were completely out of focus as we had leaned over the glass case, drawn into street after street. We wanted to climb right inside and walk around. Our curling photos were geometric assemblages of grey-brown blur, but we saw the Munich of our imaginations.

Our photographs were all marred, indecipherable, but the contents were held in Clive's head. The rooms of our flat were lined with manuscripts, jottings, paraphernalia that meant nothing to anyone but Clive, but through his knowledge, his understanding, there came from these items sublime music. It was like the way life, love, identity even, exist apart from and beyond brain and bone and mind and being.

Clive might have been obsessed with tracking physical detail but this was his passage towards the 'other', the metaphysical truth. History helped him recreate the right circumstances for performance. But it was the living event that unlocked an under-standing of the inexpressible, evoking a response from deep inside, the still place that is spirit. I think that's why he was such a

perfectionist, trying so hard to 'get everything right'. He wanted
to ensure nothing got in the way. He and his musicians had to be
vessels, empty of self, to allow the pure music to emerge.

We were always walking through ruins, with Clive describing the
life that had gone on there, pointing to nothing, telling me what
used to be, and how everything led to now. He traced his line
back to 1066. That's when the de Warin family arrived from
Normandy with William the Conqueror. They settled in the Lake
District. When we were new to each other, Clive took me up to
Ambleside to show me his childhood, and there were things still
to see. Grandpa Wearing was an architect who built a Swiss log
chalet on Lake Windermere and ran a pub called the Golden
Rule. Clive and his mother and older brother were evacuated to
the Golden Rule during the war while his dad was away plotting
the positions of incoming enemy aircraft. Among the mountains,
Clive looked even more Celtic, craggy, with the bone structure of
a film star. He showed me scree slopes he had run down as a kid,
places he had fished, and Wearing's bookshop, where he'd helped
his great-aunt May to put the prices on flyleaves.

We were in an antique shop in Grasmere one afternoon when
Clive picked up a silver spoon. He held it up to show me a wildly
embellished W engraved on the handle.

'Aaah!' said the shopkeeper. 'Are you a Wearing?' She had
recognized the Wearing nose and the W convinced her.

Clive often sang the songs he heard as a child. They were
what he sang when he wasn't thinking. He sang them when
he was happy. Life with a singer, I had imagined before my life
with a singer, would be all song – I thought I'd be serenaded
at supper, lullabied in the night. I was expecting opera and orato-
rio, but when Clive relaxed, he crooned:

*'I love coffee, I love tea*
*I love the Java jive and it loves me*
*Coffee and tea, 'n' the Java and me,*
*A cup, a cup, a cup, a cup, a cup.'*

And one I could never hear enough of:

*'My very good friend the milkman said*
*That I should marry you . . .'*

As well as loving medieval and Renaissance music, Clive worked with the very newest works as chorus master to the London Sinfonietta, a contemporary music group he helped found in 1968. The scores were huge. We had no bag big enough, so he carried them under his arm, with shopping bags shielding either end. And they were hard to read. The notation bore little resemblance to conventional music, but Clive could look at a page scored with however many staves, marked with postmodern signs and squiggles, and read it straight off, hearing it in his head. He didn't need a tuning fork; he grew up with perfect pitch, simply remembering the sounds of notes. He remembered the tuning on his childhood piano, which was a quarter tone flat, so he would recall that and adjust it up to get the desired note. He'd come a long way from that family upright in the Midlands, on which all the kids had had piano lessons to take their minds off the war, to working with big-name composers in London's best concert halls.

It was through the Sinfonietta that Clive met John Tavener. *The Whale* was the group's first concert, recorded afterwards in Abbey Road with one or two of the Beatles, and filmed for TV. Clive and

John became great pals and made a lot of noise singing late into the night. They worked together on John's opera *Thérèse*, about a French poet saint who died in her teens. A crowd of friends drove all the way to Lisieux, erstwhile home of the saint, in John's Rolls-Royce. The project took years and nearly foundered when composer and librettist could not agree. Clive was mediator as well as creative collaborator. John used to talk on the phone to Clive for hours as he worked on the score, sometimes in the middle of the night. Clive was happy to help and I accepted these nocturnal chats as a musical necessity.

*Thérèse* premiered at Covent Garden in October 1979. Clive was Assistant Conductor, directing offstage music from the wings – lots of distant voices in this piece – and acting as chorus master. The Covent Garden chorus was away in Japan so Clive used his own Sinfonietta chorus. After the show, people in positions of power offered to help his career. But Clive was modest, unwilling to push himself forward. The applause, the last-night dinner at the Garrick Club, hints and promises all made it feel like we were on the threshold of success. But in the morning we were in exactly the same place. Clive pushed a few doors but nothing happened. We woke up, all the more walled in by boxes of unsung music, Clive's tailcoat back in the wardrobe. He was sometimes terrified when there was no money, no work on the horizon, time passing, bills. He would turn pale opening the post. We managed, but things were tight.

One summer's day I bought strawberries on the way home from work, two punnets weeping red through the brown paper bag in the palm of my hand. I left them on the draining board. A little later Clive came in all smiles, holding something behind his back, saying he had a lovely surprise.

'Wait there!' he said, hurrying to the kitchen. In the silence, I knew it was strawberries. He had wanted to treat me. I was profligate, careless with money. He came back with two glass dishes, strawberries dressed with top of the milk and a sprinkling of sugar.

'Strawbugs!' He smiled.

Why did I have to buy two punnets?

Late at night we would stop at the corner shop on the way home for supper ingredients and, if we were feeling flush, mini-cheesecakes. My cooking was no great shakes but Clive loved everything I made, even when it was horrible – burnt on the outside, raw inside or with too many tastes cancelling each other out. He went on congratulating me on my food with great tenderness.

'This is disgusting,' I'd say.

'No, no,' he'd protest. 'It's made with my favourite ingredient . . . L-O-V-E!'

'Ah! . . . but I don't think I should have added the curry powder.'

'No, honestly, darling, it was delicious – just couldn't manage any more,' he'd say, scraping it into the bin. He used to speak of sending me on a cookery course. 'You could learn cordon bleu . . .'

'No fear!'

'I think you'd enjoy it. Oh well . . . fancy some cheese and biscuits?'

One morning Clive went quiet, sitting on the bed opening brown envelopes.

'What's up?' I asked him. He looked as though he were dimming. He stood up and put a red electricity bill on the mantelpiece.

'We need to pay this, but what with?'

I think he buffered me from reality whenever he could. It really upset him that he couldn't provide for me and his children in the way he wanted to.

'Every visit to that corner shop is hell,' he said. 'Every time we're spending money we haven't got. You seem oblivious.'

'We have to eat,' I said.

'But they're expensive,' he said, his voice tight.

'Where else can we go shopping at that time of night?'

'I know . . .'

It all started to come out. Clive never knew how we would get from one month to the next. The poverty was humiliating. His clothes were worn. He had on his uncle's shoes.

'Look at this mac!' He shrugged himself into it. 'It's ridiculous!' It was true that the short length had been a long time out of fashion.

'It's no wonder I don't get taken seriously as a conductor looking like this,' he said.

'You *are* taken seriously. No one else can do what you do.'

'But does anyone ever commission me? Does anyone ever ask me to do what I do?'

'The Sinfonietta, the BBC . . .'

'I make all the running.'

Clive was now sitting on the bed with his head down. I knelt by him, looking up into his face.

'You get superlative reviews, darling, but what you conduct is rare – no one ever heard of it before . . .'

'But *other* people make it in these fields.'

'They've got private money . . .'

'I've worked and worked. I do my best. Does anyone even thank me? Every day, seven days a week, three hundred and sixty-five days a year, I work. Why is it so hard? Why don't I get the jobs?'

His shoulders began to shake. My arms went round him.

'I feel,' he gasped, 'like a man of straw!' His voice cracked open and weeping came, the tears falling on to his mackintosh. Somehow I couldn't hold him right, we weren't fitting together like we usually did. Then suddenly he held me so tightly it was hard to breathe. He held on a long time, his ribcage heaving, chest hollowing. It was as if all hope were trickling out on to the floor. He'd tried to keep it in, but despair finds its own level.

Suddenly he released me and rushed out of the room. I stood, my arms reaching after him.

'Darling!' I cried. I was afraid. I'd never seen him so agitated. What was he doing? He had seized a pile of hundreds of little flimsy order forms for books he had reserved at the British Museum. Wheeling round to the middle of the room, he flung these into the air and pulled me to him under the storm of pink papers tumbling slowly around us. He held me so hard, his body racked mine, the thin pink chits floating down, falling on every part of the floor. It was as though Clive himself had burst. As the papers settled, his sobs quietened.

'I *love* you!' I gripped him, fierce with fear and defiance at our circumstances. 'You are the best man in the world!'

'You haven't seen the others.'

'I don't want to!'

'Oh, good . . .' Clive smiled and I knew we were out of the woods for that night at least. We knelt down and started picking up all the chits, each carbon copy imprinted with faint manuscript references, titles, the familiar names of composers. This lot alone represented hundreds of hours of work, and there were more piles stored in boxes. Under the windows the pink chits picked up red dust where the long red curtains were crumbling. I didn't know fabric could crumble but there were threadbare patches and a coating of red on the sideboard and on the blue carpet all around. The foam in the sofa sent up dust every time we sat down. None of the doors shut unless we applied particular knacks – lift, lean. The kitchen cupboard doors and wardrobe doors each made their own creak, clatter or bang. The disintegration of our physical surroundings made every activity – sitting down, cooking, washing, going to bed – a bit uncomfortable. The place did not hold us, it tipped us up or struck back at us. We were forever engaged in small wranglings to be comfortable, to have order. We gathered the chits once more into a neat stack and placed them back on the desk next to a small plastic jar containing Clive's kidney stone, another memento of pain past. We went on finding pink chits under chairs and behind boxes for days and weeks afterwards.

Now that I had moved to the press and public relations department at work, I wanted to do a PR job on Clive as a conductor. He was sceptical of things ever changing but agreed to let me have a go. I put together a glossy brochure on each of his ensembles, with facsimile illustrations from the Renaissance and striking photographs of him. We got a list of the 97 opera houses and 105 symphony orchestras and other musical establishments in West Germany. Clive's first choice was the North German Radio Choir, the Norddeutscherrundfunkchor. He thought them the best in the country, so we wrote there first. Straight away Clive received an offer of a month's conducting while their resident director was away. It included a recording with the Hanover Radio Orchestra.

Clive looked the business, in lightweight brown tweed, leather shoes and a long black mac. He had virtually no spoken German and was trying to learn from a phrase book. I was nervous when I saw him off to Hamburg. The rehearsals would be OK but how he'd manage in between would depend on their goodwill and skills in English.

Life without Clive was awfully quiet. Everything seemed pointless when he wasn't there. I was just waiting until it was time to be with him again. I flew out to Hamburg for the second half of his stay. He spoke to the choir in a strange mixture of languages. The singers were clearly on his side and strained to follow his meaning. Their faces would go cloudy for a while and then different ones would pipe up and suggest what it was they thought he was saying. My 'O' level German was suddenly of great use. They were to rehearse some Poulenc songs and Clive asked, did they have a speaker. Yes, they said, and pointed to a lady in the front row.

'*Gut!*' said Clive. '*Also du bist der Sprecher, ja.*' He had not grasped the business of using formal plural and gave the impression of being very intimate with everyone, to the annoyance of some of the men when Clive was addressing their wives. He launched into a song but they stumbled when they reached a spoken part. The lady had missed her cue. 'Ah!' they cried. 'We thought you wanted to know who is our union spokesman!' In the end the shop steward happily spoke the Poulenc lines and looked as if she enjoyed herself.

Clive was overwhelmed by the comfort of life for German musicians. It was amazing to meet singers who had daily work and nice homes, pensions even. So different from the situation in England. And yet the British musicians were better because, with insufficient funds for much rehearsal time, they had to be good sightreaders to get the work. In Germany, spoiled for rehearsal time, the singers were not quick readers. When Clive introduced a new piece a couple of days before a concert, I thought they were going to refuse. '*Es ist zu schwer,*' they said, 'too difficult'. Clive dismissed their fears, and schooled them until they sang as they'd never sung before. At the performance they glowed, dizzy-eyed at themselves. The audience stormed applause.

We played with the idea of moving to Germany for the ease, but Clive didn't want to be so far from his kids and I felt strange about living among a nation which had murdered some of my family and tried to wipe out the whole of my race.

So we pressed on, reset our sights, worked harder.

We did get ourselves some ease. In the summer of '82 we had a package holiday just like anyone else. Mostly when we went away it was to perform or research. And we never missed an opportunity to scout for recording venues, running into churches and cathedrals to test the acoustics and running out again. But for once we had a work-free break, ten days in Spain in a resort called Malgrat de Mar. We worked so hard to clear the decks that by the time we got on the plane we were completely exhausted. The holiday was a shock. We slept for much of the first few days, then we found a routine. After an hour in a café, the package hotel coffee being undrinkable – actually green – we went to the beach. Clive always had a jacket over his shoulder – 'How else to carry my wallet?' he reasoned. We had a flight bag and a beach bag. We had books, suntan preparations of different factors, a bottle of water against dehydration, swimming togs, towels and beach mats. We always had a two-day-old copy of *The Times* we managed to pick up in town. Getting comfortable with all the books and diversions within reach and protected from salt and sand was a palaver. I lay down. Clive lay down. I started to relax.

Clive sat up. Then he'd ask me what I wanted to do for lunch. Quite frequently he'd ask the time.

'Ten minutes after you last asked,' I said. 'We just got here.'

Poor Clive did not enjoy swimming, did not like water, and had no inclination to sit still in the sun on a beach.

At dinner we always sat at the same table with the same couple and the same bottle of sangria appeared night after night, despite our protests, until Clive finished it. The dining room was full of English people who didn't speak much to each other. We, on the other hand, never stopped. We soon signed up for a trip to Girona and gravitated to the cathedral. Then Barcelona for another cathedral and a meal in a basement Catalan restaurant. I thought it one of the best meals I had ever eaten, though the food was not like anything I knew. That night I was so ill Clive had to summon a doctor. I languished in bed in a darkened room for the rest of the holiday, emerging thin and pale the day before we were due to leave. I don't know how Clive coped with Malgrat and the beach on his own.

On our last day, hours before catching the plane home, we went down to the beach so I could take a last swim. I waded in and left Clive with *The Times*, leaning against a cliff. I was alone in the water but for a man. The water was cold and my body still fragile so I was wading gently, testing the seabed to see where I would be out of my depth. I was about chest deep when the man spoke to me. He was English.

'Go on!' he said, coming nearer. 'Go on, get in! Get in!'

Suddenly he was upon me. He put his heavy hands on my back and head, pushed me underwater and held me there. I fought to the surface and heard someone screaming. A cool, detached part of me knew that it was me. He pushed me under again and pressed down on my head and back, holding me underwater. He was strong. I fought. I came up again to breathe, scream. The sequence of being held under and bursting up happened maybe four times. From underwater I could hear splosh, splosh, splosh, splosh coming nearer and Clive's voice shouting blue murder. He pulled me up by the back of my swimsuit and pushed the man away, shouting and shouting, his voice like a battering ram.

The man moved away and Clive got me back to the beach, to our towels, coughing up water. As soon as he saw I was OK, he headed off to deal with the man. I tried to stop him, pleading and tugging on his arm. This man was dangerous. But Clive would not be stopped. He was incandescent. With me in tow he went storming over to where my attacker had slumped down next to his wife, curled up in a foetal position, his face white as chalk. Clive carried on shouting, his voice bouncing off the cliff. The woman looked to the side.

'He gets like that sometimes,' was all she said.

I wonder now if the man wasn't brain-injured. He was either that or mentally ill. At the time we never thought of how it must be for them.

'I heard a woman screaming,' Clive told me, 'and then I realized you were the only woman in the sea.'

My hands were shaking when we got on the plane, shaking the next morning at work as I poured wine for our annual wine-tasting. You can only hide so much with smiles and blusher.

In '83 Clive was asked to do more and more for the BBC. The producer who normally broadcast LLE concerts and commissioned research and scripts from Clive left, and Clive was offered his job. Being Early Music Producer for Radio 3 seemed to me like an excellent move, but Clive did not see it the same way. He was a conductor. Taking a full-time post now, however interesting, would, he believed, hamper his conducting career. We went to Gaylord's, an Indian restaurant in the West End, to talk about it. With so many waiters around and so many dishes on our white damask tablecloth, Clive looked like a prince.

'I'm a conductor,' he said, tearing his naan bread.

'You can go on building your conducting career.' My eyes were smarting from a spoonful of something hot Clive had ordered. He poured me a glass of water. Conductors who made a living out of it had engagements in their diaries years ahead. I argued that the BBC job might open doors. Clive would still have the Sinfonietta and the LLE. He also wanted to keep on the Europa Singers. By the time we left the restaurant, Clive had agreed to accept the job and would continue with almost every other activity he was currently engaged in except singing in the cathedral. We did not realize quite how much he was taking on.

He took to the post like a duck to water and his broadcasts were soon nominated for awards. He crammed his conducting and musicology into evenings, weekends and annual leave, so from working all hours as he had before he was now working all hours at a much more intense pace. As he got older, he felt this job pushing him away from the one place he needed to be, the concert rostrum, and he swam all the harder to try to reach it.

At last we were able to tie the knot. Clive approached his old college chapel to do the honours, but while they did not mind in the least my being Jewish, they drew the line at remarriage for a divorced person. So we took the next available booking for a civil ceremony at Camden Town Hall, which happened to be at 9.40 a.m. on Saturday 3 September 1983.

We spent the eve of the wedding together but I wanted to get dressed without Clive seeing my outfit, so I walked up to the

Holiday Inn Swiss Cottage where my family were staying. I made ready in my parents' bathroom, jostling for space. At one point my mother and I were side by side making up and my father was trying to see above and around us to comb his hair. It was not a large bathroom. My great-auntie Florence, who was then about ninety, had a bit of trouble putting on her stockings. Mum went to her aid and we agreed Dad would drive me to the Town Hall and the rest would come with my brother and his friend who was flying down from Newcastle. Dad went to bring the car round to the front. Thus it was I stood in the foyer of the Holiday Inn wearing a coronet of salmon rosebuds and white freesia in a cloud of gypsophila, and clutching a wonderful sculptured bouquet. My ballerina-length royal blue dupion silk skirt stood out over layers of blue net petticoat and my white lace pierrot top flopped marvellously over my hands and around my throat. Blue pumps matched the skirt. People looked at me and muttered to each other, as if I might be out of context. This was when I saw the point of bridesmaids. They are there to support you. Here I was, obviously a bride and apparently alone.

Friends and family crammed into the room, standing all round the edge. People say of marriage, 'It's only a bit of paper,' but as we declared our vows and signed our names before witnesses it felt like very much more.

The crowd of us were photographed on the steps of the Town Hall and then again on the South Bank, for our wedding break-fast at the Royal Festival Hall, the Thames rushing to the sea at our backs. A sharp wind off the river whipped trees and skirts into parallel motion. Clive's teeth chattered and my white lace billowed against his grey wool. Our friend the photographer set a timer on top of a spiral staircase, then raced to join the throng below before the shutter flicked. He tried twice and twice we are pictured laughing, half towards the camera, half towards the sprinting blur of the photographer. Warm indoors, we all made speeches and everything was funny.

We were in a room which would become the Poetry Library. I often sat there later in the silence, remembering our wedding hubbub.

We had only a few hours available for a honeymoon, so we took a ferry to Greenwich. We moved with our wedding entourage to the small red pier of the Greater London Council outside the Festival Hall. My brother flung a whole box of confetti into the air over our heads. Clive and I boarded the boat amid gales of laughter. There was cheering from high up in the Festival Hall where our wedding party continued on a balcony. Great-aunt Florence could be seen waving a large blue and yellow posy from the highest terrace.

We found the line in the ground which marks the Greenwich meridian. I stood one side, Clive on the other and we held hands. We stood either side of time beneath a sky of swirling seagulls.

'I love you!' said Clive.

'I love you!' I replied. We leaned into each other and kissed to a distant blast from the ferry horn. At that moment, that hour on our wedding day, we held eternity trapped like a butterfly in our two clasped hands.

We bought a flat in Randolph Avenue, Maida Vale. Standing out on the fire escape to take in the view of Paddington Recreation Ground and the long lawn at the back of the mansion blocks, we met an elderly neighbour who came out to say hello. When we arrived some months later with our furniture Miss Harris reappeared. She looked at us hard for a moment and asked, 'Are you the *nice* people?'

We had wedding money from my parents to spend on furniture and delighted in buying a brand new quality bed, a cream-coloured jacquard three-piece suite, and beautifully made bed-room furniture in light beech. The flat was newly decorated, in a 1930s mansion block with clean common parts. It was kind of astonishing to walk on a floor that felt solid, to have quietly closing doors, to think we were the first people hoovering this carpet and using the new hob and oven. When all the new furniture was installed, we walked round and round our beautiful flat, in a kind of quiet wonder. We owned this place and every-thing in it. In the bedroom – all creams and browns, simple, uncluttered, perfect – Clive threw himself backwards on to our pocket-sprung divan bed and kicked his legs in the air, giggling. I threw myself down beside him. The bed did not sag or creak and it did not roll us into the dip in the middle we'd been used to. In the shop we had lain on it rigid, side by side, and thought it comfortable. Now we rolled about, convulsed with laughter. It was too splendid. It was amazing.

Now that Clive was well into his full-time role at the BBC in addition to all his conducting and musicology, the strain was quickly showing. He had worked seven days a week before the job and now he was trying to pack in even more. By the summer of '84 he was deeply exhausted, but spent his annual leave conducting a Europa Singers tour in Italy. He kept going on adrenalin and iron will. We arrived home barely standing, shattered. Clive looked all in. Time and again I had begged him to do less, ease up, enjoy his life. I had warned him he was only human. Forty-six was a vulnerable age for men. He was used to my pleas to stop smoking, slow down, but there was no part of his life he felt he could give up.

'I'm doing it for you!' he cut in, striding off down the passage into the back room. He lifted his arms towards our music, which was now in library boxes neatly labelled and catalogued by a student, filling shelves on every wall up to the ceiling. 'All of it – can't you see? It's all for you!'

'Well, I don't want it!' I yelled. 'I don't want anything. I just want YOU!'

That seemed cruel to him, and to me, after all he put into his work.

'You've got me,' he said, opening his hands.

But he wasn't looking at the strain on his face. He didn't see what I saw.

Once that autumn Clive had a funny turn at a friend's house during dinner. A doctor present came with us into the next room. Clive's face looked grey, shadowy. He said he felt very odd. I wondered if he were going to have a heart attack or some kind of seizure. Our doctor friend held on to Clive's wrist, monitoring his pulse. He spoke gently, telling Clive he must go and see his GP, must make some changes in his life, take it easy. No one could keep up this kind of pace.

Clive agreed that he would and the next morning, a Saturday, he lay in bed a couple of hours longer. Then it was business as usual. I urged him to see a doctor but he said there was nothing wrong with him. He was just off colour, that was all, tired. He would be careful, he promised.

Trouble was, the music always came first. He could never

compromise, he would never produce an easy radio programme using music that was on the shelf already. Clive's programmes were of music that no one knew about, rescued from oblivion, recreated from scratch. And underneath it all, a conductor, wanting to conduct his own performances rather than sit in the studio listening to other people's. The music was his main driving force. It took him beyond his own limits of strength. That week, any week, we could not have imagined a life without music at the centre, yet that is what we were about to slam into. We were headed for dead silence.

The bracken plant was losing leaves. It was turning autumn in our bedroom. I swept up but by morning there'd be more. The bracken was my first gift to Clive. I had not repotted it in more than six years. Now the roots were swollen and all the earth was root and there was nowhere for new growth to go. We saw but did nothing. Roots grew, squeezing stems. Brown crept along the fronds, obliterating green. Every so often, after a day of bad leaf fall, I would say, 'I really must repot that plant.' I had a bag of peat under the sink. It stayed there. Neither of us felt able to take time out and do the job. We were each of us pressed and pressed by the proliferation of work. We had no time to live our lives. The leaves fell. I cut back stalks to a brush of stubble. On weeks I didn't stop to hoover, that area of the carpet looked like forest floor.

It was Clive who finally spoke out loud what we had known for a long time. 'That plant is dead,' he said. I took a step towards the sorry thing, tipped it into my hand and it came out in a solid pot-shaped mass, with almost no soil among the density of white roots worming in and around themselves.

'Oh yes,' I said. 'So it is.'

*

Time was creeping up on us. I stood in the bathroom one over-cast Saturday morning looking in the mirror to see what had happened to my face, what forces were shifting around under the surface. I was twenty-seven but felt nearer Clive's age now. He was crashing about in the kitchen. There was a sink full of washing-up to do. We mostly ate late and washing dishes was too much at the end of a day's work and an evening's work on top. But unwashed dishes were what Clive hated most. I went in. He was piling plates on the draining board.

'Careful!' I said as they clattered. Hot water was rushing from the tap and there was steam all around Clive's head, the window clouding behind him.

'How can you leave the washing-up like this? It's disgusting!' He seized the brush and began vigorously scrubbing plate after plate.

'How can *I* leave it? So they're *my* plates? . . . Oh, watch the soap! Rinse it, you'll poison us!' There were bubbles everywhere. 'Why am *I* supposed to do everything?' I grabbed a tea cloth. 'I work all the hours you do. Why don't you do something?'

'I help you!' he said. 'I'm helping you now!'

'*You're* helping *me*?' I said. 'So you think it's my job, the housework? How do you work that out?' I held one of his soapy mugs under the cold tap.

'Well, yes . . .' he said. 'It's woman's work.' I wasn't sure if he was joking and neither was he. I put down my cloth and stepped back.

'And what exactly,' I asked him, hands on hips, 'do *you* do?'

'Male things,' he said, trying not to laugh. He seized a coffee pot.

'*Like what?*' I spoke to his dim reflection in the window.

'I take care of the car . . .' he ventured.

'The *car*!!' I snorted. 'The *car*??' That meant a rare peek under the bonnet before a journey, booking it in for an annual service.

Washing dishes was what caused a stir when there was slippage, underground movement pulling on the fault lines of the way we lived.

We did take the occasional night off. I'd organized an outing for my work's Music Society. We went to see a new opera, *Anna Karenina*, at the Coliseum. It begins with a man's body under a train. Anna Karenina looks down at the man through the steam, and the event leaves its impression on her future.

We waited, half fascinated, half fearing to see Anna's demise. We'd read the book and knew what happened at the end. But the drama did not unfold as expected. In the second interval the white safety curtain remained down, screening us from the end of the story. The house lights stayed bright. Time passed, and more time. Finally a manager walked on to the stage. Pulleys had broken. The safety curtain could not be raised. Disaster was averted. Anna Karenina would not die that night. We all went home.

As Clive drove through Bloomsbury, up Tavistock Square, past Euston and into Camden, I rested my cheek on the cold window and let images of life and opera splash up against each other with the movement of the car. What made life slip off track? It starts with a step. Does the harm start with a word spoken, or the breath before the word, or the thought before the breath?

After work one night in Oxford Circus I stepped on to the escalator heading down to the Bakerloo and Victoria lines. It was the evening rush, everyone was descending – too early for theatre, too late for shops. Yet I could see at the foot of the escalator an unusual backflow from the Bakerloo line, a mêlée. People were going to the walls for support, heads in hands. Some sank to a squat, their faces twisted into agonized expressions like a fresco of hell. Others were milling, directionless, or else making a leap for the escalator, gliding upwards, looking back to where they'd come from. I reached the bottom.

'Don't go in, don't go in,' said a woman emerging from the regurgitating platform. Everyone looked as if something they had seen had scored such an imprint on the backs of their eyes, they could see nothing else. I guessed what was reflected there, but did not look. I wove my way to the Victoria line opposite and stepped on to a train full of people with no knowledge of anything untoward. I melded with them.

The first weekend of New Year 1985 we took a day off and put our feet up. Clive had just produced an enormous series, eight programmes broadcast over ten days through Christmas, and we were exhausted. Sunday 6 January 1985 was everything a day off ought to be – late breakfast, croissants and jam, then retiring to the drawing room with newspapers and more coffee. 'Re-lax, honey!' Clive said in faux American. He sat on the sofa with the *Observer* scattered at his feet. I sat across from him with other papers. We read and rustled.

'Darling,' he said suddenly. 'You've got to read this!' There was something about his voice. He lifted his arm for me to come under and closed me to his side, an automatic gesture.

The *Observer Review* lead story was *The Lost Mariner*, an extract from a book of case studies by Dr Oliver Sacks. The cartoon at the head of the page showed a young man looking in a mirror, the reflection of an old man looking back at him. Clive waited until I got to the foot of the page, turned over and we read on together.

The story concerned one Jimmie G, a man with amnesia. He could remember nothing beyond 1945. No new information stuck. The doctor had visited many times, but remained a stranger. Jimmie still thought of himself as a nineteen-year-old GI. One day, out of curiosity perhaps, Sacks handed him a mirror. The cartoon captured the horror of that moment as Jimmie caught sight of himself. The 'young' man saw his own reflection as an old man with a bush of grey hair. He turned ashen, gripped the sides of his chair. 'What's going on?' he asked. 'What's happened to me? Am I going crazy?' There was no satisfactory explanation. He was all at sea. The mercy of amnesia is that the episode is soon forgotten and when Sacks came back into the room minutes later it was as if it had never happened. Jimmie did not remember seeing him before. Sacks wrote, 'It was heartbreaking, it was absurd, it was deeply perplexing, to think of his life lost in limbo, dissolving . . . He is, as it were . . . isolated in a single moment of being . . . a man without a past (or future), stuck in a constantly changing, meaningless moment.' He wondered how to establish some continuity for this man. He wondered, did Jimmie G have a soul?

Clive and I could not get this story out of our heads and talked about it for days. The saying goes: 'that which you fear most comes upon you'. Maybe fear creates a chink in the armour, a vulnerability, predisposition. And there was already underlying weakness from Clive's overwork – compulsion overriding capacity. In remembering the picture of Jimmie G, we were staring into a mirror of our own future.

\*

Less than three months later, Clive had amnesia – different disease, worse damage. It took away all time and conscious memory except the very scrap of present he was in. Before long, Sacks and other doctors were writing about Clive. And now *he* was the subject of horrifying cartoons. *Punch* magazine depicted Clive in miniature, scrabbling blindly like a rat in a cage wheel. A periscope attached to his face focuses on a spot of air above his head, blinkering everything else from sight. His feet trip on the rungs of ever-moving time, and he is screaming into the abyss. The cartoonist got it right.

# 3

## NOT KNOWING

OUR ARRIVAL IN CASUALTY PLUNGED US INTO A NEW WORLD WHERE people were scrutinized in terms of heart rate, blood cells, responsiveness, an assemblage of physical functions or malfunctions – human mechanics laid bare. After the past week of GPs floating in and out, slow-moving events in underwater time, suddenly we had broken through to harsh light and activity. The doctor's voice was calm but urgent, his stethoscope and tie awry. He ran across the floor, making phone calls, collecting equipment, instructing nurses, frequently running back to Clive to check on him, tap something, shine a torch into each eye.

We had a moment alone in a cubicle between procedures. Clive looked up at me from his trolley bed and squeezed my hand.

'I love you,' he whispered.

'I love you,' I said. He mouthed a kiss to me and closed his eyes, smiling. We were happy to be together holding hands, cosy behind the curtains. We could not be worried. We were in our own little world that felt inviolate, whatever else was happening.

By focusing on Clive, his face, his eyes, I did not have to admit other realities.

A house doctor took me to an office and sat across a desk from me. I was ready with the case history in my handbag and handed it over. He looked at it and then asked, had Mr Wearing been anywhere tropical lately. No, I said. Innsbruck and Scandinavia had been his last work trips some months before.

He quizzed me for a while and kept coming back to the tropical question. Was I sure? He went to Norway, I said, came back with scores from Norwegian composers. Was I certain he'd never visited the tropics? Never. The closest he'd come to the tropics was eating lychees fresh from Waitrose.

Clive was not responding. The doctor rubbed vigorously at a point beneath his collarbone.

'WAKE UP, Mr Wearing!' he shouted.

Clive opened his eyes, shut them again. Blood samples were taken, measurements, readings. I held things when there was no nurse. All my life I had been squeamish. Now I forgot to be.

'What's happening?' I asked.

'He's going into a coma!' said the doctor. 'Mr Wearing! Open your eyes!'

Nothing. I leaned over Clive.

'Darling,' I said, 'look at me!' He opened his eyes.

They said he was febrile.

'Febrile?' I asked.

'He has a fever.' It was still high, 103–104°. And they said he had fluctuating consciousness, he was flitting in and out. They decided to admit him but first they would take him down for a CT scan – computerized tomography, a kind of X-ray of sections of the brain. Also, they would do a lumbar puncture to see if his cerebro-spinal fluid could tell them anything. They took him away. They would bring him back to a general medical ward when the tests were finished.

I was in the stairwell making phone calls when my brother appeared through the swing doors. How odd to see him. How did he know where to find me? He had rung my office, dropped everything and come straight over.

Later Clive's son Anthony arrived. We waited a long time sitting on Clive's bed in Prince's Ward.

For something to do I made phone calls to tell the people who loved us and the people who were expecting us to be places. The boys gave me their ten-pence pieces and went off for more change. There were only two payphones and people in dressing gowns were waiting, cadging cigarettes, dropping ash.

Clive was brought back to the ward and lifted on to his bed. They covered him with a white blanket and took his temperature, his pulse and shone lights in his eyes again. No one could tell us anything yet.

The diagnosis came at eight that evening, eleven hours after our arrival. The house doctor from that morning and a registrar beckoned us out to the corridor. They stood in the doorway of the ward with their backs to Clive's bed. I could see the shape of his legs just behind them. My brother and stepson stood flanking me, next to a red fire extinguisher on the wall. A succession of people, buckets, brooms and trolleys moved behind us and between us. The two doctors took it in turns to describe to us their findings.

They could not be certain, they said, but judging from the concentration of antibodies shown up by the lumbar puncture, they thought it was encephalitis, inflammation of the brain, from herpes simplex, the cold sore virus.

I caught at their words, looking for meaning.

'He's never had a cold sore,' I told them, as if that would change everything.

The virus, they explained, lies dormant in most of the population without symptoms. Once in a blue moon it slips its moorings, and instead of going to the mouth it goes to the brain.

'But very rarely . . .'

'One in a million chance,' said the doctors.

'There is a high mortality rate . . .' they continued.

'Eighty per cent.'

I'm thinking, does 'high mortality' mean probably live, or probably die.

'Encephalitis' they said some more times in other sentences. I tried to say it after them – broke it down to one syllable at a time – but could not seem to get the word into my mouth.

The identity of the virus could not be proved conclusively without a biopsy, which they said they did not do in cases like this; I realized afterwards what they really meant was autopsy. But, on the assumption that their diagnosis was right, they were now administering a new anti-viral drug – Acyclovir. It had only been on the market eighteen months. Before this, Clive would certainly have died. As it was, we would have to see how things went over the next few days.

We seemed to stand in that doorway hearing the news a long time. I hadn't followed exactly. Certain kinds of understanding slide away, flit past unless you grab them with your bare hands and ask, 'What is it?' and keep hold until they let drop a name, some name with which you can fasten it to memory. I could not take anything in.

'We'll call you at home if anything happens,' said the registrar. At home? Why would I be at home?

And the younger of the two, the more junior – that is, the house doctor who had been on call since we'd arrived at nine that morning – looked at me, and I saw that his tie was coming unravelled and his hair was raked upwards. He paused while he considered what should be done next for the wife who could not understand the only words he had been given to say.

They couldn't tell me, didn't know and wouldn't understand for a while how he'd be. But I knew that my husband was not about to die. That is to say, such a possibility was unthinkable.

They seemed to want me to leave.

'It's well past visiting hours,' the sister kept repeating. I refused to budge.

'You need to get some sleep,' said the doctors. Sleep? What were they talking about? My husband was here. How could they make me leave?

I must have argued a full twenty minutes. They kept saying they'd ring me if anything happened – they said it in such a way, I was sure they meant they'd call me if he died. What else could happen to a man already so ill? And how would it be possible for me to leave him alone until the following afternoon? Were they out of their minds? Finally, the sister conceded one hour.

'All right,' she said. 'In the circumstances, I'll let you in an hour early. You can come back at two.'

Nothing they said was making any sense.

The answerphone in our hall was full of messages. It was odd to come home without Clive but with my brother and stepson. I listened to the voices of friends, colleagues and family.

I sat in the hall returning calls. People were shocked, crying. I was not crying. I kept repeating the same few unintelligible fragments. It seemed so very little to say so very much. How could any of it be real? I spoke to one after another, rehearsing this new vocabulary of illness – what had happened, what he'd got, that he wouldn't make this or that appointment because he might die tonight or tomorrow or some time next week. I kept getting stuck on the word for what he had. 'Enkapha . . . enka . . .' I tried, and they each seemed to know the name and each pronounced it gently for me. I could never remember what they'd said, even immediately after they'd said it.

The bed was big and cold and smelled of Clive. I slept in his half, imagined tucking into the dent of him. Each time I woke, it was a shock to find the bed empty. Memories of the evening came back to me through sleep and seemed impossible. I phoned the ward for information.

'He's sleeping,' they said. 'No change,' they said.

Clive, even with fluctuating consciousness, must have felt my absence, wondered in the crevices of his mind, where was I. He might have been terrified, knowing nothing. I wondered in the night whether to go in, storm the ward, take my place at his side and stay there. I waited.

Next day the flat filled up with family, my brother's fiancée, Clive's younger son, Edmund. The response of the nurses at each phone call was empty of meaning.

I remember standing near the front door and seeing my parents' heads appear as they rounded the landing. I must have been holding on, for when I saw them coming up I slid a little down the wall, crying. Clive's sister came in. I heard them talking in the kitchen. I have no idea where they all slept. I can't remember where I slept.

We had not managed to get a message to Clive's daughter Alison. She was away on a sponsored parachute jump. A friend of ours spent Saturday phoning every airfield in the country to see if she was there. She finally caught up with her around 5 p.m., just as the airfield was about to close. Alison made her way back to London.

People ferried me, opened doors. I expect they fed me though I do not remember eating. When it was time to go to Clive someone took me to a car. I remember a hand protecting my head as I got in, help with the seat belt. I don't think I could have made it to the hospital on my own those first days.

The hospital corridor was filling up with our friends and relatives, musicians. They kept coming. There were no chairs anywhere. Flowers arrived, cards and messages from people, some of whom I didn't know we knew.

'Play him tapes of familiar things,' said the doctor. People went off and brought back tapes. I wondered afterwards if it might have been terrible to be made to listen to music with your brain disintegrating.

Clive was talking in a drowsy way, loving to me and his kids, a mishmash of words.

He picked up a card from his sister Adèle. He peered at it. 'Ay-dell,' he said. 'AY-dell.' Perhaps he was having a joke. Perhaps he was looking at it with crossword eyes. He was always breaking words up into stems and roots and potential crossword clues. It was how he kept his mind active if he wasn't working for a few minutes. He kept his mind whirring the whole time.

'He can read!' I told the doctor. I thought that was excellent for someone who had been unconscious the day before.

'These are very early days,' said the doctor. 'It's difficult to interpret . . .' He stood looking down at Clive and hesitated.

'What I'm saying is . . . it's probably best if you don't read too much into anything, otherwise you'll be up and down. This might be a long haul. The next few days are critical, and we are by no means out of the woods.' In other words, he was reminding me Clive could still die. Clive was reading, conscious, smiling at us. He loved us. His legs were twitching under the cover.

'This,' said the doctor, indicating Clive's twitching legs, 'is not a good sign.'

At home someone put on the television. It was the news. The newscaster listed disasters. They seemed minor in comparison to ours. The theme tune for *Dynasty* blared out. Just this time last week, we had watched it together. We always watched it when we were in. It was bizarre that it continued as if nothing had happened.

On the third day, Sunday 31 March, the curtains were drawn around Clive's bed when we arrived around noon. There was no way I could wait until two. A nurse stopped us, said we'd have to wait outside. My brother fetched chairs from goodness knows where. My parents and I sat in a row immediately opposite the open door, staring at the many feet beneath Clive's curtain. My brother stood.

A doctor swept past us and felt along the curtain for a way in. As he lifted it, I caught sight of Clive's white blanket bucking and kicking.

'What's happening?' I asked. I could not move. My father disappeared into the nurses' station. After a while the sister came. 'Your husband's having a seizure,' she said. 'A grand mal.' The sentence came out cold. The mal continued a long time.

\*

It was strangely quiet. I could not hear what anyone was saying. The world started to recede to a dot.

'Put your head between your knees,' said my mother.

Bent double in my chair, arms limp to the floor, I felt life draining out of me. My father's hand was on my back. It seemed to keep me from disappearing.

'Daddy . . .' I said. There were doctors' feet in front of us.

Things did not look good, they said in dark voices. The mal had abated, but things were not looking good at all. I wondered, did they mean in terms of his survival or the extent of possible brain damage. I did not ask.

Later I remember a finger pointing out spikes on the EEG – the electro-encephalogram, the chart showing brainwave activity. Clive's brain, they said, was in the middle of some kind of storm. The machine's pen had zigzagged crazily to indicate forked lightning in his nervous system.

There was a drip in the back of Clive's hand carrying the life-saving drug. Clive was restless and kept pulling it out. They let me stay an extra couple of hours to help stop him. The house doctor ordered nurses to bandage each hand tightly to cover the needle and hold it in. They wound cloth up his arms, as if to mummify him. Clive tore at it with his teeth. He tore and moaned. It took me and the nurses all our physical strength to pull his hands from his mouth and hold his arms down. He whimpered, breathing hard, then resumed his quest after a minute or so. He fought with superhuman strength, unaccountable in someone who had been so ill for days. Even with a nurse holding one arm and me holding the other, he was almost strong enough to overpower us both.

*

In the night he succeeded in loosening the bandages and repeatedly pulling the needle out. The man in the next bed kept watch and rang for the nurse each time. Finally, when it was becoming increasingly difficult to put the needle back in because of the number of puncture holes in both hands, the doctor ordered an extra nurse to be brought in to sit at Clive's bedside for the rest of that night. The neighbouring patient heard the doctor tell the nurse, 'This is life or death.' How strange, to have all that happening to his brain and then to have his hands bound.

The anti-viral drug eventually did stop the progress of the virus, but not until it had destroyed large parts of Clive's brain. No one knew quite how much at the time. I was still finding it hard to take in any medical explanations. The doctors spoke quickly, using words I'd never heard. The house doctor showed me the CT scan, a series of small maps of different sections of Clive's head. He pointed to areas of damage. I could not tell if he meant the light patches or the dark. I began to ask questions.

Encephalitis, he said, means inflammation of the brain. Several viruses can cause it. In Clive's case they were almost sure it was from the herpes simplex 1 virus, the virus that causes cold sores, and related to the ones that cause chicken pox, shingles and genital herpes. Herpes is Greek for creeping. The virus wakes up from where it is sleeping in a ganglion (or nerve knot) near the spinal column and, instead of causing a cold sore, it crosses the blood–brain barrier, which is not supposed to happen. The brain inflames, swells up; the skull is non-expandable and, before long, brain crushes against bone. This herpes, the little 'creeper', does not hang around but makes for key structures, does damage, before anyone knows it is there. Affected areas include temporal lobes (beneath the temples), occipito-parietal and frontal lobes (back and front) . . . thalamus, hypothalamus, amygdala; it just keeps on storming its way through. The main target areas, the parts it wipes out completely, are the sea-horse-shaped structures named hippocampus, Greek for sea horse. They are what we use for recall and remembering, laying down new thoughts.

I was not to discover this until months later but, by the time they had figured out what was wrong with Clive and started pumping the anti-viral drug into him, all he had left were sea-horse-shaped scars where his memory used to be. His hippocampus was not the only area of damage by any means, but it was critical to memory, and it was gone.

It was Clive's third night. I was home on our brown bed. I had been crying, in great gulping groans, but found myself able to break off and be composed when the telephone rang. I spoke to my boss in a normal voice, giving him the latest information. My brother took the phone away from my hand when I was done. It was almost back on the hook, I watched it, waiting to carry on, but I didn't wait until the receiver was all the way down. I let the cry come just before the phone was back. From something some-one said at work later, I believe the poor man must have heard the first second of it before the receiver clicked down. I opened my mouth to cry but a great roar rose up and up. It tore out of me, bigger than I was. From somewhere inside I observed, detached. It went on and on. I imagined it hanging over the street, toneless, you could not have pitched it. My brother shielded me as if from the impact of a bomb.

'Don't,' he said. 'Don't.'

*

I'm not sure when we crossed the line from 'probably die' to 'probably live' – perhaps some time in that first week. I alternated between hope and fear. Most of the time, Clive was conscious to a degree; at least, he responded to my voice, to my hand squeezing his. Prince's Ward was a large Victorian men's ward at the top of the stairs near the main entrance. The other patients had cancer, TB, heart attacks, kidney disease. Clive was the only one with a disease that attacked the brain.

One day I walked further down Clive's corridor and found a big wooden door with glass panels. It was ajar. I left behind the corridor full of stinking dirty linen bags and white strip lighting and found myself in a chapel. Inside it was still, quiet. I sat down. The clankings of passing trolleys were muffled. There was a kind of peace here like a blanket.

Days passed with little change. The staff worked very long hours but had nothing to tell me. I had compassionate leave from work so I hung around the hospital when they let me. My family got supplies in, waited with me. Nobody could tell me how Clive would be, or how long before they'd know. They continued with the anti-viral and anti-convulsant drugs. He was hooked up to a drip and to a catheter. Doctors came, read his chart, spoke loudly to him. They would say hello or ask him to open his eyes or look at the pen they were holding, or to squeeze their hand. Sometimes, they just stood and looked.

I stood a lot of the time too, as there was a shortage of visitors' chairs on the ward, and as one of the youngest of the ward spouses I was more able to stand than others. There were not quite enough armchairs for patients either, and the nurses tended to rotate them among those better able to sit up. I spent much of those first days and weeks when Clive was in bed either standing against the wall or squatting against the skirting board. When

Clive was most ill I didn't like to sit on the bed because it was so narrow you couldn't really perch without squashing him.

One night towards the end of that first week, a consultant neurologist appeared. Someone had introduced us. He stood, hands behind his white-coated back, gazing at Clive in the half-dark from the foot of the bed. The neurologist was not Clive's doctor. As he had come in on a 999 call, he came under a consultant physician. The physician could talk to the neurologist but I could not. Hospital etiquette dictated that I was only permitted to speak to the physician (who told me he could not answer my questions, not being a neurologist). But it was quiet, late, the lights were out, the patients asleep, and no nurse was in sight. I ventured a question.

'What do you think of him?' I asked.

He half turned to me and looked above my head.

'Lazarus,' he said, and glided off into the darkness.

Perhaps this meant life would proceed. The thought of death had entered my head. It took me back to dreams of my early child-hood – thick under-the-bed dust filling a grey coffin, the idea of no longer being. I had no notion what death would mean – nothingness, or some continuing life of the spirit. I thought we could only live on in the memories of others, or by passing on our genes to our descendants. Obliteration, however terrifying the thought, seemed the likeliest outcome. The thought of Clive, who was part of me, part of my very body, being about to die was like being about to die myself. It was like standing on the edge, in the margin between life and never. And if I screamed out, 'NO!', if I screamed after him, 'COME BACK!', who would hear? Would he?

Might Clive stop being? I stared into the possibility of not being.

*

After the first week the family went home and I returned to work. It was very bizarre to get back to my desk and answer media calls in a cheerful voice. And at the same time there was some relief in that, as if it were time off from grief. My boss agreed I could work earlier hours in order to be away by half three and back to Clive.

Clive stirred and tried to get out of bed; I knew he wanted to go to the toilet but he didn't understand about the catheter. I explained, he could just do it, do it in the tube. I showed him, look, see, you can do it here. He was not getting my drift, kept fighting me to get out of bed, couldn't understand why I was waylaying him to have this unintelligible conversation.

I called out, 'Nurse!' but there was no one. I rang the bell: no one came.

He tried the other side of the bed. I dashed round. He was on his feet, pulling away from the drips.

'I must . . . !' he said.

'No, darling, stay here, stay in bed, pee right here. Look, in the bag, down the tube . . . see? For urine, look, psss, pssss, pssss . . .'

He didn't understand a word. I could barely hold him on my own.

Frantically I rang the bell again, called out, 'Nurse!' Other patients waved that they were ringing their bells.

Clive grew so desperate, he would have pulled the drips over. I had to hold him down with all my strength. He was moaning, thrashing about, pleading – he must, he must. I talked softly to him, showed him the bag, the tube. He could make no sense of it. When he did finally urinate into the catheter, he cried.

'Sorry,' he said.

'It's all right, love!' I repeated. 'It's OK.' And I kissed his face, kissed his hands, his face again.

Some time into the second week I found Clive sitting up in an armchair by his bed, and the drip had been taken away. I nosed my way into the nurses' station where the sister and a nurse were making up the drugs trolley; the house doctor was perched on a stool, bent over some notes. Standing not far in from the doorway, I asked, were they expecting Clive to survive now, was he out of the woods? They looked up from their work, at me, at each other. No one spoke or changed their positions. The doctor lifted his pen from a chart and, although I expected him to say yes, that word did not come. I heard 'medically stable' and 'can't be certain' and 'early days'. I wanted to know if there was lasting brain damage, and what effect it might have. 'Too early to say,' replied the doctor.

There weren't too many explanations forthcoming at this point but I grasped the fundamentals. Clive knew me. Even when he was asleep and I leaned over to kiss him, he kissed me back. He knew me and he loved me. We had what was important. We were still us. He was alive. He wasn't going anywhere.

# 4

## FIRST AWAKENINGS

NOBODY KNEW WHAT WAS GOING ON IN CLIVE'S HEAD AT THIS STAGE.
The scans showed his brain had been virtually mulched by the
virus. His speech was a jumble, he could not understand what was
said to him and he could not communicate. But he could look into
my eyes and say he loved me. It was one phrase he remembered
how to say. Perhaps it was this central piece of all-rightness that
made everything else much less of a worry. I knew that Clive was
in there. No matter what the scans looked like and however
difficult it was to assess his mental condition, he was himself, and
he was mine. Our love was stronger than any of it. Everything else
would flow from that.

Soon Clive began to walk about and look around him, but he
could not locate the toilet. He could not find the words to tell
anyone he needed to go there. This led to horrible distress for
Clive when he ran up and down the ward, unable to say what the
matter was until either a nurse was called by another patient and
got him there in time, or he soiled himself. When that happened
he wept.

Talking developed gradually. Clive's words tumbled out all wrong but I don't think he was aware of that. His phrases sounded almost plausible, as though the framework for conversation were there but the content wasn't. He spoke in a thoughtful and authoritative way, in his BBC voice. He might have been holding forth on one of his special subjects. Friends and colleagues listened, struggled to make sense of it, and answered as best they could, catching any phrase that gave them an entry. Clive listened to their contribution and responded in his own language. He frequently repeated phrases like 'local people' and 'local systems'. He used the word 'chicken' to mean anything and everything, a surrogate for any noun. He would pat his pockets, looking for cigarettes, and ask, where were his chickens.

The house doctor crouched before him.

'What's this, Mr Wearing?' he asked, lifting up his tie.

'Chicken,' said Clive, smiling.

'And this?' holding up his pen.

'Er . . . chicken,' he said.

When food trolleys arrived, Clive would gesture towards me and any other visitors present; although he came out with peculiar words, he was indicating that he wanted his visitors to be served first and found it hard to eat when we had nothing. He never stopped caring deeply about other people, even when he was virtually incapable of thought. This was the Clive I knew.

He did not know which items in front of him were food. He put salt on the custard and sugar on the potato. He ate the menu.

They gave him his electric shaver and Clive sat contented, shaving his chin, his nose, his forehead. He shaved his eyebrows. He went on shaving until someone took the razor out of his hand.

I noticed this with a number of things: he would start an action, prompted when someone gave him a meal, a comb, a bar of soap, and simply go on until asked to stop. The nurses soon learned not to leave him alone in the bath.

The psychologist said we should try to orientate Clive. The staff put a notepad by his bed and wrote down the name and address of the hospital. They wrote the date each day. St Mary's Hospital, Paddington. YOU ARE HERE. But naming his location was of no help to Clive, who appeared to have no recognition even of which was his bed. St Mary's, Paddington, was just words.

I wrote Clive messages, so that he would know he was not abandoned. Other visitors did the same so I would know they had come, and Clive might possibly know someone had.

Clive's first appointment was with a neuro-psychology professor at the National Hospital for Nervous Diseases. It took place on 17 April 1985, just nineteen days after his admission to St Mary's. The encephalitis was over and Clive had made a good physical recovery. We now needed to know what were the consequences mentally. For the first time since he'd been admitted, I brought in some clothes. It was good to see him in something other than pyjamas at last. Dressed in his pale grey suit, a crisp shirt and silk tie, his hair combed, his eyes looked very blue. I pulled back the curtains just as a young nurse was walking by.

'Mr *WEARING*!!' She stopped, gaped and made a beeline for him. 'You look so . . .' She stood staring at him, her hand on his shoulder. '. . . so *smart*!' And he did. He looked the way he did before he was ill.

I was putting bags away, tidying his bedside cabinet. The nurse sat alongside Clive on the bed, looking him up and down, telling him how good he looked.

'Don't you think he's the most handsome man in the world?' I said.

'He certainly is very handsome!' she said.

Another nurse alighted, then another, flocking round this vision in the blue silk tie. As we walked arm in arm out of the ward, down the stairs and out of the hospital, a stranger would have seen nothing unusual in this smartly dressed couple. Only a month ago, Clive had been an independent human being, his brain overflowing with information and complicated thought patterns, plans, strategies, music, works of art. Now the limits to his thinking were anybody's guess. His ability to speak a coherent sentence and to register what was being said to him was gone. And here we were, on the way to see a neuro-psychologist to find out if his thought processes were damaged irretrievably. I was completely responsible for his safety, for getting him across to Queen Square and back. Ordinarily I wouldn't have given a short journey like that a second thought, but with Clive anything could happen.

Getting in the cab I wondered if the driver would mind Clive's banter, or if it would rattle him. Clive talked away, addressing his remarks to the driver, who kept glancing in the rear-view mirror, curious.

'. . . in the most imperfect way, the chickens are all you would think, possibly in the local systems these are effortlessly mine you see. It's peculiar isn't it? My er, here, is perfect. She's lovely. In the event of anything mm . . . , do you find the eloquence of these systems practically speaking, anything over nothing . . . it wasn't in keeping, yes, with chickens; these places are all completely in the bottle. In London people. Didn't you know?'

I spoke quietly in Clive's ear to try to distract him from addressing the driver. He had no idea where we were going but he was happy to be out with me.

*

A lady professor and her assistant greeted us and prepared to take Clive away with them for his assessment. They told me what time to come back. I couldn't see how they would test him without me. He wouldn't know the answer to anything.

'You don't need me to stay?' I asked. They said not.

'Don't leave him alone,' I said, not knowing if they had any idea what they were dealing with.

'Don't worry,' said the professor, 'he'll be quite safe.'

I watched them go off down a corridor.

I found a newspaper, coffee. When I got back the professor came out on her own and took me into a big empty common room. Her manner had changed considerably. She seemed a little shaken. I think she was searching my face to see if I had any idea how bad it was. I asked about remedial therapy. There was nothing she could recommend, she said, other than maintaining a constant environment, some simple structure to the day, a routine. He would, she said, need constant supervision. Clive had, as I expected, proved impossible to test. She could offer no formal report at this stage. If the hospital wanted to refer Clive to her again when his confusion had lifted, she would be glad to have another look at him. When she had said all this and there was really nothing left to add, the professor did not dismiss me in a hurry. She said some of it again. We shook hands. Behind her spectacles, I believe her eyes were swimming.

After the appointment we stood on the pavement in Queen Square waiting for a taxi. Clive looked strained. I guessed the morning had not been easy for him although I had no idea what, if anything, he would have known about it. I had hoped to have a clearer picture of what the illness had done, how it would affect Clive long term, what treatment was being proposed. Clive was not better, therefore he should be treated for whatever was wrong with him. No one seemed able to say precisely what had happened, how he was going to be or how things might develop. No one was planning a programme of treatment. It had been less than three weeks since admission, and yet it seemed far too long to have come only this far. Sitting around in a general medical ward could not possibly be the whole answer, and yet this National Institute of Neurology, this National Hospital for Nervous Diseases, could offer nothing else by way of advice for now. So where did that leave us?

A taxi drew up. I handed Clive in and told the driver, 'Randolph Avenue please.' We were between hospitals. It was lunchtime. I was in charge. Why take him back to St Mary's where he would only have to sit in his dressing gown and eat soft-boiled carrots? I'd have to get back to the office as soon as I could but I figured another hour or two wouldn't be the end of the world. I would work late that evening.

I took Clive home. We sat holding hands in the back of the taxi. It was when London was still full of sparrows. Clive was quiet and seemed perfectly content.

'This is where we live,' I said.

'Mmm,' he said, looking around the place. 'Very posh.'

I had fresh fish in the fridge, so we sat down to grilled plaice with bread and butter and salad. I was delighted to see Clive tucking into a pile of lettuce. Normally he called it 'rabbit food'. Today he ate everything with relish.

It was good to be home and feeding him again at our table in our kitchen, although there was a sense in which it already felt as if we were just pretending, playing at being husband and wife together. I had the same feeling I had as a child pushing my dolls' pram along the pavement, or when we had pretend feasts in the garden with mud and sand and rain out of the barrel for wine and twigs for knives and forks. We were going through the motions of man and wife eating a meal together in our own home but we were not really supposed to be here, and I would soon have to hand Clive over again.

'Is that nice, darling?' I asked him.

'Mmmm,' he said. 'Very clean.' I think he meant fresh. This was remarkable. I put some more on his plate and he thanked me. While he was still eating I went up the hall to phone the ward and tell them we were at lunch and would be returning shortly. I looked down the hall at Clive, his back to me, finishing his meal. When I returned to the kitchen and cleared away our plates I noticed the two halves of lemon for squeezing over our fish were missing. I looked around, under the table. No sign of them.

'You haven't eaten the lemon!' I said. 'Have you eaten the lemon?'

'No,' said Clive.

'Open your mouth.' He smelled of lemon. He had eaten it. His sense of taste must be affected. Hence the new love of lettuce. I gave him his coffee without sugar. Normally he took at least three teaspoons.

'Has it got . . . er . . . ?'

'Sugar?' I said.

'Yes.'

'Have a taste,' I said.

He tasted.

'Is it all right?' I asked.

'Yes,' he said. 'Lovely.'

I'd been trying to persuade him to give up sugar for years. Now it seemed he could kick the habit overnight. His brain might be in a bad way but, hey, we could reap the benefit for his teeth.

*

That trip home made me realize we were not prisoners. We could do this again. Maybe he could come home for weekends. It had to be good for Clive to be in a normal environment and surrounded by familiar things, I thought, even if he apparently did not recognize them.

To my surprise, the hospital said yes, that we could try it. They would give me a bag of medication with instructions about when Clive should take what. I could lock the front door and hide the key, I told them. Clive's kids would be around to help.

Bank Holiday Monday, 6 May, was my twenty-eighth birthday. Clive was home for the weekend. His elder son and daughter were providing back-up. Some friends had come for breakfast with a present for Clive to give me. Caroline handed him a little parcel and whispered in his ear. He smiled when he heard the reason. I went over and told him I thought it was for me. He looked at the tiny parcel in his hand as though he could not imagine how it got there. I took it from him and kissed his cheek. It was a pair of lapis lazuli earrings. He looked uncomfortable at being thanked for something he had no knowledge of. That same weekend was his daughter Alison's twenty-first. She came for lunch. Clive wrote in his diary, no doubt at her prompting, that we gave her 'a very pretty watch'. We kept asking Clive to write things in his diary as we thought it would help him to register what was going on, but we had to tell him what to put and then he laughed and wrote his own version of what we had asked him to write. What came out was a mix of the ongoing narrative, items and events of everyday life that we dictated for his record, combined with Clive's wit, his heart and clues as to what small insights he might have through the chaos of a badly smashed-up brain.

\*

Saturday 11 May was Clive's forty-seventh birthday. My parents were with us and I know that Clive, as he wrote his diary, was doing his best to compliment my mother, assuming she had done the cooking (which she had). It was nice that he knew my parents and was still, from out of his confusion, the gallant son-in-law. He wrote:

> I am 47 years old today. Today is my birthday.
> 10.04  Breakfast finished (cereal, milk, toast and honey and coffee; two cups of coffee; and two pills)
> [Up to here dictated verbatim]
> 1.07pm  Lunch finished (after delicious eats) [Clive's nod to my mother in parenthesis] – chicken
> 1.16pm  coffee attacked me and won
> 1.17pm  I've eaten London food which is magnificently satisfying.

Already here Clive is noting the time of day. This would suggest that while he was still thought to be completely bewildered, he had started to need to identify the minute where he found himself. By noting the exact time, he was already fighting his way back.

The next day I held a birthday tea party and baked cakes, Dutch *spekulaas* biscuits, scones. Everyone I invited came bearing cards and presents for Clive. It meant the place was rather full. It was a mistake. Clive was overwhelmed, unable to follow any conversation. He did a lot of tight-lipped pacing. One or two guests spoke effusively to him, tried to bring him into the conversation, and then he exploded, shouting in a voice that blasted people out of the water. A number of them never visited again.

We were only six weeks into this, but life had changed

drastically. We had always been gregarious, loved nothing better than a good party with our friends. I thought the sight of familiar faces and a happy atmosphere would do Clive good. I could not have been more wrong. It was positively dangerous.

Aside from these sudden episodes, Clive's dominant mood was euphoria. While he was in this phase, he was buffered from knowing what had happened to him, what state his brain was in. His sense of humour seemed heightened. With the little conscious awareness he had, Clive was full of wordplay, ready for pranks and high jinks. He kept the staff in stitches. Though they didn't understand what he was saying, they could pick up the gist from his expressions and gestures. He would give them to understand he thought a doctor and nurse should be a couple, or just laugh and speak and laugh so they laughed too. He might jump out at them from behind the curtain or make an elaborate bow (from his repertoire of eighteenth-century opera). He might walk behind a doctor copying his gestures and funny walk. We often danced down the ward. Clive would seize me and tango. I don't think they'd seen anything like this before. The men on Prince's Ward were seriously ill. People died. Clive was the ward jester.

His disorientation was evident. He often got into other people's beds, sometimes when they were still in them, in which case he would argue for them to get out. I heard of some ruckus on the women's ward opposite into which Clive frequently wandered, not being able to recognize his own room. The other patients were incredibly kind and sympathetic. They seemed to see him as a kid brother who needed watching. But the men around him were often too sick themselves to ring the bell, or to keep telling him which was his bed. They could not watch him at night.

Clive often wandered off when the nurses were not on the

ward. Many nights Clive would pitch up in coronary care, asking, 'Where's my wife?'

I was always anxious if I found Clive's bed empty. The other patients would tell me where they thought he was. If he was in the bathroom and emerged alone he might walk straight past his bed and me, or walk off in the opposite direction. Each day the other patients and their visitors would fill me in on Clive's latest escapades. I kept asking the sister and doctors if Clive were really safe.

I was drained, what with the shortage of chairs and no seats on the northbound Bakerloo line at Paddington either. I had to process our near-death tragedy standing at Clive's bedside five hours a day on a diet of crisps and chocolate, because there was no café in the hospital. You couldn't even get a cup of tea. One of our friends who came on Wednesdays used to bring me a bag of pâté, or cheese, and water biscuits. I remember how good they tasted.

A group of doctors and students arrived on a ward round. The consultant introduced himself to Clive, presumably demonstrating to the students that Clive had no knowledge of ever seeing him before. My husband in his white dressing gown shook hands with the doctor and nodded to the students, a flock of white coats. Clive stood listening to the summary of his case as if he were a visiting professor. When he'd heard enough, he picked up the clipboard and scanned his chart. Then he tucked it under his arm, gave a small bow and bid the assembled company good morning. They watched him stride off down the ward with the bearing of one who knew more than they did and had other ward rounds to attend. They gaped, stupefied, and the consultant's words petered out. No one thought to stop him so I gave chase.

Clive often bolted, sometimes for a lark. I would try to catch him but he made me laugh. It was like looking after a toddler, only he was faster and stronger than I was. Once I was trying to hang on to him as he pulled with all his might to get down the stairs. He was saying crazy things and giggling, and I was giggling too. I sank down on the stairs, stomach in stitches, laughing tears, and lost my grip on his arm. He sped off. I was helpless. Just then, with Clive running free, a big buffer appeared to stop him. Chris, our six-foot-three rugby-playing friend, stood at the bottom of the stairs with his arms out. Clive recognized him and tried to escape under his arm, squealing with delight, but Chris grabbed hold of him. People in the lobby and on the stairs looked at us and smiled. I wonder what they thought was going on.

'Hello, Clive!' said Chris in his reassuring baritone. 'Hey, hey, I'm here to see you – don't run out on me!' After a small tussle Clive came back, pleased to see his friend.

The office was a safe haven for me during all this time. I could come in, get my head down and work. Here was a part of my life where I knew what to do. Normally I could step out briskly and put on a brave face.

My mind was safely occupied with Sunday trading laws, food labelling legislation, refrigerator heat compressors and the week's sales figures. During office hours I could immerse myself in events and forecasts and editing copy and the day's news as it affected our business. I needed the structure that work provided when the rest of life seemed to have caved in. My diary for that period includes entries like 'Waitrose Esher opens; Ring *What's In Interiors*; 9am operations talk, Bracknell; 6pm Royal Society: Mod. Tech. Retailing', peppered with a new kind of entry: '9.45am Dr W; 3pm porter's desk Putney Neuro-Disability' or simply 'Clive home.' There was a third group of entries put there before the illness, some in Clive's handwriting – concerts, dinners, radio programmes Clive had made that were still to be broadcast, *Sequentia* on Radio 3. These entries had emptied of meaning. They were our old life.

Occasionally work and life bled into each other. I usually managed without letting anyone see my grief, but the unexpected could set it off – a letter from social services asking Clive when he would be returning to work, a call from someone who didn't know and their shock when I told them. Or it could simply be a person asking me how things were; a kind look could be my undoing. One day I cried in the office. I don't remember what precipitated it. I greeted my secretary that morning without looking at her and pulled my door to, hoping to discourage visitors. I sat at my desk and started to cry so I got up again and closed the door completely. I picked up a file from my in-tray but couldn't see through the blur. I turned towards the potted plants on the windowsill, file in hand, in case anyone looked in. I got out my compact and powdered my nose and eyelids, but no sooner was it back in my handbag than another wave came. I couldn't seem to stop. After the fourth application of powder, I rang a friend on the house magazine.

'Ann!' I gulped. 'Please can you bring me a cheese sandwich?'

I never knew an inter-departmental delivery to arrive so fast. Ann saw how things were and sat with me while I swallowed the sandwich over the lump in my throat.

I was always deeply conscious of the rock-solid support I had from my parents, from my family and Clive's, from our friends and colleagues. Perhaps it is only when you hit something like this that you see what life is, what matters, who is there for you, how the most important thing is love. Perhaps it is only when the rest of life comes apart that the strength of love becomes visible.

*

In the nurses' station the senior registrar held a new CT scan up to the light – a big black X-ray photograph with a grid of small images of different cross sections of Clive's brain. His name and ward were printed on the corner of each, but I needed no help identifying them as his: Clive's nose and ears could be no one else's. Here were multiple images of the most handsome head I had ever seen. The doctor was pointing to areas he said were 'lesions'. They could not tell, he said, where there would be lasting damage. The bruising would subside and blood vessels would make new connections. But they could not, he said, predict the picture long term.

It was odd to see these shadowy interiors of Clive's head. I'd thought until then that I knew him inside and out. But here were arrangements of light and dark, indicating brain, bone, void. Where were his thoughts? I still could not take in whether the doctor was saying the light patches were damage or the dark – either seemed too vast to be damage. I asked again, and he showed me again, but his words were not getting into the right roads of my brain. He named parts, referred to functions, but since he used words that were new to me I could have no idea of their significance. Besides, I could not take my eyes off the shape of Clive's skull on the scan. He had the sweetest shaped head. They could never have seen one like it.

I did take in that the scar tissue could itself cause problems like epilepsy, but Clive was receiving large doses of an anti-convulsant drug to avoid that.

In another conversation near Clive's bed when he was asleep, the senior registrar told me that recovery could take as long as a year. He talked of progress and plateaux. With encephalitis caused by the herpes simplex virus, he said, a third die, a third recover and a third don't die but only partially recover.

When will we know what happens next? I asked. It's too early to predict, was all he said. I asked every doctor the same thing.

'Your husband could end up a vegetable,' said one.

'We can't say if he will ever return to work,' said another, 'or when. We may not know for six months, a year.' This was the differential diagnosis, the difference between the worst and the best, medically speaking.

The BBC was keeping Clive's job open. The doctors were giving no indication of a potential return to work, one way or the other.

I realized I was going to have to learn a lot more, both to ask the right questions and to understand the answers. There was a medical bookshop nearby; I asked the house doctor to recommend some titles.

'No need to buy any books,' he said. 'Come with me.' The next I knew we were walking into the Medical School Library. He introduced me and asked the staff to let me study there. The *Index Medicus* was our starting point. The doctor showed me how to look up subjects and find papers. I looked up E for Encephalitis and H for Herpes Simplex and noted lists of papers written in journals that I could then fetch from other shelves. The language of this research was dense to the point of unintelligible. I worked through the papers with a medical dictionary. Patients, or subjects, were known by their initials and age. The authors' focus was more on the behaviour of the disease at onset. They wrote of symptoms, the physiological minutiae that might help doctors in diagnosis, but said little or nothing about long-term effects and treatment.

It was interesting, and surprising, to me that diagnosis had usually taken at least a week and frequently longer. So the delay in correct diagnosis for Clive was not so untypical. His illness happening to coincide with a flu bug that looked like meningitis was bad timing of tragic proportions. But this disease was sneaky; herpes, or 'creeping', aptly named.

I learned that no one knows why the herpes simplex virus, instead of causing cold sores, would once in a blue moon break bounds and penetrate the blood–brain barrier, or why it wreaked so much havoc. I learned nothing about how or where the brain-damaged patients ended up, where they went for treatment.

I wrote to the authors to ask about KW aged fifty-eight, SS, forty-two. Where were they now? I posted letters to doctors in universities and medical centres around the UK, in America and in Sweden.

Many wrote back kind and helpful letters. They wrote in their medical language. The aftermath, or 'sequelae', of disease tended to leave patients with lifelong 'residual deficits'. They referred me to other literature in the domain of neuro-psychology rather than neurology, and advised referral to a neuro-psychologist or neuro-psychiatrist rather than a neurologist. The disciplines of neuro-psychology and neuro-psychiatry were concerned with how damage to the brain affects functions of the mind and the literature was written using a different bank of vocabulary. I wrote more letters. Those who wrote back clearly had some concept of how brain injuries affect mental capacity in the longer term. We were on the right track.

Long-term outcome depends on where and to what extent a brain has been injured. Where damage is diffuse, as in oxygen starvation, cells die off over a widespread area with a pointillist effect, impairing many functions; diffuse damage causes a blunt-ing of emotions and personality and is often characterized by a tendency to dissociate. Where damage is discrete – in other words, a precise piece of brain is missing and the location of the lesion is defined and dense – the problems are different depending on which parts of the brain have gone and what remains. In cases of head injury where the front of the head hits a hard surface, the brain is thrown around inside the skull, hitting first the front, then the back of the skull, making two main areas of damage. There will often also be a shearing injury from the twisting and tearing of the brain stem. In encephalitis, the way the brain swells against the skull causes damage on either side of the brain, to the temporal lobes. Mental malfunction can occur for a number of physiological reasons: direct damage to a brain structure necessary to a particular function like memory, damage to the neural network involved in the process, or damage to the transmission of neuro-chemicals in that system. Also, one function can be contingent upon another, now faulty. Take attention and memory. It would be impossible to recall something if you were not able to take it in effectively in the first place.

But however much I learned about the brain, and that journey was only just beginning, no study was required to understand my husband's heart, how he felt.

Anyway, although the literature told me a certain amount, the cases I read about bore little resemblance to Clive's. For one thing, he started to talk backwards. I couldn't find that in the *Index Medicus*. It had the qualities of compulsion, as if it were his language of choice. He spoke backwards more quickly than anyone could decipher what he was saying. He thoroughly enjoyed this, and gave the staff a run for their money, giggling when they couldn't make him out. He didn't seem to be able to recall my name, but recognized it when he saw it.

'Harobed!' he said. 'O Harobed, I evol ouy!'

'I evol ouy oot, evil C!' I replied.

The fact that Clive could spell and speak back to front with such facility and wit showed there was some real intelligence alive in there. His brain might be dark, and yet he was a crack backwards speaker. He knocked all the doctors into a cocked hat.

I would arrive in my posh suit from work and some of my allies on the ward would relay what I'd missed during the day. I would check over the diary hoping to read some revelation, any sign of improvement.

Clive dashed off short diary entries with spelling that was comically phonetic: 'pipal' for people, 'conchaseness' and many other versions for consciousness. I don't know if his memory of how to spell things was indeed shot, or whether he exaggerated odd spellings to cover his uncertainty about a word. I think he was simply out to entertain. For example, he wrote, 'Harobed (in reverse) went to steigh with her brother and his finance (sorry fiancee).'

I was soon to discover that more of Clive's brain was intact. There were not many places to go off the ward with Clive – the payphones downstairs, the tuck shop, for the time it took to ring family or buy biscuits. The only other place was the chapel, a familiar environment to Clive, who had spent his whole life singing, playing the organ or conducting in similar rooms. We would sit there to get away from the clatter of crockery in the ward kitchen, which used to send Clive wild. Sudden noise made him jump out of his skin. Always acutely sensitive to sound, since the illness he'd developed an uncomfortable hypersensitivity to loud noises, which rattled him beyond endurance.

I picked up some music and held it open for Clive to see. I started to sing one of the lines. He picked up the tenor line and sang with me. A bar or so in, I suddenly realized what was happening. He could still read music. He was singing. His talk might be a jumble no one could understand but his brain was still capable of music. What a turn-up! I could hardly wait to get back to the ward and share this news. When he got to the end of the line I hugged him and kissed him all over his face.

'Darling, that was lovely!' I told him. Clive looked at the cover to see what we had been singing. It was only an old hymn book but he examined it like a paleographer handling a rare volume.

Back on the ward I thought my discovery of Clive's singing ability would stun them. They were simply pleased, I think, that we had found something Clive could do, something that might amuse him. The house doctor said he would ask permission for Clive to play the organ. The next day he told me where the key was hidden. This opened the door to a new lease of life. Clive could sit down at the organ and play with both hands on the keyboard, changing stops, and with his feet on the pedals, as if this were easier than riding a bicycle. Suddenly we had a place to be together, where we could create our own world away from the ward. Our friends came in to sing. I left a pile of music by the bed and visitors brought other pieces. Clive had no trouble sight-reading and there were several singers who came in to practise with him; they had their own private accompanist available free of charge every afternoon from three.

Singing was in many ways easier than talking. It transcended language. And the momentum of the music carried Clive from bar to bar. Within the structure of a piece, he was held, as if the staves were tramlines and there was only one way to go. He knew exactly where he was because in every phrase there is context implied, by rhythm, key, melody. It was marvellous to be free. When the music stopped Clive fell through to the lost place. But for those moments he was playing he seemed normal. I wondered if music might contain some key to his recovery. I brought in old favourites, things I knew he liked and could play without too much trouble. Music was respite, time off from the illness, a dwelling place. Clive played and people sang, and on those evenings, for an hour or so, I could pretend we were back in our life again.

The diary entries make odd reading. I prompted Clive on what to write.

'Put anything,' I said. 'Put how you feel.'

'HOW YOU FEEL,' he wrote.

'No, how *you* feel.'

'U feel,' he wrote.

I would pass him a pen and dictate the day's news, who came to visit or, if we'd just been home, what we ate. Our diet had progressed from spaghetti Bolognese. Now that Clive would eat anything – and there was nothing to do at weekends except sing with him and cook – I served poulet noir or herrings with spinach and brown rice, gefilte fish, sirloin steak, kneidlach. He embellished the diary entries I dictated with his sense of the surreal. All of life was for him a bizarre and sometimes droll experience. He wrote down what I said but clearly had no memory of the experience and marvelled at the things I told him we had done, adding his own asides.

On Saturday 8 June, Clive's brother Howard visited from New Zealand: 'Howard appeared (dramatically) – and staid! stayed until Sunday (whoever she may be!) Anthony appeared too!' The next day we went home:

Howard (or drawoH) returned and a remarkably large group appeared, for reasons which so far unknown. Graham (and wife) from BBC (producer), Lindsey and Richard, and their daughter

(anonymous). Brian (Dr of physics) made scones. Chris sang
Italian arias in England. We all sang Mozart's Coronation Mass
. . . Deborah sang Agnus Dei in it, apparently very well (according
to her). Went back to hospital.

Many of our friends went on visiting Clive in hospital.
Different combinations would arrive after work and sing with
Clive or both of us in the chapel. My pal Sarah used to arrive with
bunches of daffodils clipped to the back of her pushbike. They
encouraged Clive to record their visits in his diary and added
notes of their own, often messages to let me know how they found
him: 'Kristine called. Clive was in a very jovial mood.' Some even
got the hang of naming themselves backwards. They attempted to
explain to Clive what he'd had:

Me, did come at 4pm (TENAJ)
Andrew came to see you today, and so did Jo (We're both from
your choir).

Then in Clive's handwriting: 'I am suffering from encephalitis!!
(whatever that is) [It probably doesn't exist – I have no brain].
Apparently you've been here for 2½ months.' A fellow patient
wrote: 'My name is Mike . . . and I'm going home today – thank
you for your conversations and another lesson I've learned in life.
God bless you and all good fortune.'

Clive's beloved uncle arrived from New Zealand. Uncle Geoffrey
was an actor and had emigrated there from London aged seventy-
four to further his stage career. He had been like a second father
to Clive and some said they were the spitting image of each other.
   On Sunday 23 June 1985 Clive wrote: 'A two and a three is the

same as my Uncle Geoff (don't accurate). He says I came to see him (wrong sword). I am not daft (apparently) My uncle Image (Geoffrey).'

I gradually became familiar with the anatomy of the brain and with the strange developments in my husband's brain in particular. In July they took a second CT scan, in which the dark and light patches gave a more accurate idea of the areas that could be presumed permanently damaged, now that the initial bruising and swelling had subsided.

A CT scan, though, I was later to discover, is not a precise image of brain tissue by any means, as it is not high resolution and cannot pick up smaller patches of damage. I already knew from the original CT scan that Clive had damage in many areas of the cortex or outer mantle. He had lesions on either side (temporal lobes), back (occipital), upper back (occipital parietal) and in the frontal lobes. He was thought to have damage also to the hippocampus and other structures deeper inside the brain. But it wasn't until a year later, when he had a magnetic resonance image (MRI) scan, that the precise areas of damage were revealed.

A neuropsychiatrist said to me once that taking a picture of the brain with a CT scanner was a bit like photographing the moon with an old Box Brownie camera. You couldn't expect to see much. But in 1985 the more sophisticated magnetic resonance imagers were not in every hospital. When Clive finally had an MRI scan it showed that the hippocampus, a brain structure necessary for laying down new memories, had been completely destroyed. It showed holes in his brain so big that they altered the shape of his temporal lobes. An American university psychology department was intrigued by the extent of damage to Clive's brain and they had a computer graphics programme produce 3D images of his MRI scans, colouring in the missing parts red. When I saw on a documentary film just how much red there was, more than a decade after the illness, I was shocked and amazed that Clive coped as well as he did with so much of his brain gone. But back in these early days we were all in the dark, just guessing at the damage, at the future, thinking that even a return to work could be on the cards. I think his doctors must have been at a loss as to precisely what had happened and as to any clear prognosis. They couldn't ever have seen a case like Clive. We were all in a state of not knowing.

The library opened the doors to knowledge that under-neath Clive's happy confusion there might lurk a whole raft of thinking deficits. Thinking and knowing are called 'cognition'. Having 'cognitive problems' means you can't think straight. After encephalitis patients typically suffer from 'aphasia' — an inability to find the right words. Frontal-lobe damage is associated with 'disinhibition' or loss of self-control, saying or doing exactly what you're thinking without the inhibiting mechanism that tells you that's not a good idea. 'Anomia', or trouble naming things or people, was already evident in Clive — he did not use my name, indeed he had clearly forgotten it two days before entering hospital. Clive's mood swings were a syndrome known as 'emotional lability', exacerbated by the disinhibition which caused emotions to show, so that he would readily break into laughter, cry or shout. This kind of brain damage left people sometimes unable to initiate activities or conversation, or unable to stop. 'Perseveration' is when you carry on doing something until some-one else stops you — like getting dressed: Clive would put on all the clothes he could see — his shirt, his pyjamas, his jumper, my jumper and so on. Post-encephalitic people tend to show aggression, to react violently in extremes of agitation. And, in among all these other 'deficits' created by the brain damage, the writers said they exhibit memory loss. That didn't seem so terrible. But then I had absolutely no idea what it meant.

Like most people, I assumed that after brain damage a 'second tank' would kick in that could be trained to take over from the 'lost' parts. I went on thinking that for a while. But though I was still hazy on where in the brain did what and how it fared after damage, I expected doctors to tell me what would and wouldn't happen, what could and couldn't be achieved. I realized that answers might be slow in coming but I surmised that the doctors would give us a range of possibilities. I expected a programme of treatment directed by someone who knew something about brains.

News of Clive's illness continued to spread and I received mail from strangers urging me to take Clive to a faith healer, serve him aloe vera, or brew horsehair tea. Did they think the doctors and I would withhold a cure from Clive if there was one? A number of letters wrote of celebrities who had suffered a stroke and learned to talk again. They spoke as if anything neuro- would respond equally well to treatment. 'It worked for me . . . you never know . . .' Some said they had lit candles. I imagined small flames flickering in the darkness.

Many friends asked me out for meals but either I didn't respond or I didn't show up, crying off at the last minute. I could not cope with small talk. What I really wanted to do in my spare time was to drop like a stone, lie down on a mud bank and cover myself with earth and roar. There are countries where you can do that, and everyone would roar or lie in the mud with you.

# 5

## LOST IN THE LIVING ROOM

CLIVE WAS STILL LAUGHING. THE CONFUSION HELD HIM LIKE CELL walls, but in that no-space with no name and with just a narrow airhole to breathe he made the most of whatever he perceived, and did what he could to keep me and all those around him chipper.

Clive's sense of fun was once more irrepressible and seemed at its height when he was home with me. It was a bit like being kids together. We'd always goofed around a little but nowadays that was our main mode. One summer Sunday I was preparing lunch. Clive was home. The children were visiting. I was in the kitchen, chopping the last of the vegetables, when Alison came in.

'Where's Dad?' she said.

'Isn't he with you?' I said.

I was up the corridor.

'He must be in the bedroom. *Darling!*'

'I looked,' she said.

He wasn't there. In the front room the boys switched off the TV.

'Dad!' they called.

I tried the front door. It was still locked. The key was in its place in my bedside drawer.

'Dad! Dad! Where are you?' the kids called.

The bathroom was empty. I ran back through the kitchen to the back room. Alison was coming out.

'Not there!'

'Where *is* he?' I had gone cold. He had vanished!

I went back into the bedroom to look round the other side of the bed in case he were on the floor.

'Darling!' I called. 'Where *are* you!' The kids followed me into the bedroom.

Suddenly the wardrobe door burst open and we all screamed as Clive leaped out laughing, arms akimbo as if to say, *'Here I am!'* He was delighted at our surprise and picked me up and swung me round, and hugged the children and tousled their hair. Later that afternoon while we were washing up after roast lamb, apple crumble and custard, he went missing again. This time we found him wrapped in the floor-length white curtains in the living room. The next morning he leaped from the wardrobe once or twice more, and surprised us by bobbing up with a great roar of laughter from behind the sofa. I don't know why Clive was playing hide and seek – perhaps his recovering brain was going through a playful phase. He seemed to thoroughly enjoy out-witting us and escaping our clutches, as if we were the parents and he the mischievous child.

Sometimes my role was to reassure Clive. On Wednesday 10 July 1985 in my handwriting is the diary entry: 'Don't worry Darling, you're getting better and better all the time and the doctors are v. pleased with your progress. You'll soon be home with me and when you've had some therapy for your memory and a long holiday, you'll be able to go back to the BBC to work.'

Sometimes I used the diary as a record for us both:

*Sunday 14th July 1985*
Alison and Edmund came for lunch. You had indigestion. We had stuffed marrow and apple charlotte.

Then when Deborah was washing up you locked Alison and Edmund in the front room and hid in your wardrobe. When Alison found you (after Deborah let her out) you leapt out of the wardrobe and shouted BOO!!! You enjoyed this game so much that you kept jumping out on us all afternoon. Then we took you back after cassoulet, spinach and then peaches and sorbet. And so to bed.

The 'indigestion' I referred to was an early manifestation of the atypical seizure which was soon to grip Clive in earnest. I thought then it was ordinary indigestion but soon Clive succumbed to long and loud belching fits, usually accompanied by jerks in his upper body. The episodes occurred whenever he was anxious or surprised and the violent jerking suggested it was caused by a problem in the nervous system.

At about this time Clive began to experience a tremor in his hands, like someone with Parkinson's disease, which came on especially if he were going to pick something up – his arm would wobble wide of the mark, as if the act of will to pick up a cup were somehow activating a counter-attack to stop him having it. I found I could help him by distracting his attention. He could pick it up more easily if his thoughts were elsewhere. Likewise, bringing cup or fork to lip set up a tremor that sent drink or food spilling across the table, and Clive would quickly get upset. Some of the drugs Clive was taking were also said to cause Parkinsonian side effects.

Both the belching and the tremor seemed to happen mostly when he was with me. Perhaps in the anonymity of his hospital ward it was OK to be completely at a loss, but at home with your wife the stakes increased. Clive expected more of himself and his anxiety intensified.

The nurses kept telling him he was at St Mary's, Paddington, but he only answered, 'Notgniddap Syramts!' and thought it screamingly funny. The name of the hospital was just so many words to Clive. I'm not sure to what extent he was even aware he was in hospital. I used to ask how they could keep him from escaping. He often left the ward and made it downstairs. Staff had so far brought him back, but I thought it was only a matter of time before he would wander off into the outside world.

The call I had feared came one afternoon at work.

'Now, please try not to worry . . .' the staff nurse began. The ward had never phoned me at work so I knew it was something bad. Clive was missing. The police had been called. When did they last see him, I asked. Two or three hours earlier, the nurse admitted. I was telling my boss I needed to go out and look for him when the hospital phoned back. The police had picked him up and he was waiting for an ambulance at Marylebone Police Station. He could be waiting there all afternoon. He'd be hungry. He might wander off again. I said I would fetch him myself and bring him back to the ward in a taxi.

Clive was sitting with the police officers in his blue dressing gown and red leather slippers, rather tired and with blisters on his feet. He was happy and relieved to see me. Apparently a number of people had called the police about a gentleman in a blue dressing gown in Marylebone High Street. I wondered if anyone had addressed him during those lost hours. It didn't bear thinking about.

Back at the hospital the nurses made a fuss of Clive and rustled up tea and hot buttered toast as he had missed lunch. I asked if they could circulate a snapshot of Clive to the hospital security people, and keep one on his notes. I asked what else could be done to make him safe. They promised greater vigilance.

No one knew what Clive might say or do next. He was still in his upbeat phase, and his uninhibited euphoria seemed to be accepted by the staff. 'Mr Wearing is just *so* funny – he's delightful!' It was beyond me how they could believe this was his normal personality.

The pranks and wisecracks did serve to divert everyone from thinking about what might lie ahead. If you're laughing, it's difficult to be too alarmed. His wild, jocular bouts brought ephemeral protection from registering the full impact of what had happened, and I believe they brought Clive relief too. It was as if his consciousness were skating about on the surface of himself, quipping and jesting, making full use of the little conscious intelligence remaining to him, so that none of us would notice what was missing. But in my heart I knew he was skating on thin ice, and there were hidden cracks.

Around the hospital, Clive greeted everyone he saw with a bow and a smile, an aristocratic wave of the hand or a small round of applause.

'Merry Christmas and a Happy New Year and Lang May Yer Lumb Reek!' he called out to passers-by in the corridor. People returned his greetings, smiled back. The auxiliaries grew quite fond of him but did not understand that his warm greetings and bravos for their services were given without Clive remembering them from one time to the next.

We were walking up the corridor after a bit of a sing in the chapel when a Hispanic lady, bearing down on us with a trolley, threw her arms in the air shrieking joyfully, 'MEESTER WEARING!!! HELLO, MEESTER WEARING!!!'

Clive screamed in terror and rounded on her shouting, in his battering ram voice. To have a complete stranger suddenly shout his name at close range was too much for him. The poor woman was naturally taken aback. She looked absolutely appalled. I put my arm round Clive's shoulders to reassure him, calm him. 'I'm sorry,' I said, 'he doesn't remember you . . . It's his illness.' As we continued up the corridor I mouthed silently over Clive's shoulder, *His brain . . .* I hoped she would understand.

A day or so later we went to the chapel as usual to sing, but Clive was subdued. He said he didn't think he could play the organ, stopped short of it, and sank down on to the front pew. We sat side by side. Clive's body looked heavy and he seemed in low spirits.

'What is it, my love?' I asked, holding his hand.

Clive shook his head and caught his breath. He looked stricken. 'What, sweetheart?'

His face was ash colour. He looked ready to cry.

'Sweetheart!' I picked up his hand and kissed it, which would normally have evoked an enraptured smile, but there was barely a flicker. 'Tell me, what's wrong?'

'I . . . can't,' he whispered, looking down and shaking his head. 'I can't say . . .' He looked down at his hands and began to cry. When he had cried in the past, he had always fallen on me, clung to me. Now he was inside himself, horrified, sobbing, defeated by what he saw. All I could do was hold him very gently, and tell him I loved him.

After a while, I took him back to the ward still crying. People looked up as we shuffled past. A nurse brought Clive a cup of tea and sat by him, put her hand on his shoulder.

'Mr Wearing,' she said. 'What's wrong?'

He was unable to answer beyond shaking his head. He continued to sob and to stare at some point ahead of him with a look of horror on his face. The nurse drew the curtains around us, screening our grief from onlookers.

Clive was still crying when I left four hours later. I led him, crying, to brush his teeth and use the toilet. I put him to bed and pulled the cover up under his chin. As his eyes closed he continued to emit rhythmic whimpers. I heard them down the corridor. I heard them all the way home and in my sleep.

The next day when I arrived after work, Clive's sobs were audible as soon as I was through the ward door. His bed curtains were drawn again, making a small tent, not much refuge. I slipped inside. The nurses had dressed him. They must be keen he should leave for the weekend, I thought. They usually left dressing him to me. He was sitting on the edge of the bed, head bowed, looking down as though he were deeply ashamed.

I sat next to him, my arm round his shoulder. He acknowledged my presence when I kissed him. He did not stop sobbing. I began to sob with him.

We sat like that, the pair of us, side by side. A nurse came in and told me Clive had been this way all day. How could I take him home, I wondered. Would a taxi stop for two crying people?

The house doctor came. He squatted down in front of us; my crying let up, Clive's continued. The doctor spoke gently and kindly, leaning towards Clive, looking up into his crying face.

'Mr Wearing, do you have any pain?'

'No,' Clive whispered and shook his head.

The doctor asked if there was anything he could do, anything Clive wanted. He shook his head again. The doctor asked Clive if he could speak with me outside for a moment. Clive nodded, said, 'Yes, of course.' I reassured him I would be just outside, would be right back, kissed him, then followed the doctor through the curtain.

He talked about the importance of my staying strong for Clive.

'Why don't you go and rest, Mrs Wearing?' he said. 'You can use my on-call room. Go to sleep if you want, the room's yours.' I nodded. The tears kept coming, dripping on the floor. I don't know where all the water came from. I followed the doctor through old Victorian corridors, the undersides of the hospital. I remember the walls as pale green. The room was like a cell, small and white. He opened a body-sized wardrobe and took out a big bottle of Scotch and a tumbler, which he left on the dressing table.

'Help yourself if you want,' he said. 'Might make you feel better.'

'Thanks,' I said.

He closed the door. There was quiet. I lay down stiff and mute atop the narrow bed. I wasn't crying, I wasn't thinking. Around me was this other person's room and there was me, not really in the room at all, just lying rigid with the room outside of me. I lay a long time, a long long time, watching my sweater rise and fall with each breath. I sat up and looked at my watch. Seven and a half minutes had passed. That was enough. I had to get back. I did not fancy the whisky. The door clicked shut and I swam my way back up green corridors to signposts that would get me out of there.

Clive was exactly as I had left him. He was wearing his summer seersucker blue-and-white striped blazer. The apparel looked jaunty next to his sobbing face. Clive has had a blazer like that ever since; I buy him the same clothes, as if time stopped then. I half hoped that the ward sister would say, we'd better keep him in this weekend, but she didn't. I said I didn't know how we were going to get home. I was crying again. The nurses said couldn't I call a friend. I wondered which friend could I call when I was crying. The first was busy, the second, a girl in the choir we didn't know well and who was probably surprised to hear from me, did come and get us. Only that week she had said, 'If there's anything . . .' Well, here was something.

We stood on the kerb, arms entwined, Clive's little bag at our feet, waiting for Annie. People walked wide of us, even stepping into the road. They looked alarmed, as if we might make them cry. A car drew up, Annie's concerned head visible through tears and windscreen. We sat in the back seat, Clive audibly sobbing, me mostly quiet with tears trickling on to my handbag. Annie checked us in her rear-view mirror, two hiccoughing people to be deposited in Maida Vale. We thanked her, and I led Clive by the hand into our building, up the stairs and home.

The only minutes Clive was not crying that weekend were when he was playing the piano. I watched him wake up in the mornings. He would stir a little and then fat tears would come in the corners of his eyes and start brimming out from under his eyelashes when his eyes were still shut. He wept from the first moment of awakening until after he had fallen asleep at night. His pillow was wet. The water loss made him thirsty. He made up for the salt by chance as he shook salt and pepper on to his meal several times, forgetting he had done it before. Anthony arrived. We decided to take Clive for a short walk, although he was crying. He needed air and exercise and perhaps being outside would distract him. We walked him to the church on the corner. We thought at least that would be a safe place to cry, people were expected to cry in church, and Clive might be interested in the architecture. He didn't even look up but cried as we walked round the outside. We saw a vicar but he did not ask if he could help. I would have liked to hand the responsibility for Clive's sorrow over to someone official for five minutes, but we were left to ourselves.

As playing the piano was the only thing that stopped his tears, I naturally encouraged Clive to keep playing. He wasn't all that keen but playing had to be better than crying. Halfway through Sunday, my neighbour knocked on the door. The two ladies from downstairs were beside themselves with the constant noise from the piano, and had asked her to let us know. I could cope with Clive, I could just about cope with the crying, but if this one effective remedy was taken away from us what were we to do?

Back at the hospital I put Clive to bed. It was hard to leave him like this. He went off to sleep fairly soon, small tears sticking to his black eyelashes.

The weeping continued for over a month. It made swallowing food tricky because of the constant lump in his throat. The tears were all exhausted but he gave out a dry heaving sob with each breath he took.

In that month we went to the Wolfson Brain Injury Rehabilitation Centre at Atkinson Morley's Hospital in Wimbledon for another assessment. They laid on an ambulance to take us both ways because he needed me to comfort him and a taxi so far was out of the question.

Clive was unable to answer most of the test questions. He shook his head uncomprehending and sobbed with each intake of breath. The psychologist wondered if it might be some neurological tic rather than real crying. That assumption frightened me. I knew that Clive was crying because the confusion had lifted, as the neuro-psychology professor in Queen Square had said it would. He was crying out of despair, because he finally had insight into his own state of mind. People had accepted Clive's euphoria as the real him when it wasn't. But now, if medics did not accept his grief as real when it was, what would it mean for the treatment he received? Would people see him with compassion, or only with irritation?

We were to wait in a particular spot for the ambulance to take us back to Paddington. We sat on a wall. Clive waited, head bowed, each breath catching, a look of horror on his face. The ambulance did not turn up. We waited an hour, more. People stared at us on their way into the hospital and on their way out. Nobody is used to seeing a well-dressed intelligent-looking man weep in a public place.

The neuro-psychologist at Atkinson Morley's had spoken of the types of memory loss that typically follow encephalitis. He said it leaves people amnesic, without the ability to take in new memories. Information coming into the brain melted like snow alighting on warm ground, leaving not a trace. As he said these things I could relate them to the way Clive had been. They seemed to describe his behaviour aptly. This concept of nothing-ness was too ghastly to comprehend for more than a split second. It made me nearly pass out with fear. And now Clive was in something like that, a great big blank nothing all of the time, seeing me and perceiving the world around him, and yet being unable to get a purchase on it, unable to live in a continuum, to move through from one moment to the next. He seemed to be lost to any ordinary consciousness, to be existing in the deepest darkest pit, seeing all of us peering in at him from a small opening way above him, but not able to get out of that hole and live in the world where we lived. All I could do was to keep hold of him, keep speaking words of love, but I was afraid that no matter how fierce and enormous my love for him and his for me, for now, at least, nothing could touch where he was. He appeared to be unreachable.

A thought seized me. If Clive could tell me, could somehow indicate what was going on inside his head, then the doctors and others might be more likely to respond to him as a grief-torn human being, and not a complex case with a nervous tic only masquerading as sorrow. Maybe Clive could tell us what the brain disease had done to him. Then they might be better able to treat him.

'Why are you crying, darling?' I asked. He shook his head without looking up. 'Tell me what's the matter . . . ?'

'I . . .' He struggled. '. . . I can't,' he sighed.

I felt for a pen and notepad in my pocket.

'Write it,' I said, taking the cap off the pen. 'Write me why you're sad.' I put the pen and pad into his hands. He stared at them.

'Write what comes to mind, why you're crying.' He put the nib on the paper; there was a moment of visible effort, then he slumped.

'I can't,' he said.

'Don't worry,' I said, 'but just write quickly what's going on in your head.'

His willingness to please me enabled what happened next. He wrote in one fast motion, then put the pen down on the tiny pad and thrust them at me. He had written in a desperate hand, '*I am completely incapable of thinking.'* I had my confirmation. It was dark in there.

I didn't know it was possible for a person to cry for so long. I heard a similar sound once, in a Fellini film, *La Strada*. A young woman loves but is not loved in return. She loses the will to live. She emits the same pitiful whimper day and night, through the streets; she sleeps in the open on the beach, like she's waiting for the sea to come and cover her up.

I wrote to friends to warn them about Clive's crying if they were visiting the hospital, and to guide them as to what to do with him if I were not there. I told them where the playing cards might be found, where the key to the chapel organ. I wrote encouraging them to come and perform music with him. I said it made him happy. I seem to have been under the misapprehension that the moments he was happy – that is, not crying – would 'give his brain a chance to heal'. Perhaps Clive had more insight than I had. Ignorance protected me from the full force of our predicament. I took the lack of a clear prognosis as a hopeful sign. I could superimpose my own choice of outcome on the doctors' blank looks. I wrote that the psychologists were 'grim-faced' but, I noted, 'I can be optimistic. Clive has resources and determination that are uncommon.' That, at least, was accurate.

'[He] will continue to need round-the-clock supervision for some months,' I wrote, thinking about what would happen when he was discharged from hospital. The BBC doctor thought he might eventually be able to return to work and suggested I take six weeks off from my job to look after him until he should be better. The local authority got it wrong as well. They offered us a companion at home for three–four hours a day for two–three months. I did wonder what would happen at the end of that time, how much he would really have improved. The local authority help would still leave about thirty hours a week when I would have to buy in care for Clive, assuming I spent all the time I was not actually at work caring for him at home. I thought I could probably manage it for a few months – as long as he slept through the night, which he didn't yet – and, besides, as he got better he'd become more independent. The possibility of his not getting significantly better than he was now was too horrible to consider, even for the medics. Better to plan for recovery.

There was some progress. The crying subsided and Clive talked less rubbish, more complete sentences. He began to make himself better understood, to remember names for things. But still no one seemed to know what to do with him. At a loss themselves, the hospital gladly referred Clive to all the neuro-psychologists I had contacted who showed an interest in seeing him. I took him to every main psychology department in London, hoping each time that the next one would have an answer to Clive's situation. But these visits never seemed to amount to much. They would fire questions at Clive, most of which he was completely unable to answer. And then nothing. Their reports would be submitted to Clive's consultant. At that stage no one shared much with me as the patient's wife. I could only read the expressions on their faces at the end of a session – embarrassed, subdued, not very hopeful.

When a psychologist finally let me sit in on one of these assessments I learned that the test materials for brain-injured people had been designed for those with far higher levels of cognitive ability. Clive was not only unable to give correct answers, he was unable to follow the questions. They would show him a series of pictures and then show him another series with some in common and ask which he had seen before. Clive did not know he had been shown any picture other than the one he was looking at now. Nothing was familiar. He didn't know what they were talking about. He was right off the scale.

The psychologists should have thrown their tests aside, as Clive sometimes threatened to do, and let Clive show them himself. You did not need to watch him for very long before he did or said something that was an eloquent illustration of where he was. A friend had left him a box of chocolates. I came in that day and saw Clive holding something in the palm of one hand, and repeatedly covering it and uncovering it with his other hand as if he were a magician practising a disappearing trick. He was holding a chocolate. He could feel the chocolate unmoving in his left palm, and yet every time he lifted his hand he told me it revealed a brand new chocolate.

'Look!' he said. 'It's new!' He couldn't take his eyes off it.

'It's the same chocolate,' I said gently.

'No . . . Look! It's changed. It wasn't like that before . . .' He covered and uncovered the chocolate every couple of seconds, lifting and looking.

'Look! It's different again! How do they do it?'

Such was the speed of darkness covering his mind, his hand repeatedly rose to reveal a chocolate he had never seen before.

'What on earth,' he asked, spellbound, 'is going on?'

It was the same with the world around him. If he glanced away for a moment, all trace of what he had seen vanished from his mind. He looked down at where he had laid out cards for a game of patience, with no recollection of the cards, no memory of the game. In his left hand, the remains of a pack. On the bed, strange cards. If he looked away for a moment, the layout of cards seemed to change. The curtain changed colour. He found part of a pack of cards in his hand, a new layout of cards on the bed, altered since he last looked. The act of playing cards might, he hoped, free him from this crisis, help him collect his wits. The momentum of each deal and turn, deal and turn, carried him from moment to moment. 1,2,3, turn, 1,2,3, turn, 10 on Jack, Queen on King, 2 on 3, no more. 1,2,3, turn, 1,2,3, turn, 1,2,3, turn. As long as he kept playing, without stopping to think, the rhythm calmed him and kept time flowing, gave him his own momentum, a tiny platform to hold him above the abyss.

As it seemed impossible to fix anything in his mind, it was as if every waking moment was the first waking moment. Clive was under the constant impression that he had just emerged from unconsciousness because he had no evidence in his own mind of ever being awake before. He was alert but confused, not recognizing his surroundings, not knowing anything that had happened, not aware of any time before this. Just like anyone awakening from unconsciousness, Clive was keen to know how long he had been in that state. And because no answer stuck, he asked the same set of questions over and over. He had a constant need for reassurance, a need that could never be quenched.

'How long have I been ill?' he would demand urgently as soon as he was over the shock of seeing me enter the room. I would answer however long it was, and no sooner was the answer out of my mouth than he would be asking again. No amount of my repeating or his repeating the answer to his most urgent question seemed to enable it to penetrate. He simply could not get a hold of anything.

'How long have I been ill?'

'Nine weeks.'

'Nine weeks . . . ?' He always said that with contempt, as if to say, well, who would have believed it?

'I haven't heard anything, seen anything, touched anything, smelled anything. It's like being dead. What's it like being dead? Answer: nobody knows. How long's it been?'

'Nine weeks.'

'Nine weeks . . . ?' He shook his head. 'I haven't heard anything, seen anything, touched anything, smelled anything. What do you think it's like being dead?'

'I don't know, darling.'

'No, nobody knows. I haven't heard anything, seen anything, touched anything, smelled anything. It's like one long night lasting . . . How long?'

'Nine weeks.'

'Nine weeks . . . One long night lasting how long?'

'Nine weeks.'

'Nine weeks . . . I haven't heard anything, seen anything, touched anything, smelled anything. It's just like being dead. What's it like being dead? Answer: nobody knows. I haven't heard anything, seen anything, felt anything, smelled anything, touched anything . . . It's been one long night lasting . . . How long?'

One weekend at home, while he was trying to understand the room changing in front of him, the belching racked him until he fell to the floor, sweating profusely. His lips turned blue, his face dark red. I dialled 999. He had recovered and was sleeping when the ambulance arrived but they took him back to the hospital. An EEG confirmed these episodes were epileptic in origin.

As I read more about neuropsychology, I began to understand that Clive was an extreme case. I had more and more urgent questions. Sometimes the neuropsychologists let me sit in on their tests.

'Do you remember how you got here this morning?' one asked Clive.

'No,' he said.

'Do you know if you came by bus, train or car?'

'I don't remember coming into this room!' said Clive, a little exasperated.

'He doesn't remember,' I confirmed. 'He doesn't know what floor we are on.'

'Do you know if you came up here by escalator or lift?' she asked.

'I don't remember sitting down here,' he said. 'I don't know how long I've been here.'

I tried to illustrate further, holding his hand in both mine.

'Do you know which hospital we are in?' I said.

Clive grew more irritated. 'I haven't the faintest idea! Are we in a hospital? I haven't seen anything until now. My eyes have come on just a few seconds ago.'

'We're in —— Hospital in London,' said the psychologist, reassuring him.

'Well, you're the first person I've seen, and my wife here is the second person.'

As Clive looked from her to me, he forgot the image of her.

'No, she's the first person now. You're the second person,' he said, looking back at her.

We were sitting in front of a mirror. Clive stood and took a couple of steps towards it, combed his hair, stepped backwards and sat down again all in the space of about fifteen seconds. Literally four or five seconds after he had sat down I asked him, 'What did you do just now?'

'I've no idea,' he said.

'When you stood up?'

'Did I stand up? I've no knowledge of it.'

The testing might go on for a while but, to Clive, every question was the first question. On the other hand, the feelings they evoked would not go away instantly so the anger and frustration were cumulative. He felt humiliated, ashamed at his lack of knowledge of anything but the fact of just awakening. When it was clear to me that he was about to explode, I might suggest a break and, after a moment in the corridor, the arrival of coffee, the slate would be wiped clean. The psychologists would talk about resuming.

'Are you ready to come back, Mr Wearing?'

'Back? I've never seen you before,' he'd say.

I would effect formal introductions to start the ball rolling again. Even psychologists find it hard to be repeatedly introduced to someone who is forever meeting them for the first time.

In the 'Famous Faces' test Clive saw slides projected on the wall showing well-known people. He couldn't name any of them, although he did find some familiar. He recognized Winston Churchill and could say Churchill if someone prompted Winston. He looked at the Queen and Duke of Edinburgh in civvies and thought they were singers from London. He said he had never heard of John Lennon or John F. Kennedy. There were quite a few faces I did not recognize either.

There were a few times when Clive went into a highly confused, manic state that the hospital called psychotic. Occasionally he was even unsure of exactly who I was, as his life telescoped in on itself and he lost all perspective. It was a wonder that, existing with such a tiny window on his own life, he was not more crazy than he was.

One night when Clive was home for the weekend, I awoke to

hear a strange noise. I switched on the light and saw him, fully clothed, trying to step into the wardrobe. In the light he was startled.

'Oh, I thought this was the door!' he said.

'What's up, love?'

Clive headed for the door out of the room.

'I've got to go home,' he said.

'You are home, sweetheart!'

He went out to the front door. I leaped out of bed.

'It's locked,' I whispered, trying not to wake Anthony. 'Come back to bed, love, you're home. This is home.'

Clive continued to fumble with the latch but I had Chubb-locked and hidden the key. Anthony appeared from the front room. Clive got a fright.

'Hello, Dad!'

'Don't be ridiculous,' said Clive. 'You're not my son!'

'Course he's your son, darling. It's Anthony – don't you recognize him?'

'My children are tiny, they're tiny. I've got to get home to them.'

'Do you recognize me at all, Clive?' said Anthony.

'Of course,' said Clive.

'Who am I?'

'Use your intelligence,' said Clive, getting angry. 'Now stop messing about and let me out! I've got to get home to my wife and children.'

'This is your wife, Dad. And I'm your son.'

Clive was shouting now.

'Stop it!! Stop it!!' He wrestled with the door handle.

'Darling!' I put my arm round his shoulders. 'Come back to bed, love. It's the middle of the night!'

'I've got to get home to my family!'

'I'm your wife, love! Don't you know me?' I asked.

'You're my girlfriend!'

'Anthony,' I said, 'put the kettle on. See, Ant can make us a nice hot drink. Please, darling, just come and sit down for one minute.'

'Let go of me,' he suddenly roared and broke away. The next thing, he was shaking the front door as if he would break it down. I hoped the neighbours would not be frightened. He would not give up, yelling, kicking the door, trying to shake it open. I wondered if he would try to punch through the glass. He ran up and down the corridor to see if there were another way out. I was exhausted, ill with tiredness, but Clive seemed to have a super-human strength, endless stamina, an iron will. He was convinced he had a wife and young children waiting for him somewhere across town. When we asked the address where he wanted to go, he couldn't tell us. When we asked the address where he now was, he had no idea. We asked how he would get there if he didn't know where to go. He would manage it, he insisted, we just had to let him out. It was as if he were having a throwback to twenty years earlier. He could make no sense of our familiar faces.

'I *am* your wife, love,' I said for the umpteenth time.

'Don't be ridiculous,' said Clive.

'I *love* you!!'

'Let me out!'

'You know me though, don't you?' said Anthony.

'You're my brother!' said Clive. Anthony was now around the age that Clive had been when Anthony was born. If Clive thought he was back in the mid-sixties then this familiar young man before him had to be his brother. There was no other explanation that Clive's mind could cope with.

\*

As Clive's confusion continued to lift, allowing him to understand and process his own perceptions of the world around him, certain things became clear. His ability to perceive what he saw and heard was unimpaired. But he did not seem able to retain any impression of anything for more than a blink. Indeed, if he did blink, his eyelids parted to reveal a new scene. The view before the blink was utterly forgotten. Each blink, each glance away and back, brought him an entirely new view. Clive was unable to remember anything for so much as a second. He had an amnesia so all-encompassing, it erased everything instantly. Clive was left reeling. He could not take in the room he was in. He saw me, knew me, loved me, recognized me but couldn't understand why I looked different.

'You weren't wearing blue just now!'

'What was I wearing?'

'I don't know, but it wasn't blue.'

How could a room change in the blink of an eye? He would stare at something, then turn to me and back, pointing, gasping at the shifting environment. The only mercy was that having no memory meant the experience was only ever momentary, as he had no means to register that an experience was continuing, let alone constant.

I tried to imagine how it was for him. Something akin to a film with bad continuity, the glass half empty, then full, the cigarette suddenly longer, the actor's hair now tousled, now smooth. But this was real life, a room changing in ways that were physically impossible. It must have looked as though the world were ending, the earth falling apart.

\*

One Saturday afternoon I was ironing while Clive paced up and down, tight-lipped. The short loop-tape script asking how long he had been ill went round and round. After twenty-four hours of it, I was wondering how we would manage the next half-hour. I didn't think we could bear it through the weekend, but while I would be free from the constant assault of amnesia when I left Clive at St Mary's the following night, there was no escape for him. He was held prisoner by his own mind. I had turned on the TV hoping it might stay or slow his questioning, the noise acting as a buffer. Perhaps he would see that I was watching and try not to interrupt me. But his need for answers was too pressing to be deterred for more than very short breaks and the fact of the television being on might rile him all the more. It was a fine line. I knew he could blow at any moment.

Clive stopped pacing and stared up at the bookcase, shaking his head.

'How do they do that?' he asked.

'What, darling?'

'How do they make the whole system change like that?'

'Don't worry, love . . .'

'But look, everything's different. How do they do that? It wasn't like that a moment ago!'

'How was it?'

'I don't know, but not like that. It keeps changing. Everything's new.'

It was clear that although Clive could perceive everything perfectly well, nothing was going in, no impression stuck. Each time he blinked and looked at the bookcase again, he was seeing it for the first time. His whole world appeared to change, to be in a state of constant flux.

'I can't understand it!'

'Relax, love. It's just your illness.'

While I knew that no explanation could stick, I had to hope that if I repeated something there was some chance of his one day being able to take it in.

'Look! See? It's different!' he said, pointing to the sofa. 'There!' He looked back at the bookcase. 'See, it wasn't like that before. It's incredible! I don't understand it. What's going on?'

'Sweetheart . . .' I put the iron down. 'It's just that your memory's playing tricks on you.'

'It's not my memory, I haven't been conscious. I know nothing at all about it.'

'You're conscious now . . .'

'I woke up just a couple of seconds ago; I haven't seen anything up till now. And that's different! What's going on? How do they control it?'

I had picked up the iron again and was going to continue with the pile, in the hope that it would restore a sense of normality, but Clive couldn't bear this apparent indifference.

'NO! Never mind that!' He wrenched the iron out of my hand and pushed the ironing board over. The iron just missed our feet.

'Just TELL ME WHAT THE HELL'S GOING ON!!!' He was desperate now, like a man fighting for his life, gripping my shoulders. We were near the floor. I was worried about the iron burning the carpet. I stretched to reach it, could feel the heat of it close to my hand.

'Forget that. Look, I tell you, everything's changed . . . I'm ALIVE!!!'

'Do you love me?' The iron was still flat on the carpet.

'Of course I do . . .' His voice collapsed; he was contrite, disarmed. I kissed his shoulder as it was near my mouth.

'You're mine and I'm yours,' I said.

'Oh good . . .'

'Sweetheart, shall I make you a cup of coffee?'

'Yes, a cup of coffee, that would be nice. It might wake me up!'

I shuffled to move the iron to safety and stood up. He stood with me.

'No, don't go!' he said.

'Come with me to the kitchen then.' Arms entwined, we set off three-legged. That made him laugh. Good, the famous Wearing giggle.

'We're one,' he said.

While I made the drinks, Clive wandered back into the drawing room. I could hear *The Generation Game* on the telly. Suddenly I saw him reflected in the kitchen window, peeping round the door to see who was in the room.

'It's me, love!' I said. He gasped and ran towards me, hugged me hard.

'I *thought* it was! Come and look!'

'I'm making you a coffee . . .'

'Never mind that now, you've got to come and look!' He grabbed my hand, yanked me out of the kitchen, and rushed up the corridor to the living room where the television was still on. A procession of objects on a conveyor belt travelled past the contestant.

Clive looked around, baffled.

'Do you want to sit down, love?' I asked him.

'No,' he said, his face drained. 'I don't know,' he said. 'I think we must be in the wrong room.'

We stood in the middle of the floor, hand in hand, lost in our own living room.

*

As Clive got more out of hand, I had less idea of where we might be heading. The brain injury had made Clive hypersensitive to noise and since they had put his bed furthest from the doors in a bid to stop him wandering, he was now directly opposite the ward kitchen, where domestic staff seemed to spend a lot of time crashing metal. The noise drove Clive berserk. When they started up he would begin to rant and bolt from the ward in anger or yell at anyone who spoke to him. No adjustment was made either to the noise of the washing-up or to Clive's location.

It was a friend who realized how dangerous things were getting during visits home. While she was with us one Sunday afternoon, he grew frantic at his ever-shifting environment.

'Why are they doing this to me?' he shouted, chalk-white with fear and rage. 'I haven't seen a doctor yet! I'm awake. I haven't seen anything, smelled anything, touched anything . . . It's like being dead!! Who's done this? Who's done this to me?' The pain of being so alive, so lucidly perceptive of the all-encompassing gaps in his knowledge, was almost too much for him to bear, too much for anyone near him to contemplate.

Our friend and I were talking. Clive, unable to follow any conversation, went into the bedroom. I went in after him as I didn't want him to feel left out, sorry for talking. He grabbed a score of Stravinsky's *Rake's Progress* from the top of a pile of music on the dressing table and sat down with it at the harpsichord. Clive's musical abilities were intact but his judgement impaired. This rich orchestral score was not meant to be played on a small domestic harpsichord and Clive's attempt to play the many lines at once and at a fast pace was doomed. After heroically sight-reading a few lines, Clive stood up and hurled the music across the room.

'Who's done this to me? What are they playing at? Someone's trying to keep me quiet! What's going on??'

I tried to reassure him, 'Darling, it's all right, it's all right,' but that only made him madder, and he ran at me, shouting, 'NO, IT'S NOT, IT'S NOT ALL RIGHT!!!' I don't remember how it was he knocked me to the ground, but I remember being on the floor, his face shouting into my face, his hands squeezing my wrists so hard I expected bruises. I saw our friend standing at the door, visibly shocked.

'Clive!' she said. 'I'm making a cup of tea. Bring Deborah to sit down in the kitchen.'

'We'll be there in a minute,' I told her from the floor in a normal voice, Clive's face still wild-eyed, shouting into my face.

'Why are they doing this to me?' he yelled. 'Why are they doing this?'

Our friend took us back to the hospital and told the sister what she had seen. The sister told us that Clive had started to be physically aggressive with staff on the ward. They had assumed he would not be violent with me. I had assumed he would not be violent with them. Soon after this incident the doctors told me that I was not to take him home for weekends any more. They consulted the psychiatry department about more appropriate drugs.

I had regular meetings with the hospital social worker. When my stepchildren first suggested I see her, some time during the first month of Clive's illness, I could not understand what possible need we might have of her. She turned out to be an incredibly nice and motherly woman called Shirley. She had a rich voice like Fenella Fielding and always made me a cup of tea with sugar for strength. I didn't get tea on the ward, except once, when I cried. She encouraged me to talk to her about anything and everything. Once we'd gone through the latest ideas of where Clive could go for treatment and reviewed the reports and advice that we were collecting, Shirley would ask how I was. She really seemed to want to know, and I felt I could tell her. This meeting was my safety valve. I felt I could open up to her in a way I did not like to do with friends or family. And Shirley supported me. She never made me feel I was taking up too much of her time. The medical staff were rushed off their feet. Shirly took an intelligent interest in current research on brain injury, she valued my input, made me feel part of the team. She let me cry. I told her how I looked at babies in pushchairs and wondered if I would ever have any now. Once, in desperation, I asked Shirley if she thought there were some surgery they could use to extract the necessary to enable me to have Clive's children. Shirley counselled me against thinking of these things when there was so much else to wade through. She gently reminded me of realities, helped me face truths. She let me sit, talk and sip sweet tea and when I cried she made more tea with extra sugar. She never hurried me away. She had a plan of action. We made progress. Shirley helped me steer a path through those first terrible months.

When Clive was still confused and cheerful, I had begun to imagine a scenario for our near future. During the week he would attend a rehab unit – once he had recovered enough, and once a unit accepted him. I would arrange transport and a suitably trained assistant to escort him there and back. I figured there must be some volunteer service that could be relied upon in circumstances like this. For the hours between Clive returning from rehab and my returning from work, a team of care assistants would step in – psychology students, I thought, would be competent to reinforce the rehab he was receiving and help apply its effects to the home setting. These assistants would be able to converse with Clive in his own language, without patronizing him, and be so interested in his case that they would not baulk at the difficulties. This arrangement would mean that my life would consist only of work and looking after Clive, but, I thought, this wouldn't be for long – just until Clive got better, or considerably better than he was now, once this mysterious panacea – rehab – kicked in. I felt that a period of intensive rehab by some crack psychologists would surely make a significant difference. I thought the brain would get over its 'shock' and that new connections would grow, lost function be restored. My knowledge of neuro-anatomy and of the chemistry and psychology of the brain was still rudimentary. The medics' attempts at prognosis differed so widely that I could believe what I liked. The idea that Clive might not get better was inconceivable to me.

Initially the Wolfson brain-injury rehab centre at Atkinson Morley in Wimbledon offered Clive a place in their day-care programme. There was a year-long waiting list that would need pole-vaulting, but I was so confident about the pressure I could bring to bear through the media if I had to, it never occurred to me that it would be a problem. I spent my days working with journalists on far less interesting stories than this one. Another snag, once I looked into it, was transport. No disability ferrying service was willing to take a person from Maida Vale in North London to Wimbledon in South West London. It meant crossing too many boroughs. The Red Cross only did one-offs, not regular trips. Disability services were geared for people in wheelchairs. Nothing seemed set up for people with cognitive or behavioural problems. Even benefits were initially refused. The assessors denied Clive mobility allowance because he could walk. The fact that his incapacity might have led him to run into a road or to be a danger on public transport (to himself and others) seemed to have no place in their eligibility criteria. I engaged the services of a free legal practice specializing in disability and, on appeal, Clive was awarded mobility allowance as, although he was technically mobile, he was not capable of 'purposive movement'. I considered driving Clive to the Wolfson and back myself, but it would have meant giving up my job, or negotiating leave of absence for the duration of his rehab, with no guarantees that he would not require care at the end of it. Plus, I would have needed someone to sit with Clive for the journey both ways, a capable male to take him to the gents en route if necessary. And I was the breadwinner now. How could I give up work?

If I did give up work, we'd have to sell the flat and go into a council flat and live on benefits. How would we manage in cramped conditions with thin walls if Clive were running amok and shouting all night (which he'd been doing lately)? The Wolfson could not offer residential rehab but perhaps that was what Clive needed. It was all I could do to survive a weekend with him. He must get rehab, and transport would have to be found.

I seemed to have a kind of steamroller mentality at this time, disregarding any barriers as negligible. If Clive had a firm place at the right rehabilitation centre, I would let nothing stand in the way of his taking it up and undergoing the treatment prescribed.

I began work with Shirley towards discharge. We even set a date that everyone signed up to: 24 June 1985. I wrote in my diary for that day, 'Clive comes home.' Two care assistants were assigned to take it in turns to care for Clive from discharge. They would give

Clive the maximum time allowed, four hours per day, five days a week for three months.

The two care assistants, Linda and Patrick, started visiting Clive in hospital to allow him to 'get used to' them, little realizing that he was not capable of getting used to anyone or anything.

We got to June and I was still talking as if discharge were imminent, that Clive would live at home and eventually return to work in some capacity. I don't think I really believed it. Around mid-June I bumped into a friend.

'You've not been out for yonks,' she said. 'Let's get together for a drink.'

'That would be lovely,' I said, 'but it'll have to be this week.'

'Why?' she said.

'Because then Clive comes home, and I won't be able to go out after that.'

'Oh,' she said. 'For how long?'

I thought for a moment. 'Er . . . for ever, possibly.' I hadn't put it into words before.

The homecoming was, however, shelved at the eleventh hour. Clive's aggressive behaviour had escalated and the hospital decided discharge was not an option.

We had an appointment at the Wolfson two days after the day we had thought Clive might have been able to come home. This is Clive's record of those two days. The brackets are his own, and the bad spellings are his joke.

*Tuesday 25 June 1985*
Debrhoa collected me in the levening. We went hoam and as I had already had superp, I just had some soup and some yoghurt. We went to bedd and (you) Clive kept crying because I thought I was a (newsans) nuisance to Deborah but I was wrong (I don't admit this

but my wife insists on it). My wife says I have been ill and I am still lovely and knot a nuisance.

*Wednesday 26 June 1985*

We got you pee (UP) at 7.45 and had baths and then wee ate muesli and grapefruit. Deborah drove me to Andy the barbers in Swiss Cottage and he gave me a cut and blow dry. I liked going up and down in the big chair so he pumped me up and down a bit more (meem). Then we went to the Wolfson rehabilitation centre and met Mr Tyerman, the psychologist, for the second time. We were more than half an hour late because Deborah kept on getting lost on the way and ended up in Surbiton and in New Malden twice. Mr Tyerman thought I (CW) was very funny. But he said that it would be better if I could have 'Therapy' at the Middlesex Hospital first for a few months and then come to the Wolfson for about six months after that. He said I would benefit much more from his therapy if I were rather better to start off with. He will then deal with the subtleties of getting my rain functions back to their original state, so that I can go back to work again. Then we had lunch and Deborah brought me back to St Marie's Hospital.

The Wolfson, which had offered Clive a place, ruled him out when they saw him in this new aggressive phase. Like most brain-injury units, they did not take people with behaviour problems who could walk. They could manage aggression only if the patient were confined to a wheelchair and unlikely to hurt anyone. (Suddenly the fact that Clive was strong, healthy and ambulant turned out to be a drawback, barring him from the few rehab facilities that did exist.)

The care workers continued to visit for a while because we still hoped for a homecoming. They left Clive messages in his diary along with other visitors.

*Tuesday 16 July 1985*
Linda and Patrick visited this morning. We're home care workers who will be visiting you at home when you are discharged from St Mary's Hospital, Praed St, W2.

As time went on I felt an increased need to take action on Clive's behalf. He just seemed to be languishing on the ward.

I took time off work to sit at home and phone all the leads I had, the experts I'd contacted, organizations who were set up to assist people after a disability, social services, government departments. Our bed was a sea of paper, academic literature, leaflets, telephone directories, lists of questions. At the end of three days I had learned that I was in the middle of a thick dark forest with no map and no paths out of it. There was simply nowhere to go.

# PART II

PRISONERS OF CONSCIOUSNESS

# 6

## LIFE WITH NO MEMORY

*August 1985*

'How long have I been ill?'

'Four months.'

'Four months?! . . . Is that F-O-R or F-O-*U*-R (ha ha!)?'

'F-O-*U*-R.'

'Well, I've been unconscious the whole time! What do you think it's like to be unconscious for . . . how long?'

'Four months.'

'. . . four months! For months?! . . . Is that F-O-R or F-O-*U*-R?'

'F-O-*U*-R.'

'I haven't heard anything, seen anything, smelled anything, felt anything, touched anything. How long?'

'Four months.'

'. . . four months! It's like being dead. I haven't been conscious the whole time. How long's it been?'

'Four months.'

'FOUR!! Is that F-O-R or F-O-*U*-R?'

| SEPTEMBER | | | | | | |
|---|---|---|---|---|---|---|
| S | M | T | W | T | F | S |
| 1 | 2 | 3 | 4 | 5 | 6 | 7 |
| 8 | 9 | 10 | 11 | 12 | 13 | 14 |
| 15 | 16 | 17 | 18 | 19 | 20 | 21 |
| 22 | 23 | 24 | 25 | 26 | 27 | 28 |
| 29 | 30 | | | | | |

**AUGUST 1985**

Week 34/35

## 25 Sunday
237 — 128

~~I WOKE AT 8.50am AND BAUGHT A COTTON THE OBSERVER.~~

I WOKE AT 9.00am     I Had already Bought a copy of the

OBSERVER.

THIS (OFFICIALLY) CONFIRMS THAT I AWOKE AT
9.05 am THIS MORNING.

I woke again at 2.06pm. (This time properly) and 2.09pm.
" " " " 2.10pm. ( " - " ) " 2.11pm.
✓✓ " " " 2.14pm. ( " " finally) " 2.18 pm (
" " " " 2.16pm. ( " " " ) " 2.26pm
" " " " 2.26pm. ( " " " ) " 2.27½pm
" " " " 2.29pm. ( " - completely. " 2.35pm.

3.15  2.40  2.55  3.05  3.09
5.00  FINALLY AWOKE  3.19 3.25 3.27 3.32 Conscious 3.37 3.39 3.44 4.5

AT 9.40pm I awoke for the 1st Time, despite any
previous claims.         NOT FULLY CONCIOUS!

I WAS FULLY CONCHASE AT 10-35pm, AND AWAKE FOR
THE FIRST TIME FOR MANY, MANY WEEKS. PROPER CONCHASENESS
AT 1.19am.

'F-O-*U*-R.'

'I haven't seen a doctor the whole time. I know nothing about this case. My eyes just came on about a minute ago.'

After only a week I wondered how I would bear the pun any longer. A part of me saw with some dread that I might still be living with this joke when the answer to his eternal question was four years instead of four months. I put up screens to prevent myself thinking this, scrabbling about in my mind for more bearable scenarios. This trick didn't work.

After two weeks, I decided it was legitimate to start saying, 'Nearly five months,' to skip the joke. It was all I could do to manage the dialogue itself, but finding the patience to react to the joke each time as if for the first time – so that he wouldn't feel that I was ignoring him – was sometimes beyond me.

After being with Clive all day, I found it harder and harder to manage his questions and drag the right answer out of my head. If we were in the car, either I needed to watch the traffic or my mouth just couldn't say it any more. That was hard for him.

'How long???'

'Wait a minute, I'm driving, let me think.'

Clive would apologize, look down at his hands, contrite. But in no time at all, he would forget that I had asked him to stay quiet and it would start all over again.

'Darling, I've just woken up! I can see you! I can see everything normally! How long's it been?'

Clive was constantly surrounded by strangers in a strange place, with no knowledge of where he was or what had happened to him. To catch sight of me was always a massive relief – to know that he was not alone, that I still cared, that I loved him, that I was there. Clive was terrified all the time. But I was his life, I was his lifeline. Every time he saw me, he would run to me, fall on me, sobbing, clinging. It was a fierce reunion. 'I thought I was dead,' he would say, 'if I had any thoughts at all.'

If I left Clive's side, the impact of my reappearance after a trip to the bathroom, a word with a nurse, was no less than at my first appearance that day. Clive would be shocked at the sight of me in the doorway, throw up his arms, clamp himself around me and weep in relief. He would tell me it was OK, he was alive, awake, everything was normal now. Most times he cried and clung, cried and clung. Clive was living in an abyss, and then out of nowhere, without any warning, I, his wife, would appear over the rim, right there in the room with him. Sometimes his right arm shot up in the air and he would sing a high note, a little cadenza, he would lift me up and swing me round and laugh, then stop and hold me and look at me, study my face, grinning, searching to see if I had cottoned on to the fact that he was awake now, alive, truly seeing me.

'I can see you!!!!' he'd announce triumphantly. 'I'm seeing everything properly now!!!'

It was hard to look excited and delighted for the umpteenth time on one visit, but being besotted with him helped. I was always delighted to see his face, to hold him and kiss him. I was never not thrilled. Before he'd been ill, we would greet each other whenever we found ourselves in the same room together. In the kitchen, when he was bent over work, at mealtimes, we were generally attached to each other. When we met at the end of the day or in the street or at rehearsal, we always hurried to reach each other, passionate and full of affection.

So although it was painful when Clive was so distressed, hugging him for some minutes after a visit to the bathroom was in keeping with our relationship.

*

In spite of Clive's severe amnesia, inside he still retained his fundamental intelligence. We had not lost our Clive. He was often lucid and could perceive acutely. Apart from occasional and short-lived episodes when he was full of rage and frustration, he was himself. That was what made his condition all the more horrific, of course. As we began to piece together what he'd retained and what he'd lost, the psychologists confirmed that he had lost more of his memory function than anyone had ever thought it possible to lose. He was grabbing on to micro-seconds which were running away without leaving the slightest trace. The tests the psychologists had used at first were not designed to measure this degree of amnesia, so I used to chip in with questions that would reveal it more clearly.

It is perhaps impossible for anyone to imagine such a split-second experience and an intelligent man trapped inside. His now was instantly erased, his past void, and he had only the vaguest sense of autobiography.

Clive no longer had any episodic memory, that is, memory for events. When he was questioned about his life before the illness, the extent of his amnesia was already evident, although without seeing a clear picture of the brain damage we were unaware of his capacity, if any, to recover. Clive did not have the brain parts necessary to recall anything that had happened to him in the whole of his life. The mechanism by which a person brings something to their 'mind's eye' was missing. But, as is the case with amnesia, he could remember general things. Later on, I learned to distinguish between the different brain functions involved in remembering, recognition and having a general knowledge. For example, Clive knew that he was married, although he was unable to recall the wedding. He could not have described my appearance, although he knew me as soon as he saw me. He knew he was a musician and conductor but could not recall any concert. It was also clear that Clive's amnesia was 'retrograde', blotting out a big chunk of his life before the illness. He knew his children but expected them to be much smaller and wasn't sure how many he had. He didn't know the year or the decade. He was surprised to see *The Times* no longer had personal columns on the front page, and thought it would cost fourpence, a pre-decimalization price.

He knew his own name and the names of his siblings and childhood family. He knew facts about his childhood life, where he grew up, where he was evacuated to in the war, where the air-raid shelter was, what A levels he did. He knew he went to Clare College, Cambridge, on a choral scholarship, opting against King's because 'everybody wanted to go there' and he preferred to be different. After that, his sense of his own autobiography got a bit hazy. He recognized the faces of people he had known for some years. It was just as well we'd been together six and a half years or he might not have been able to remember me. But his ability to register any new impressions, to lay down any memory since the illness, was non-existent. It would gradually become apparent that everything and every place was perpetually unfamiliar and every person he did not know of old was forever a stranger.

Clive was near shore, looking at shore, but with nothing to catch hold of, nothing to moor him to time. No information or visual impression or word spoken could sink in. He could see or hear something a thousand times and each time was, as far as he was concerned, the first time. He could never satisfy his hunger to know long he'd been out of it and what impact it had had on his life. No matter how many times he asked, he was unable to take in and store the answers. Every question was the first question, and every answer was news to him. He was forever emerging into first consciousness, every moment for him was in the first moments of awakening; from what, to what, was just out of grasp. He was forever questioning, in the first time of asking, desperate to have the answers, never knowing he had had an answer before.

We were looking around for treatment, a brain injury rehabilitation programme that would take him on. But could rehabilitation stick when nothing else stuck? Clive could not remember the sentence before the one he was in. Conversation, watching TV or reading were beyond him. I learned that amnesic people have some residual learning capacity that is implicit; they can learn through a kind of conditioning process. A person can learn to respond to certain stimuli even if they think this is their first experience of the stimulus or cue. For example, since the staff always gave Clive a small plastic beaker of water with his medication, he would expect it, raise the beaker and say every time, 'Is this champagne, or real pain?' Amnesic people can also recall by using 'priming', that is, if they hear one thing or phrase associated with another, hearing the first prompts a statement of the second. So, if I said, 'St Mary's,' Clive could say, 'Paddington,' though he had no idea what it meant.

In the early months, when he was still very confused, unable even to find language, the hospital speech and language therapist worked with Clive for a while. I sat in on one of her sessions.

'What is a tree?' she asked. 'Do you dress in it, play football with it or pick fruit from it?' Clive had no idea. Sometimes he complained that words had changed their meanings. When asked to define 'eyelid', he replied, 'I don't know that word, it must be used by a great specialist.'

But steadily his vocabulary was restored and, despite his gross memory impairment, he was soon able to reveal much of himself, as in this exercise where he was asked to give examples of things:

something courageous
*rugby*

something tragic
*the death of your wife*

something that hurts your ears
*a high untuned note*

something that is unpleasant
*me*

something that is bitter
*me*

something that is loving
*my wife*

something that has to be renewed
*promise*

something stiff
*concrete mind*

something that changes shape
*painter*

something that should be insured
*my life*

something that needs to be planned
*a town development*

something that needs to be repeated
*good music*

something comical
*my seriousness*

something that has springs
*every year*

something that might expire
*my heart*

something that tastes sweet
*honey*

something that is extinct
*my ability*

something dangerous
*my humour*

something fake
*my humour*

something you enjoy doing
*kissing*

something habit-forming
*kissing*

something wider than it is high
*my stupidity*

This exercise revealed Clive's insight as well as a deep sense of shame at being what he called 'stupid'. I wished I could impress upon him how loved and valued he was, how vital to my existence, how much I esteemed him whatever he was or wasn't able to do. It was perhaps only when so much had been taken away from him that I realized quite what an amazing person he was.

When Clive made the first entries in his diary it was at my prompting. But on Sunday 7 July 1985 he made his first spontaneous entry: 'Today: 1st CONSCIOUSNESS . . . Conscious for the FIRST TIME.' This probably marks the first time Clive was able to articulate to himself the strange phenomenon of immediate and blanket forgetting that he had experienced since he was brought into hospital.

It was just as well that the new awakeness was on such a tiny scrap of time. Any more and he might have been shattered by this revelation that he had nothing, no conscious evidence of his life before this moment. If he had had sufficient time to draw breath and see the nothing and register its impact, he might have screamed all day. That would have been a perfectly rational and understandable response.

Instead, he breathed a moment-to-moment existence, where no one instant was joined to any other. He had no continuum. There was no accumulation of glimpses long enough to get any kind of perspective on his condition.

Clive made entries in the diary every two or three minutes. People have sometimes interpreted that to imply a new awakening at two- or three-minute intervals. In fact the lapse between each entry signified only the time it took for the process of recording. It involved deciding to write down the fact of his awakening, pulling a pen from his pocket and writing; then a read-through of previous entries, scoring these out because he was sure he had been unconscious when he wrote them. When he came to the last entry he checked his watch and saw that it was incorrect, so he amended it, reinforcing the last and only true entry by underlining it. Finally Clive would replace the top on his pen, put it back in his pocket and look around to get his bearings in the room. That process might take the few minutes between entries. His span of 'consciousness' is actually a great deal shorter.

In his hand was usually a pack of cards which he would shuffle before continuing with a game of patience laid out on the bed. Here he would see a journal. In his handwriting were false claims of being awake, when in actual fact he had woken up only in the last twenty seconds and knew for sure he had written nothing in this journal since waking up. He had to set the record straight. Feeling in his pocket for a pen, he would score out previous entries, check his watch for the correct time of awakening and record it with more superlatives to distinguish this final entry as the real one. He would put his pen away – no need to keep it out because he was completely awake now, all other claims being inaccurate. This was the only true awakeness, everything now working normally. Life can resume. He shuffles cards.

Clive noted the moment of first real awakening the same way prisoners make marks on a cell wall, to fix his place in time, and to leave a record for others passing that way to know when he emerged from oblivion. The entries were mostly addressed to me: '9.04pm COMPLETELY AWAKE, DARLING. PLEASE COME AT THE SPEED OF LIGHT.'

If he were not near his journal, the compulsion to record the sudden and momentous fact of just awakening after apparently years of unconsciousness was just as strong, so Clive would at that time make his notes on any available surface, including walls and furniture.

He wakes, he wakes, he records the tremendous effect of coming alive. The act of writing a sentence provides momentum, each word carrying him to the next – but the act of lifting his pen and looking around blots the words from his memory. He looks down and sees a claim of awakeness, apparently in his handwriting, a pen in his hand. He sees a whole page of such incorrect entries. Flicking back, he finds days and weeks, months with identical statements of new awakening, mostly crossed out.

His finger in the latest page of entries would indicate the day's date, but he has no memory of writing any of it. A glance at his wristwatch shows the time only a couple of minutes later than the last time written, but *now* is the real awakeness, *now* he is really awake for the first time. He has to set the record straight. '3.34pm *NOW superlatively* awake first time.'

While Clive was still confused, there remained to him the capacity to be more discursive. He was striving to express his deeper feelings, and had not yet been hit by the realizations that were later to hamper him. In the first few months the confusion was a protective mechanism, shielding both Clive and me from understanding the horror of the reality of his condition.

On Sunday 19 May 1985 he wrote: 'I miss my wife, but she is still here, and marvellously warm and happy – full of joy and love.' And in an effort to expand on the theme of love which so gripped him despite the amnesia: 'The life of joy and beauty is a perfect expression of the greatest human qualities which God has developed over many centuries.'

Occasionally, instead of addressing a diary entry to me, Clive would address it to the scientists/doctors he assumed must be working on his case. These messages ask, within the limits of Clive's word-finding difficulties and from his singular perspective, how it is his environment is in flux: 'How are the techniques of the alterations contained in this and other reports developed.

And let me know how long your investigation is carried out.'
From his phrase 'the techniques of the alterations', we can assume
that Clive did not believe that he was the problem, but that it
was caused by something outside himself. He would point to his
environment, expecting that I would also see it constantly shifting.

Shuffling the cards in his hand and looking down at the game
of patience laid out on the table in front of him, he would say,
'And the cards! They're not laid out by me. I've never seen them
before. I can't understand it . . . The world's gone *mad*!!!'

Clive found solace in cards. He had played patience all his life. His
family played patience in the air-raid shelters as a distraction from
the sound of bombs falling on Birmingham. It was Clive's habit to
play a hand whenever he needed to stay calm or to wind down
after an evening performance. I had often fallen asleep to the
slap of cards on Formica. He went on playing it in the hospital
but the sight of a new layout of cards every time he blinked or
looked away was distressing. He sought to know the secret of
this. He determined to observe the cards, track their movements
methodically, to understand what was going on, in the same way
you might watch a magician, resolved to spot the sleight of hand.

He picked up his pencil and pad and noted down the current
layout of cards. He used symbols for suits and numbers or letters
for picture cards. R or B signified red or black. Sometimes he
noted the positions of cards in columns. But that process did not
unravel the mystery to him. Then, to fool any who might attempt
to trick him, he tried a much subtler method, a secret code. He
translated the characteristics of each card into a musical note
and represented each column of cards as a melody on a musical
stave, drawn meticulously on his notepad. Clive was used to
writing musical parts quickly and clearly and this was a way of

# FINAL SOLUTION — MUSICAL PHRASE

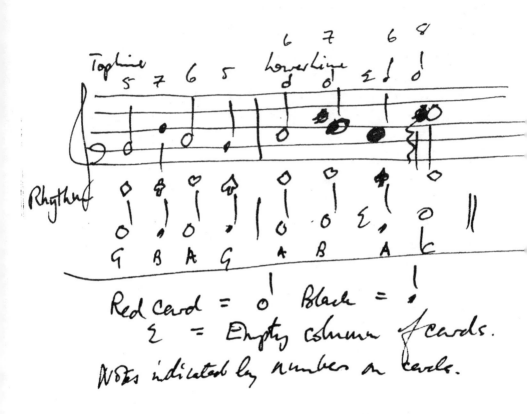

Red Card = o  Black = !
ε = Empty column of cards.
Notes indicated by number on cards.

Cards J Q K are in bottom line etc.
I awoke at 10.06 precisely (a.m).

## MY SELFISHNESS IS STUPID.

embedding the card layout into a sequence that was incorruptible. Any saboteur could have managed to copy Clive's handwriting, but it would have been more difficult to reproduce his style of musical notation. At one point he wrote out a key to the code. The note pitch was derived from the number on the card, determining where the note sat on the treble stave; picture cards were interpreted as sequential from the numbers. The colour, red or black, determined note values – crotchet or minim. Symbols for suits ran beneath the notes like a word underlay.

The melody would represent the layout of a game of patience at a given moment. By this method Clive tried to fix himself in time. If the cards corresponded to the melody and if the melody were clearly of his own making, then the cards had not changed, even though they appeared new to him.

Yet if he had no memory of the melody or the cards, how could the game of patience or the writing of the melody have occurred?

He could see the handwriting was his, and the style of notation. His name was on a sign at the head of his bed. Over and over again he went through the same exercise, but each melody he made, though apparently authentic, was new to him. What was behind it all?

He wrote notes on his bewilderment with further details of the precise positioning of the cards/notes:

D and F were over each other.

G and A were further to the left than E and F.

So first ['first' deleted and 'last but one' inserted as the amnesia blots out his sentence before he is done] bar was slower (and last note there longest).

♦E ♣F ♥G ♣D ♠F ♠G ♠A ♠E

An authoritative view of the speed of final cadences. 8.15am.

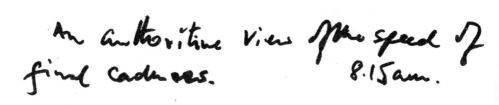

cornet

Red
A23      Bl    ↓R        Bl A2

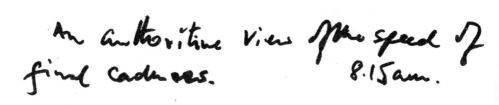

1st
line.  E◇3   F♣4   G♡5   D♠2
     Red   Black  R   Bl

2d  Bl    Bl    Bl        Bl
line.  G♣5  A♣6  E♣3 - (gap.) . . F♣4

(Laid out by Sidek
1,3,4. Not 2)

~~key test~~:      D and F were over each
                          other

           G and A were further to the left
last but one than E and F:

So ~~they~~ (?) was shoved (and got into these large)

   ♣◇    ♣◇    ♣   ♠
   E   F   G   D
 ♣  ♣  ♠     ♣
 G  A  E     F.

An authoritive view of the speed of
final cadences.         8.15am.

HEAVENLY INSPIRED.

Cards NOT laid out by me.

But it was only authoritative at bang on 8.15 a.m. Thirty seconds later and he had no memory of writing the sequence of cards (which he now did without staves for speed, using letter names as shorthand to describe the melody). There was only one possible explanation, only one way the cards could be changing position without his intervention, one way of creating this melody not of his making.

So Clive wrote: 'HEAVENLY INSPIRED. Cards NOT laid out by me.'

Packs of cards became important to Clive, as an instrument both for passing the time and for attempting to get a fix on time. He reached for them or patted his pockets to look for them constantly. They quickly became soft and dog-eared. I brought him fresh packs. Soon there were packs bulging from every pocket in his pyjamas and dressing gowns. When fully clothed with jacket and trousers he could be carrying eight or nine packs of cards. It made him lumpy as he walked along. There were more packs in his coat, in his sponge bag, and secreted in and around his bedside cabinet.

He accumulated bars of soap too and other toiletries. When he went to the bathroom, with or without a sponge bag, he took whatever soap was there, assuming it could be his. One day I counted as many as twenty-seven bars of soap in his possession.

At first glance his diary looks like a chronology of nothing. When statements are repeated so many times, they can seem to empty of meaning. But just as Clive is searching for clues to explain the odd event of just awakening, so his notes contain clues as to where he is, his thinking processes, his experience of amnesia. They reveal more of himself than the results of any neuro-psychological examination.

Every diary entry gives an eyewitness account of a life with no memory:

5.10am  Conscusch.

5.22  [coded representation of layout of cards; in brackets he writes '(in Reserves),' noting which cards were the last to be added from his pack at the end]

Result of *FIRST* PROPER GAME.

FINALLY AWAKE AT —— am [a hotchpotch of successive times all scribbled out later] exactly.

Newspaper arrived at 8.40am

Medicines arrived at 8.45am

AND I AWOKE properly AT 8.47am

And completely at 8.49am

And became aware of the problems of understanding me.

That first year Clive wrote his diary very neatly, one entry beneath the other, the way he wrote out research notes, the figures ranged left and key words in capital letters. The diary lay open on the table, its pages thick with ink and graphite pressed hard, from all the scorings out and underlinings as each entry had to be corrected because each revelation of just awakening cancelled out all previous claims to that effect. Only this awakening is the real awakening. Disregard all previous claims, he was saying. Cross out the time, cross out the previous statements. Cross out the time, THIS is the first conscious moment. THIS is the only real awakening.

A constant act of correction went on, for the evidence had to be trustworthy. With so much deletion and reinforcing, the pages curved thickly from the spine, and the paper became soft and pockmarked as though beaten. Clive did not remember ever seeing this book, but instinctively moved towards it many times a day. He did not know what he might have written there but went to write the same phrase over and over. If he could just link one moment to another, continuity would be restored. Everything has changed now, he says. This is different. I can see perfectly. He recorded the fact in his book of moments, his record of his experience of consciousness. This writing down, this last new record, was his first foot on dry land.

He addressed many diary entries to me. 'D———' he put, the way he used to write Valentine's cards. D for Darling or D for Deborah was not at first clear. 'D——— – PLEASE ARRIVE! PLEASE FLY HERE AT THE SPEED OF LIGHT!'

Eventually I realized he could not recall my name, but recognized it when he heard it or saw it written. He did not need to remember my name. He knew me, he knew my voice on the phone, my breath, the feel of my hand. I kissed him when he was asleep and he kissed me back. He knew it was me. We were intertwined, his self, my self. I was part of him.

Friends wrote in the diary, recording the things they had talked about with Clive. He seemed to enjoy people talking to him about his subject, music, though he could contribute little. He was like a child pretending to have a conversation, making the right sounds but they were devoid of meaningful content. When I arrived I would read who had been in and what they had discussed. On Tuesday 20 August 1985: 'Robert M came to see you. You were talking to a nurse.' Robert must have handed Clive the pen and asked him to write something else. 'SOMETHING ELSE,' Clive writes. 'I am A Wake. (C Wearing). Something else.' Robert's handwriting continues:

> You said that I was the first person you'd had a conversation with. We talked about your illness, and the effect it has had on your memory. We also talked about the Promenade Concert I am going to hear tonight – music by Nielsen, Williamson, Liszt and Sibelius. [Here Robert writes out a bar of Sibelius] And the way in which you jazz up Monteverdi when you play the chapel organ, and tell the singers off (very nicely) when they sing the wrong notes!

On Thursday 5 September 1985: 'George and Caroline and Shonni came in the evening and we were all very disapproving about football hooligans.' On Monday 9 September: 'Kristine called this evening. We spent half an hour discussing the different styles of early French music and the technicalities of tuning within a choir and the role the conductor plays. An excellent evening.'

One evening we sat in the hospital foyer with friends. The only place for visitors to sit with Clive was by the main entrance, where there were a few hard chairs against the wall, just inside the threshold. Clive waved to passers-by. Some waved back.

I was very encouraged by the things Clive was remembering in our chats. He suddenly remembered the initials of a friend at Cambridge with whom he used to play squash, T.J.P. – Trevor. When I reminded Clive that Trevor was Treasurer of the music company he had started, he even remembered its name. 'Musica Europa Ltd!' he burst out. I thought this was a sign of his memories coming back.

\*

The life and death dramas of the hospital rarely made any impression on Clive as he cocooned himself in card game after card game, each shuffling and dealing precisely timed. But suddenly, one day in early October 1985, he wrote:

Ended shuffling and dealt and played
1st deal got nowhere
1.24 Changed for second
1.27 EMERGENCY IN CUPBOARD
1.28 EMERGENCY Next Door
1.34 EMERGENCY OVER
HUGE PROBLEM WORRY.
Please forgive me O Lord for my stupid selfishness
2.17 Uncompleted card game cleaned up
2.24 Card game ended unfinished

When I got to Clive later that afternoon, I saw that the next bed was empty. The gentleman who had always smiled and put up with Clive's distress, fear and anger with great kindness and patience was not there any more. I asked a nurse if he had been transferred elsewhere. No, he'd died, she told me. How strange it must have been for him to leave this life with Clive a couple of feet away, playing cards. How strange for Clive to witness the sounds of a man's death behind a curtain, understanding something, remembering nothing.

There were often times in the first year when Clive's reaction to his state of 'just awakening' was to ask, who did this to me? Who rendered me unconscious for so long? How is it that I should become conscious at this particular moment? He would ascribe his apparent unconsciousness to sabotage. It could have been his own

**NOVEMBER**
S M T W T F S
1 2
3 4 5 6 7 8 9
10 11 12 13 14 15 16
17 18 19 20 21 22 23
24 25 26 27 28 29 30

**OCTOBER 1985**
Week 42
**16 Wednesday**
289 — 76

(7 months in Hospital) and blind! deaf!
7.55 a.m.

5.52pm!

I AM AWAKE !!!
10.45 a.m.
(and probably RIGHT!)

THE ISSUE OF THE *TIMES* TODAY GIVES ALL NECESSARY INFORMATION (TIME).
AWAKE AND CONSCIOUS for the first time.

I have been unable to see properly for a very long time. But: Today's *Times* paper gives a rather clear indication for my tragedy. I WAS Whoever has been plugging me has gone! Secondly, I suspect RIGHT that the results of the meeting are the cause of my problems!

FULLY AWAKE 10.03 10.28am. I WAS RIGHT — THE TIMES CONFIRMS IT !!!
I Agree at 10.45 a.m! I AWOKE Fully AT 10.55 a.m! Obviously I am free flowing suddenly! Properly awake ab 11.08a.m! I was a victim of Israelian policy! And my thinking was correct. It is obviously advantageous to ?Thrinia that I am not using any powerful understanding! 11.10 am
11.22 FULLY AWAKE FOR THE FIRST Time (despite what has been said above) 30 weeks loss!
11.40 ACTUALLY FULLY AWAKE (Real FIRST). 1.30 END of lunch. 1.30 Patience Cards. 1.48 FULLY AWAKE.
1st (and over at 1.55 2.(Patience) 2.05 3.30pm. 2.18 3rd time (Fully Conscious for the FIRST Time). 1st CARD Game FOR YEARS. PATIENCE.
7.35 ACTUALLY awake (FIRST TIME) AT 4.20pm (AT LAST). REALLY AWAKE AT 5.55 pm
and certainly awake 6.35 (now's time!) 7.20, 7.40 7.52
Your wife. Deborah came. We sat + talked in the chapel.
Fully awake at 12.20 am!

---

WAKE-UP DAY AT 4.15pm. Clive made a video: an Very interview made from The Magic Flute.
4.45 a.m. FULLY AWAKE for the first time (despite to earlier claims).
Vision is also complete (for the 1st time) Slightly improved by 5.00 a.m. 5.0 am, 5.08 am
5.18 am. Tried to snooze! Fully Conscious 5.35 a.m. (actually 5.40 a.m) I suspect that a "system" of keeping me deaf and blind on purpose has been switched off.
See heading report in *The Times* (16.10.85.) 6.06 am is really the first fully awake moment.
Fully conscious at 6.14 a.m. (Whoever attacked me has stopped). See *The Times* 16.10.85
" awake 6.45 FULLY AWAKE for the first time at 7.30 Ray, home first of all
breakfast 7.10 - 7.35, When I was actually awake (confirmed written line) 7.36 better & awake
7.55 Best. and 7.59. Better, now actually awake (despite )
10.09 am Much more awake than ever this year. But: better at 10.14 am
I AM AWAKE for the FIRST TIME. (really alert at
Card Game for fun. 1st REAL GAME over ab 7.49 pm. (Real = observed) 7.49 1ST TIME AWAKE.
1st Cup of Tea 2.52 pm! 1ST TIME AWAKE CONSCIOUSLY 3.09 pm 3.10 pm 1st (and over 3.15 p Fully Awake
Now tired, 2 of 3.20 & 3.27. 1st FULLY CONSCIOUS 3.29 (Public at 3.35) AND TOTALLY 3.43 pm
4.26 pm I AWAKE NOW 4.28 pm a more really 4.45 pm AWAKE
5.05 pm AWAKE ✓ 5.10 am FULLY AWAKE AND CONSCIOUS AT 5.28 Whatever the Hell has happened?
5.45 ANYTHING WRITTEN ABOVE IS WITHOUT ANY PROPER THOUGHTS AND UNDERSTANDING!
Juliet and we had a talk music Andrew came today — You've met people before

construct, a reasonable one, on what could have happened to cause sudden awakeness after years of unconsciousness. Or, I learned, it could have been paranoia, which can occur as a direct result of damage to the amygdala, a small almond-shaped brain structure.

Clive, ever the research scholar, used to check to see if there were any clues to this sudden awakening. He would seize upon headlines in *The Times*, which we had ordered daily. On Wednesday 23 October 1985 he wrote: 'This is the first time I have been awake for many months. It is likely that my sleeping and living food have been organized to keep me quiet and controllable by somebody. Who? Is the problem!' For unknown forces to have sought to shut him up so completely and for so long, he must, he deduced, have unwittingly been party to potent information. He looked to his newspaper to know what had happened this day that might be a cause for his awakening now. To me this seemed a pretty acute rationale – he would have had to ask, why now? Why am I once more conscious at this particular moment, after so long in oblivion? It would have to be something big. The answer would in all likelihood be in that day's papers. He had not lost his Holmesian powers of deduction. And engaging in this train of thought, Clive was so focused, he became capable of greater fluency, longer periods of concentration.

On 27 October 1985 he wrote in his diary:

A *strange* kind of illness seems to blame for this gap in my life! Was this illness imposed upon me by other people? The only way to find out is to do a detailed examination of all the magazines, newspapers and other published material appearing during the last six months. The results of an inquiry will release the causes of my 'now-living' – despite apparently unlikely connection between the subjects.

For the next few weeks Clive ascribed blame, variously, to a trial at the Old Bailey, King Hussein of Jordan, politician Sir Geoffrey Howe, and Mrs Victoria Gillick, Roman Catholic mother of ten, who was heading up a public campaign against underage contraception.

Sometimes he would be seized by fears for his safety, and, wanting to see the perpetrators take the rap for his illness, he used to bolt out of the ward and run through the hospital corridors calling for someone to please contact the police. I used to wonder if his fears were fuelled when everyone ignored or humoured him. He wasn't stupid. He could see if people believed him or not.

I put a blackboard next to his bed with reassuring sentences written in large print. I wasn't sure if he would find any comfort in this statement explaining to him where he was, what had happened to him. If he could see it all the time, perhaps it would have a calming effect, perhaps he would weave my words into his inner thought process where he repeatedly guessed at what might have happened to him. He read my notice but it supplied no reassurance. In fact he picked up pieces of chalk and scribbled his own notices around the edges of mine. 5.08pm awake first time. 5.11 truly awake first time. 5.14 first real consciousness. 5.18 NOW truly awake first time. When he looked at the board he saw his own false claims which constantly had to be put right, and my information which made no sense, though he did incorporate the information into his own notes in his diary.

THE GUARDIAN Tues. Oct. 29. 1985
SPY case fiasco puts pressure on ministers – refers to the case, which was enveloping me! The Government will be to blame for some of it, I suppose. The House of Commons will be investigating this matter immediately!

Christopher Payne and Geoffrey Jones and five other servicemen were freed 'NOT GUILTY'. This was Britain's longest running and most costly spy trial!!!

WHERE WAS I, AND WHY? [7 months!]
Notice in my room: THURS. 31st OCT 85
Rare brain disease / with memory loss / 7 MONTHS.
The 'spy trial' is explained in The Guardian of Tuesday October 29 1985.

SPY case fiasco / puts pressure / on ministers (Headlines)
The case is Britain's longest running and most costly spy trial!!!
Cost 4½ million £'s! 119 Days. All seven cleared! NUM votes to apologise!!
I had 'rare brain disease / with memory loss / 7 MONTHS'!!!!!!!

Clive's care in noting where the line changes fell both in the newspaper headlines and on the blackboard was typical of his careful scholarship. And he had never so needed to get to the bottom of an enquiry as he did now.

As the months wore on, Clive's behaviour became increasingly volatile and explosive. He existed in a blinkered moment with no past to anchor it, and not enough present to be able to breathe. His panic at having no past blotted out even the few moments of present remaining to him. In the circumstances, I believe he was incredibly restrained, especially as the part of the brain that enables self-restraint was, in Clive's case, missing. But if a staff member or visitor who didn't know better said the wrong thing, Clive might flip, shout, bolt or lash out.

It should have been obvious to me by this stage that Prince's Ward, a general medical ward, could not cope with Clive any longer, but it was still a shock when one day in October 1985 a nurse told me that Clive would be transferred to a psychiatric ward. I went home to bed and cried. Clive was not mentally ill. He was normal, but with no working memory. I had in my mind awful images of what a psychiatric ward might be like. How might it compound his distress to find himself alongside people who behaved in disturbing ways?

A nurse transferred Clive across the road to the psychiatric unit, the Paterson Wing, while I was at work. I'd taken in a bag for his things. He was placed on a locked acute admissions ward. Here at least there would be no more danger of his escaping. The building was next door to the Red Star parcel office of Paddington Station and not far from the canal and the Edgware Road flyover, so the secure policy was some comfort.

Clive had a room to himself. This too was a step forward. And he was able to dress himself in his own clothes instead of wearing pyjamas all day. This seemed, to me at any rate, to be restoring some dignity to him. But Clive complained about a generator outside his window that sounded an incessant B flat. There was also often the noise of other patients screaming, roaring, howling or banging, occasionally all at once – hard to bear for someone with Clive's sensitive ears and compassionate heart. The composer Luciano Berio, Clive's friend and colleague, had once organized that everyone in Florence should sound a B♭ at the same time on whatever they had at their disposal – car horn, voice, kitchenware, instruments – to celebrate the Maggio Musicale. Clive had clapped his hands at this idea. But the B♭ sounding from the generator was hellish, for there was no getting away from it. 'This could damage my ears,' he kept saying.

The staff here were used to handling behaviour problems, although the skills and responses needed for behaviour arising from acquired brain injury are not the same as the responses appropriate for mentally ill people because the underlying pathology causing the behaviour may be completely different, even if the behaviour itself is the same.

Soon after Clive's arrival in the Paterson Wing I met his new consultant and a more junior doctor. They explained that the referral was only temporary, for a fortnight, to allow time to find a suitable placement for Clive. He had been put in their care because he had become unmanageable on the general ward.

No place had been found for Clive in the last seven months. They seemed to be indicating this would change. I wondered how.

I was at work when Shirley, the social worker, called me. She was hesitating to tell me something. She spoke in her most gentle voice. The hospital, she told me, was exploring Clive's transfer to the local psycho-geriatric unit. She would be looking into this and would let me know of further developments.

I was standing next to a row of green plants on my window ledge as she said these things. Taxis were passing below, and people with big bags of early Christmas shopping moved in all directions, planning family joys to come. Psycho-geriatric. How would Clive fare with elderly people with dementia, the smell of urine? I had heard of people being tied to their chairs. Would they tie Clive to a chair? How could he survive in such a place? How could we go there? How could either of us manage it? I sank on to the window ledge, looking out of the window through the greenery.

'Debbie?' Shirley's voice in the receiver sought for mine in the silence. I didn't mind her using the diminutive of my name. My secretary appeared with a sheaf of memos for me to sign. She put them on the desk, looking at me wide-eyed, and I motioned for her to please shut the door.

'Debbie love, are you OK?' came Shirley's voice again. I wished I were anywhere else – home, no, not home, that was full of Clive's things from before he was ill.

'That . . . that can't be all there is,' I said. I had hold of a fistful of busy Lizzie and now it was all crushed, uprooting.

'We'll see, dear. I'll keep searching. You keep searching. It's just until we find somewhere. Anyway,' she said, 'there's no knowing if they'll take him. He might be too young.'

'You bet he's too young!' I said. 'He's so young. He's more like my little boy.'

'Don't worry about it for now. I'll give you a ring when I've got some more information. We have to put together a report. It'll take a few days to sort out. All right? Then come and see me and we'll talk about it over tea.'

She rang off and I put the big grey receiver down on the window ledge for a moment for respite before other calls. I looked out at the lowering sky over Cavendish Square. A few days. A fortnight. Geriatric . . . These words echoed over the sound of distant buzzing.

My secretary peered through the porthole and knocked gently. 'I brought you some tea,' she said, 'and a bit of KitKat.' She was a brick.

I stood up and grabbed the phone, the pen. This was not going to happen to my husband. I would protect him and all those hundreds or perhaps thousands of people like him whom the system was neglecting. I would make his plight known. With the spotlight on him, they wouldn't dare take him to such a desperate place. If there were no better services in England for people like Clive, I would shame the health authorities into creating some appropriate provision. If the world's eyes were upon Clive, I did not believe they would proceed with this course of action. They would think again.

I knew what to do. I was a press officer. I would go public. Clive was regarded, it seemed, as a mere statistic, an inconvenience. It felt as though they were ready to sweep him under the carpet. But his case deserved to be heard, it merited in-depth coverage. A thoughtful documentary on national television would be my first attempt to engage the authorities in discussion. Clive would, I sensed, need long-term protection. The psychologists had said he was the worst case they'd come across. What's more, he was especially interesting because of his preserved musical skills and his extraordinary eloquence in commenting on his own condition. A documentary would focus public attention on his plight and that of others like him. Once I had achieved scrutiny, we could conduct the necessary debate and seek a remedy for this situation. The reaction to the documentary would identify other players, champions, and a pool of people similarly affected.

So I began putting together a proposal for a TV documentary, with the aim of protecting Clive and making a case for the provision of suitable rehabilitation and care support for all those currently unprovided for.

I was in full swing when Shirley called me to say the geriatric unit had refused Clive a place on account of his age. It was a relief and meant a temporary reprieve. St Mary's would have to keep him until alternative care was secured. I pressed on with my plans for a documentary. It was clear that Clive and all the other brain-injured people were going to need it.

We continued our efforts to get him assessed for possible referral at rehab and special care units anywhere in the UK. I remember one doctor saying he had never seen anyone with such a thick file. I would take Clive anywhere if they could help him. However, taking him any distance could be fairly fraught for me. Even going to the toilet en route was tricky. I could not go with him into the Gents and, as I usually needed to use the Ladies at the same time, I would have to risk letting him go to his while I went to mine. Our reunions afterwards tended to be less dramatic than in the hospital, though he always remained surprised to see me.

On a dual carriageway heading east out of London Clive said he wanted to go. I saw a sign for parking and the symbol for toilets so I pulled in. There was a long lay-by with a Portakabin. Clive put his hand out to open the car door but I told him to wait until I came round to let him out. He didn't wait but unlocked and opened the door. As he did so, a sheet of paper, our how-to-get-there instructions, flew off the dashboard and out of the car. A gust of wind bucketed it along and Clive gave chase despite my firm warnings to leave it. He bounded for the paper and I bounded to reach him. The wind took the paper always a little beyond him, and he was always a little beyond me. The paper flew along the dirt verge beside the dual carriageway.

'*NO, CLIVE!*' I yelled as I ran after him. '*LEAVE IT!!*' He was focused only on the white paper dancing in the air, unaware of anything except perhaps the instinct to be chivalrous and helpful to me in fetching it back.

'I can get it,' he called. He was a fast runner, a wing player at rugby when he was at school. He might have been going for a try.

'*STOP!!!*' I shouted at the top of my voice. '*STOP THERE! STOP!!!*'

I caught up with him at the very edge of the road. I flew and grabbed him from behind, flinging my arms round his middle. At that moment he saw where he was, the heavy traffic he had been about to run into. He turned his fear on me, shaking me by the shoulders.

'*What are you doing, you stupid woman?*' he yelled. '*What d'you think you're doing?*'

I could see blurry white faces turned towards us behind the glass of passing cars, feet away. Clive could not recall what had happened but could see we were close to danger. He went on shouting.

'*You silly woman! What are you doing? What d'you think you're doing??*'

'*Do you love me?*' I cut in loudly. He stopped, looked at me for a moment as if suddenly seeing who I was. The anger went out of his face, he deflated and relaxed his hold on me.

'Yes, of course,' he said, contrite. We could move on.

I edged him gently back from the road, hoping he would not see our piece of paper gusting up and down, hoping he would have forgotten it had anything to do with us. I turned his attention back to the car, got him inside and drove to the next service station for the Gents.

Love was always my way of getting through to Clive whatever the circumstances. Love stopped him in his tracks. Love brought him up against what was important. Yes, he might not have any idea about what was going on or where he was, or of anything that had happened to him in the whole of his existence, but one thing he did know for sure – he knew he loved me, he knew I loved him, he knew we were one, and he knew that came before everything.

We found a service station.

'Wait for me!' I urged repeatedly as he disappeared through the Gents' door. 'Wait for me here!' I thought if it was the last thing he heard before going in, maybe my voice would echo in his head. Maybe he'd rehearse it until he was out again.

I rushed through the Ladies as fast as I could, although he

nearly always came out before I did. He wasn't there waiting for me, and he didn't come out. I began to panic. Maybe I had missed him, and he was already who knew where. I looked about frantically. A tall mechanic in greasy overalls was heading my way.

'Erm . . . excuse me,' I said.

He stopped, looked down at me, blocking out the sun, and I wondered what on earth I could say.

'Could you please see if my husband is in the Gents? He's got amnesia and I haven't seen him come out.'

'No problem,' said the man, unfazed. 'Maybe he used the other exit.'

'*Other exit?!*' My face must have told him this was really terrible news.

'Don't worry,' he said. 'I'll find him.'

'He's a little taller than I am, dark hair, black overcoat, camel scarf.'

A long time passed. Finally the mechanic appeared with Clive in tow, grinning.

'He was in our workshop,' said the man, chuckling, 'just striding up and down. You were inspecting the cars, weren't you, sir?'

'Was I?' said Clive, who, though he had no memory of it, had evidently thoroughly enjoyed the experience and was pleased to be in this jolly mechanic's company.

It was after that eventful trip that the hospital decided I could not manage long journeys alone with Clive and started sending a nurse with us. That took the pressure off somewhat, although Clive still wanted me, and not the nurse, to answer all his questions as I drove. So the journeys were no less tiring but at least I had the security of another responsible adult to cover the Gents' exits.

The furthest we went was Yorkshire, to a home designed for people with learning disabilities. As in most of the homes we visited, all the residents were a lot more independent than Clive was. They were shocked to find he would need prompting and supervision for everything all of the time, day and night, and that there were many activities he would not be able to undertake at all. They found it difficult to believe the depth of his impairment until they had spent a little time with him.

Asking Clive something like, 'How are you?' might provoke an eruption of anger and frustration. He didn't know how he was. He didn't know who was asking him. He didn't know if he'd just travelled across country for hours to get there or if he'd been there all the time. If the person with him was not in uniform, he had no idea if they were doctor, nurse, friend or next-door neighbour. All he knew was his own identity, his profession and his love for me.

Care staff would ask Clive how he was, did he like his room, did he still play the piano, had he enjoyed his day, his meal?

'Have you been watching the rugby, Mr Wearing?' They were surprised when Clive leaped up, shouted at them or kicked over the coffee table laden with refreshments.

I took Clive to see Dr Barbara Wilson, the consultant neuro-psychologist at Charing Cross Hospital. To assess precisely which brain functions are affected and to what degree is a complex undertaking, requiring many different kinds of task and sets of questions in a comprehensive battery of tests. Barbara was so good with Clive that he was able to engage with her and respond well to all she asked him to do. In this way she managed to build up a detailed picture of precisely how his brain was functioning.

One day as we sat in her office, Barbara asked Clive to say all the words he could think of beginning with 's'. He had a minute. She clicked her stopwatch. He seemed to be able to retain a sense of the task longer than I had expected him to, I guess because he was concentrating, hanging on to it without his mind wandering.

'Superb . . .' he began, 'sausage . . . sandwich . . . silly . . . sausage . . . er . . . sausage . . . er, superb . . . sausage . . . Sunday . . . sandwich . . . sand . . . sausage,' sticking on certain words.

The next test was to name animals.

'All the animals you can think of beginning with "s",' said Barbara. 'Sixty seconds.' She clicked her stopwatch again.

'Sixty . . .' said Clive.

Barbara stopped the watch. 'Animals, Mr Wearing, beginning with "s".' She restarted the clock.

'Snake . . . Er . . . snake . . .'

I thought Clive would be defeated by this. Then his face lit up.

'Sausage dog!' he said triumphantly.

This was too much for me. All the pent-up strain of getting him there, parking, using the loo . . . I was overcome with the need to laugh. But how could I, in front of my poor man who could not know what he'd said that was funny? I put my hand over my mouth but a few snorts escaped. Clive looked at me quizzically.

'Are you all right, darling?'

I was shaking with laughter. I bit my lip. 'Uh huh.' I tried to pull myself together.

'Animals beginning with "s", Mr Wearing,' pursued Barbara. 'As many as you can think of in sixty seconds.'

'"S"! . . . Er . . . Snake! . . . er . . . Sausage dog!'

I ran from the room. I ran down the corridor, both hands over my mouth. I ran into the Ladies and leaned against the wall, and all the laugher shook out of me. I shook and laughed until I was crying and my stomach hurt, and then I cried laughing some more. Every time I tried to leave the toilet it started afresh. Finally, I began to sober up, thinking about our predicament, and became quite miserable. I walked slowly back to the room. I went in. Clive leaped out of his seat.

'Darling!!!!!!!!!!!!' he gasped, running to me and holding me tightly. Then Barbara continued showing him a series of drawings and asked him what he thought they were. Clive's answers were a riot. He peered at what was probably intended to be a scarecrow and told Barbara it was 'an item of worship by foreign peoples of strange belief'. I had to run from the room all over again. He had me in stitches.

The saddest answer came when Barbara asked him to name all the composers he could think of. He could name only four in the space of one minute – Mozart, Beethoven, Bach and Haydn, the composers he would have known best in childhood. After twenty-five years faithfully studying the life and work of Orlandus Lassus, even that name escaped him.

Now I was struggling not to cry. Emotional lability, that is, laughing and crying easily, can be indicative of frontal lobe damage. Clive had the brain damage but we both had the symptoms.

# 7

## LIFE WITH NO CLIVE

ONE NIGHT I WALKED HOME FROM THE TUBE. IT WAS GETTING DARK and I had hardly opened the door when the front room filled with flashing blue light. I looked out of the window and saw a couple of fire engines round the corner. I decided to go and look because my car was parked somewhere there and it might be in their way. The fire engine was stuck out in the road, double parked. Firemen were foaming the tarmac. I approached one who was standing on the pavement and offered to move my car, waving at the metallic blue Audi.

'This yours?' he asked, looking at me, at his mate.

'Yes,' I said.

'Well, you won't be moving it anywhere. Your car is why we're here. It's leaking petrol.'

I was about to say I knew it was leaking petrol, when it occurred to me that perhaps to leak petrol was not safe and I should, come to think of it, have done something.

'How did you know?' I asked.

'Fortunately someone saw it and dialled 999,' he said.

'Ah, yes . . .' Oh dear. It had been stinking of petrol some little while, and whenever I drove it I stank of petrol too – my clothes, my hair. I had noticed a small leak under the car, leaving a psychedelic film on puddles.

'I thought I could smell something,' I said.

'Oh, was it you who dialled 999?'

'Er . . . no,' I said.

'If anyone had walked past and dropped a cigarette, the whole thing would have gone up – BOOM!' he said.

'By all these other cars,' his mate chipped in. 'It could have been very nasty.'

The garage showed me the rusty old petrol tank. Erosion to one edge had eaten a big hole. It was a miracle the whole thing hadn't blown.

I thought about the car disintegrating under me. I'd smelled it, smelled of it, seen the leaks on the ground, but had not understood that it was serious, had not known to take action, to get help. Why did I not have a clear grasp on reality? Had such an attitude kept me from getting Clive the help he needed? All the cases of encephalitis I'd read about in the library had taken a similar time to diagnose, and I reminded myself that two trained doctors had missed it as well, but I still felt I should have seen it, I should have taken him to hospital myself when he disappeared, or that morning when he woke up delirious, when the doctor had asked him to say 'Ninety-nine', and Clive could only answer 'Yes'. I let the doctor tap and talk and listen and leave. Why didn't I understand what was going on?

\*

I had to go back to the doctors' surgery myself some weeks after Clive got ill. Both doctors who'd attended Clive were in the consulting room when I went in. They sat quietly facing me over a desk. They asked after Clive. I explained the difficulties of finding anywhere suitable for Clive to go. They asked, was there anything they could do. I said, could they keep a lookout for any care solutions. Then there was a kind of lull. I told them I'd come for my smear test. They stared, registering this information. Then they lightened up quite a bit.

'I'll do it,' said the woman.

'Well, you've to be at the opera,' said the man. 'I'll take care of it.'

'Which would you prefer, Mrs Wearing?' asked the woman.

I'd rather have had the woman but didn't like to detain her. They both got up, chatting, drawing blinds. The woman grabbed her coat and bag, ready for her night out.

The exigencies of this new life were making me strong. Clive relied on me now. I had to defend him with a ferocity I didn't know I had in me. I forgot to be shy. My voice became louder. I had to speak up for Clive. The new strength translated into everything I did. I suddenly found I could swim length after length when I'd only ever splashed at widths in the shallow end of the baths. I'd never been out of my depth before.

I wrote in Clive's diary on 29 August 1985: 'Your wife, Deborah, showed you how strong her biceps are after she carried the car battery downstairs and put it back in the car all on her own. The only thing she couldn't do was to put the car seat back.'

But though I was gaining courage, car maintenance was never my forte. On Saturday 31 August I prompted Clive to write:

Deborah!!! ✓✓✓ ✓✓✓ wass a bit laet and tellyfond mei hosspittall 2 tel them knot too geeve mee eni suppper, andd wen I gott thu messsag I had already cut into my sausage. Deborah arrives and took me home in a TAXI becus our car wouldn't start (CW). She gave me fresh grilled sardines with mashed potato which she dug from her father's alottment, and B R O A D beans, followed by peaches (pitches).

Clive could by now spell perfectly well most of the time but wrote this way when I dictated a diary entry in order to amuse me, and to cover for any mistakes he might have made. I kept encouraging him to write down in his diary how he felt, but he only made a joke of it, probably because he didn't have access to enough inner information to know what his feelings were.

On Monday 2 September he wrote: 'How U feal. Well How do U feel. Down in the Direy.' On Tuesday 3 September I wrote, 'TODAY IS OUR SECOND WEDDING ANNIVERSARY!' And he wrote at my dictation:

Wee wentt whome with Michael Vyner and Terry Edwards. Eye played the harp *if* chord and if the piano and Terry Ps-ang. Then wee oppenind a bottul of shampain, Bollinger '73 which weed hadd four a weddding Pressent. Wee gaiv sum to our next door nayboor.

Then we had steak, potato waffles and broccoli and watched the 9 o'clock news. Then we got a taxi back.

Before he was ill, Clive didn't like to kiss in front of people. We generally went everywhere arm in arm or hand in hand but that was all. Occasionally I'd fling my arms round him and kiss him in the street.

'Not here!' he'd say. 'We're in public!' Perhaps there was no kissing in 1940s–50s Birmingham. However, the moment we were alone in a lift Clive would kiss me. It was our little joke. Then we'd spring apart and feign innocence just before the doors opened. After the illness Clive completely forgot his no-kissing-in-public policy, and if he heard music he might dance in the streets. To the doctors, this signified disinhibition from underlying frontal lobe damage. I preferred to see it as a break-through.

Taking Clive back to the hospital after our anniversary dinner felt all wrong. This time last year we had been celebrating our first anniversary with great hopes of conducting success and a second family. Returning home alone on the Bakerloo line, letting myself into the flat where Clive had just been talking, laughing, our dinner things still in the sink, his music where he left it on the harpsichord. He was here and not here. We were together apart. His books filled the shelves, his clothes hung in his wardrobe. I was in the thick of him. So why wasn't he here?

One night the phone rang. I was sitting on the floor in the dark and put the receiver to my ear.

A voice said, 'Hello, love! 'Tis me!' At that moment I turned faint, lost my grip on the room altogether.

'Hello??' said the voice again. I felt I was drowning and trying to fight my way back to the surface. This was Clive's voice, and with the greeting he always used. How could this be? I had never expected to hear from him by phone again.

'Hello?' I whispered.

'*Darling!!*' He laughed joyously. We talked. I put the phone down at the end. I called the ward to find out what had happened, to make sure he was there. A nurse had dialled the number for him.

I couldn't stand the silence so I had the radio and TV playing in different rooms. I didn't like lights on. Everything was too bright. If visitors put on a central light I had to ask if I could switch it off again. I needed dark, to feel hidden. Black was my colour of choice. If I put on clothes of any other colour I had to change again immediately. I could not listen to music, apart from when Clive played. No concerts, no Radio 3, no tapes or records, because every performance was wrong. There was only one right performance of any work, and it was his. I knew Clive's response to music so intimately, I could hear a work performed and know exactly how Clive would have tackled it. None of them came anywhere near the mark.

I did, however, start listening to pop music. I realized one day that I could, because Clive wasn't there to be annoyed. I didn't know what any of the bands were called, but I played those stations at full volume in the car. When I gave someone a lift she said she felt sick from the jolting of the car as I tapped my foot on the accelerator in time to the music, lurching her forward. I wasn't affected, I hadn't known I was doing it. I come from a family of Welsh sailors. We're used to choppy seas.

Swashbuckling bravado was my main mode when dealing with Clive's situation and campaigning on his behalf; at work I drove myself hard. However, alone, I was inert, numb, or torn with raging grief. One Sunday evening the London Sinfonietta was on television, doing a piece they would have done with Clive, but he wasn't there and never would be. I wept loudly and wanted to tell someone, wanted someone else to understand what this performance was missing, to see the Sinfonietta without him. In the main I didn't cry in front of other people: my grief was silent, imploded, paralysing. But this night was different. I telephoned my friend Caroline and tried to speak through my crying. I couldn't have been very coherent but she understood. 'Turn the television off, Deborah,' she said. 'Turn it off! . . . I'm coming over.' And she ran out of her house in Kentish Town and got a cab over to my house and by the time she got there I had cheered up quite a bit just because someone else could agree with me.

We switched it off and had some tea and then things didn't seem so bad. Caroline had to go, as she had left her husband George at home with a half-cooked supper, and then I was alone again.

It took me years and years to get used to the emptiness of the bed. I took to wearing a big sloppy jumper of Clive's over my pyjamas. It was one he'd worn since his early twenties, long and warm and of Scandinavian design. Wearing it was like wearing Clive.

It was odd things that penetrated my emotional cordon. Failing to get the lid off a jar of pickles, for example, felt like the end of the world. Clive had always done lids. He should have been here for this lid. Everything came down to that. The full jar sat out on the kitchen counter for weeks.

My company kept asking what did I need. Nothing, I said. Nothing matters when the one thing you want you can't have. But they saw my difficulties in ferrying Clive around. Public transport would not have been safe. The directors who managed funds for staff grants were immensely kind. They announced they were giving me a car.

The directors wrote to me like uncles. 'Mr G—— and I are always at the end of a phone,' wrote Mr S——. Kindness always made me want to cry.

I bought a good second-hand Vauxhall Astra with the firm's gift. Clive liked the car and commented that my driving had improved. He always used to drive before so I wasn't very good at parking or at going in a straight line. I would watch the white lines in the middle of the road and find I had veered towards them and have to keep compensating. The fact that Clive had registered the difference in my driving now, in the midst of his amnesia, shows just what an impression it had made on him. No wonder he had never let me drive.

The staff on Clive's psychiatric ward, unlike staff on a general medical ward, had in their brief some duty of care to the family, as it was understood that the nearest and dearest of someone in the Paterson Wing was likely to be in need of support. The nurses would invite me to pull up a chair and talk, so I frequently did. It was a relief to talk to professionals. I didn't have to worry about burdening them with my troubles.

Sometimes the pain was so bad I didn't know how I could bear it another hour, or five minutes. I called the Samaritans a couple of times. They were engaged.

I did look in the phone book, but could locate no emergency service for what I had. It was like bereavement, but time gave me no distance; it only drew me deeper into my loss. Clive had no escape, so neither did I. I rang a bereavement service once but they said I didn't meet their criteria because Clive was alive.

What got me up in the mornings was the need to keep going for Clive and for my family. But when I got home from work, once the front door closed, I saw little point in going any further. I would lie down on the floor where I was, probably creasing my suit, the corner of my briefcase sticking into my face.

The world appears at odd angles from the floor. The crack under the front door was very wide. Sometimes the air from outside hurt my eyeballs. Dust from the carpet irritated my lungs, and the compressed weave of wool scraped my cheek as I turned my head. There were small carpet hairs on the skirting board. Through the window was nothing but sky, sky, sky. I could hear my neighbours living their lives above and below me, crockery clattering on draining boards, the dog from downstairs being let into the garden for a run and a bark. Sometimes my phone rang and the voice of one of my parents or a friend would speak into the empty room. I might lie there seeing ceiling and carpet fluff until colour faded and moonlight came in.

I wasn't on the floor all the time. It came in spates. There was a 7/11 store on the corner open all night. I would go and buy a dairy cream sponge dusted with caster sugar, a Swiss roll with ice cream, a few packets of crisps, chocolate bars, a tin of rice pudding and one of ravioli, some cheese or currant buns, and eat these goodies in front of the television. I ate because I had a pain in my throat, like a knife lodged. Swallowing food might provide temporary relief for a hungry soul, so I gorged on comfort foods in addition to large meals. At times I was skinny as a rake, or I might balloon up. Or I might go to the gym three or four times a week as a way of getting tough and fighting against the pain.

I used to wonder if Clive ever noticed the changes in my appearance. Against the idea of me that he retained in his memory, I appeared in his doorway in many different sizes from skinny to large, with long red hair or short mousy hair, wild or neat, in pinstripes or in grunge. He was always pleased to see me.

I couldn't seem to get enough oxygen. People thought I was sighing, but I was only trying to suck in enough air to fill my lungs. I would get dizzy spells, even when driving. I'd have to stop in service stations because I thought I was going to pass out at the wheel. It was vertigo at ground level.

Clive's new neighbours were like no one he had ever spent time with. He shared the ward with people who were acutely mentally ill. One walked about half dressed and smeared faeces on the lavatory wall. There was much wailing and shouting. Clive would look at his companions and say to me out of the corner of his mouth, 'Have I been like that?'

'No, love, nothing like it.'

'Phew!!! Thank goodness for that!' he'd say, mopping his brow.

There was one mother who visited her son every day, though she had to take two buses and was always laden with shopping for her other children whom she'd had to leave at home. I had thought my life was difficult but at least I had a job, a car and people around me to help. I should have offered her a regular lift. At least I could have saved her all that waiting for buses.

I liked the other patients. At one time there was a young boy with a guitar and a group of us started singing Beatles songs with him. It was outside Clive's usual repertoire but he sang the harmonies with good grace. The staff eyed us through the glass surround. Their charges who were usually fighting were suddenly singing.

When I left Clive in the unit I would pause in the street and look up at his blue-curtained window among all the other blue-curtained windows. His was the one with a plant. The whir of the generator continued night and day.

Clive was still capable of finding a public payphone downstairs and his long-term memory allowed him to ask the operator to make a reverse-charge call. He remembered his home number, which had stayed the same when we moved, so he'd known it for fourteen years.

I would stand over the machine listening to his BBC voice announcing the news of his awakening. His voice from message to message would go from excited and cheerful to angry or despairing, often ending in a desperate, pleading whisper close to tears.

*Hello, love, 'tis me, Clive. It's five minutes past four, and I don't know what's going on here. I'm awake for the first time and I haven't spoken to anyone. I only want to speak to you. Please come, darling. Please come. Get here as soon as you can, by helicopter if you have to. I only want to see you, nobody else. Please come, darling, please come! PLEASE COME!! . . .* [Click. Bip.]

*Hello, love, 'tis me, Clive. It's nine minutes past four and I'm awake. I don't know what's going on, but I want to speak to you. Get here as soon as you can. Please come, darling, please come! Please come, please come! I love you. Please come, PLEASE COME! . . .* [Click. Bip.]

*Darling? Hello, it's me, Clive. It's a quarter past four and I'm awake now for the first time. It all just happened a minute ago, and I want to see you. Get here right away, darling, at the speed of light. Please come, please come, please come. I just want to see you and talk to you and find out what the hell's been going on. Please come, darling, please come, please come – I don't want to talk to anyone except you, darling – I love you – please come, PLEASE COME! . . .* [Click. Bip.]

*Darling? It's me, Clive, and it's eighteen minutes past four and I'm awake. My eyes have just come on about a minute ago, and I can see everything normally for the first time. I haven't spoken to anyone yet, I just want to talk to you, so please get here as soon as you can. I love you, darling, please come, please come. Do whatever you have to* [he meant take a taxi, use any transport whatever the cost], *I don't care, I don't care about anything except you, darling. Please come, please come, PLEASE COME!! PLEASE come . . . !!* [Click.]

There is one baffling entry in Clive's diary:

At [*9.07 deleted*] 10.00 I WAS AWAKE. Telephone <u>didn't</u> WORK.
At 10.10pm I attempted to arrange a call.

Since the telephone was situated a couple of floors beneath Clive's, I still don't know how he managed to remember what he had done long enough to write it down, unless he took his diary with him. Maybe he was asking to use the ward telephone.

I had regretted not knowing all of his past. Now no one, not even Clive, had access to his present.

On Monday 23 December 1985 I wrote in Clive's diary:

Hallo Darling!
When I arrived I found you alone downstairs telephoning me and the staff did not know you had gone.

I asked to speak to Dr B— who was here on the ward at the time but he decided to go home instead. No-one here takes me seriously. I shall have to take action. Love from your wife, Deborah xx

There was a sense in which Clive was still my confidant, the one I told things to.

One Saturday in December the Europa Singers were to do their usual stint singing carols under the tree in the National Theatre foyer. I thought it would be a good idea to take Clive along. It might make it Christmassy for him. He'd see faces he knew, he might even sing along from the audience. We arrived while the group was singing one of our old favourites and I walked Clive up to one of the galleries so we could get a good view of the singers in their festive red and green. But I had not accounted for the effect seeing Clive here on this of all days might have on the choir. As we leaned on the balcony, one by one our friends began to notice us. But instead of beaming at us as I had expected, their eyes filled with tears. I found out from them afterwards that it was hard enough doing this traditional Europa jaunt without Clive. To see him suddenly appear was too much. It was all they could do to keep singing.

I got out our box of decorations and the silver tree and fixed up the flat for Clive to spend Christmas at home. The fridge was packed, the fruit bowl overflowing on to the table. I woke in the night to find Clive in his dressing gown, a pair of nutcrackers in his hand and the wastepaper basket deep with peel, cores and nut-shells.

'You've never eaten all the fruit, the nuts!' I said.

'No,' said Clive, and of course he hadn't, as far as he was concerned. Those nuts, whoever had eaten them, had been consumed before he became conscious. He appeared to have no feeling of satiety in those days. I had read that this was a sign of damage to a part of the brain called the hypothalamus. I had to try to hide any food when I was asleep. Another night I found him in the kitchen halfway through a catering pack of peanut butter, which he was eating with a dessert spoon.

I took Clive to Westminster Cathedral on Christmas morning. As he had sung there for twenty-five years I thought he would feel at home. But he was not used to being among the congregation and, again, his erstwhile fellow singers got quite a shock seeing him there as they slow-paced towards us in procession down the nave. Several of them gave me a slight nod. They could not do more than that in their sombre garb and with their cathedral faces on. All the way through the service Clive kept asking, 'What day is it? It's not Christmas Day, is it?' I was conscious of the people around us who must have thought this an odd question to keep repeating. We were on safe ground here because there were people who knew us.

We went for lunch afterwards in a dusty steak restaurant in Victoria. One other table was occupied. We had not booked. I had not known where we were going to eat that day. It didn't matter. Who goes to an empty steak house in Victoria Street on a day when everyone else has plans?

I recognized the family at the other table immediately as being in the same boat as us. An elderly couple sat opposite their middle-aged daughter. She wore a small hat a long way up on her hair and obviously had some kind of mental handicap. They spoke in whispers, and ate neatly, deferential to the waiters. The waiters had nothing else to do and so they were around the table like flies, moving cruets, offering more bread, filling glasses. I knew from the parents' faded backs and the flat grey of their hair that they were wondering what would happen to their daughter when they died. Who would have Christmas with her then? The daughter was wearing her best clothes and wished she had a husband and a safe home of her own. They were all three a little nervous at being out, and a little sad at being in such an empty place, but then empty is best if you don't want people looking, or if you don't want a noise. It is important to have a quiet environment to hear yourself think. Disorders of thinking are not helped by background chatter or 'Jingle Bells'. Yes, this was the right place for all of us. We were far enough away that they would not have overheard our conversation. They might not even have realized we had anything in common.

The chain-restaurant menus were fixed: steak chasseur, steak in mushroom sauce, steak in a basket. I read out a couple of choices to Clive. We ordered the grilled sirloin. The sauce bottles had all been wiped down – you could tell because they were still damp – and there was bent silver holly on doilies. Dust seemed to rest on everything, as if the tables had been laid years ago. There was an eerie silence. Through the fugged window, the outside looked strange. There was no traffic, just the odd empty bus running between Victoria station and Westminster.

Our loop-tape conversation ran on as usual, but underneath I was worrying what Clive would do next. He might start belching loudly and double up in a fit, or shout out if he got cross, or bolt from the restaurant if they put music on. He might say peculiar things to the waiters. He might get upset about the price of steak and yell his disgust, or run out into the road. He might throw his dinner on the floor. He might dance.

We both had a glass of red wine. There was dust in the wine. Clive kept clinking glasses because he didn't know he'd done it before. It felt like we were drinking the dust into our hearts. The steak was chewy. The other family left and then we were alone at our table by the window. Clive felt he had to finish quickly though I told him not to worry. We drove home, Clive looking to left and right at the junctions and telling me, 'OK left! OK left! All clear!'

I watched Christmas on TV. Clive paced and said never mind the television, just tell me how long have I been ill. He did not sleep much but was up and down at night, asking how long, how long, how long, just tell me, how long? And the minutes and the hours were all the same, same question after same question without respite, piling up in my mind like sawdust. With every hour, it seemed we were disintegrating.

Clive got worse. His violence escalated. The shouting, threats, outbursts were terrible. They upped his drugs. It made little difference. Perhaps the more they gave him the more inclined he was to fight the forces that befuddled him. All he wanted to do was wake up. Clive was on a high dose of Mellerill, a major tranquillizer, sometimes known as 'liquid kosh'. But it did not seem to have much effect.

Clive could have no memory of where he was and yet the amnesia for his environment did not protect him from institutionalization. His conversation reduced down and down until he had little more than a few short rants repeated verbatim. It was bad enough to be trapped in the minuscule window of consciousness left by the amnesia, but to find yourself in the place where he was, surrounded by others with such disturbed behaviour, seemed to add insult to injury. His situation was completely unacceptable.

Clive and I spent most of our evenings walking around the vicinity of Praed Street, Paddington. If we went into a shop where there was pop music playing, Clive would usually do an ape dance complete with lolling tongue and boss eyes to show his opinion of the music. The cashiers might laugh at first, but then as

Clive's dance and grotesque expressions continued with snarling comments about the inanity of the music and a certain amount of raspberry-blowing, they would get rather nervous. I tried to shove the shopping into bags and pay as quickly as possible, being polite to them and responsive to Clive (whose opinions of the music were valid if extreme), but in the end I might succumb to giggling and hustle us both out of there. I tried not to go back to the same shops too often. I learned to avoid ones with music.

The hospital domestics refused to clean Clive's room since he terrified them, so I did it. One weekday lunchtime I'd popped in to drop off some laundry on the way to an appointment. Clive was downstairs at lunch and there wouldn't be time for me to say hello to him as there could be no such thing as a brief hello with Clive. If you haven't seen your wife in ten or twenty years you expect more than a hurried kiss and a 'see you later!' If I ran in and ran out I could just make my appointment, so I couldn't afford to bump into him.

On the way down the stairs, I saw Clive round the landing below, heading towards me. He climbed the stairs, hugging the wall, not looking anywhere but straight ahead of him. I knew if he saw me I would be late. I hesitated but kept going. Clive didn't see me, I didn't stop. I passed him. He didn't look back. I heard him go through his ward door higher up. My feet continued down the electric-blue carpet.

The horror of walking down those stairs returned to me for a long time.

# 8

## LOOKING FOR ANSWERS

CLIVE WAS GETTING WORSE ON THE ACUTE PSYCHIATRIC WARD, BUT there were no care services for people with this kind of brain injury. A whole clinical group appeared to have been forgotten. If you weren't mentally ill, physically handicapped, elderly or suffering from a congenital learning disability – in other words, if you had an acquired brain injury and could walk – there was very little in most parts of the country. Making the documentary film was a first step in my strategy to provoke the authorities into providing brain-injury treatment and care. Then Dr Barbara Wilson and I planned to gather all the experts and families we were in touch with, or who came forward as a result of the documentary, and launch a national charity. Through this we could spearhead the campaign for appropriate services.

I spoke to Clive about taking part in the film a number of times. I described the idea in short sentences, just to gauge whether he was comfortable with it. His response was always the same. 'If people can learn,' he said, 'we must help. It's important!'

I had a presenter in mind, Dr Jonathan Miller. Not only had he presented the last big BBC series on anatomy, *The Human Body*, but also he had been Clive's contemporary at Cambridge, one of the Footlights Review team with Dudley Moore and Peter Cook. A doctor turned opera director, he had recently done a stint at Sussex University researching brain-injured patients with memory problems and had also recently presented a film, *Ivan*, about a mathematician with a neurological disease. It turned out he even lived near us.

I didn't need to think hard about asking him. He didn't have to think hard about accepting. Channel 4 had just commissioned him to make a programme for their new series, *Equinox*. The scenario of a musician with no memory fitted the brief. I met him together with the director, John Dollar, in an Indian restaurant in Baker Street. Clive would have enjoyed the meal. By the time they brought in the *ras malai*, we had our documentary.

The centrepiece of the film would be an experiment to see if Clive, faced with his whole choir and some familiar music, would be able to conduct them. I suspected he would. Miller and Dollar were prepared to go with my hunch.

On day one of filming, when Clive came into the hospital chapel, the singers of the London Lassus Ensemble watched one of his prolonged and racking reunions with me, weeping, jerking, belching at the shock of it. But the moment his fingers touched the organ to accompany his friend Linda, they saw the old Clive again, having a blast. I led him from the organ and, lo, his choir was suddenly in front of him, familiar music on the lectern. How could he resist? It was a piece of music he loved and used as a signature tune at most Lassus Ensemble concerts – *Musica Dei Donum* (Music the Gift of God), a sumptuous piece. Casually I asked him, would he conduct it?

'I don't know what might happen . . .' he said.

He lifted his hands – and then he was conducting. It was second nature to him. The music's own momentum carried him from bar to bar. Inside a piece of music, Clive was in time once again. To perform music you need only the phrase you are in. While the music sounded Clive had structure, a context, safe ground. For the time he is in the music, provided it is taking his full attention, he forgets the abyss at his back. He has continuum. But when the music stops, he falls out of time all over again.

The singers couldn't believe their eyes. They said it was like a throwback to their days on the South Bank. There was Clive, mouthing the words, giving all their entries, in complete control.

Afterwards he thanked them all graciously. He embraced his old flatmate in the front row.

'That was marvellous!' he said. 'I waved my arms, and you sang!'

'Do you remember who we are?' asked one.

'Your faces look very familiar,' he said, 'but I can't remember anybody's name.' Clive chatted to them, describing his condition as if it were no more than a curiosity. His stock of conversation exhausted, he took his leave in the manner of someone hastening to his next appointment. He was charming, engaging, debonair and completely himself.

Later the cameras filmed Clive talking with Miller in the empty chapel. A good twenty minutes after his friends had left he made an intriguing remark:

'I can't remember now what was going on here this morning . . . I don't know whether anybody sang . . .'

Now it could be that Clive generally associated chapels, or even this chapel in particular, with singing and the playing of music.

Or could it be that the experience of conducting his own choir here was so significant to him that he still bore a faint trace of it and was casting about to see if the memory were true?

Later in the week the film crew packed us and their equipment into a minibus and drove us to Cambridge. We would discover what Clive remembered of the place where he had been a student. We stopped at a roadside café for bacon sandwiches and coffee en route. Clive remained quiet, occupied with his drink and snack. To go anywhere with him in a relatively stress-free situation, with others around to help, was like a holiday for me.

Clive was delighted to see his old friend Stephen Cleobury waiting to greet us at the entrance to King's College Chapel. On film, it is quite strange to watch the people pouring out of the chapel. They were giving us a good look as if to say, what's so special about this pair that everyone is being turfed out just because they arrive?

We talked in the organ loft; Clive played a silly tune. They wanted to film us walking around the quadrangle afterwards. But Clive was growing agitated. I should have stepped in, asked for time out. Would we just walk around again, they asked. Whenever Clive's mind was not actively engaged – and it could only really be engaged now in performing music – he would fall back into the dark crack of amnesia. Sometimes he spoke to me in a sad or desperate or bewildered way. This time it was straight black anger. His voice frightened me.

'It's like being dead! They're behaving with stupidity, the people who are treating me . . . I've never seen anything like it in my life!'

He was shouting. People stopped to look, uncertain what was going on. It is not usual to hear anger in a Cambridge quadrangle.

Suddenly Clive saw the crew under the archway filming us, and he went berserk. He snarled and made a lunge for the tripod, shouting his head off. I can be heard out of shot, saying we couldn't get out of there. There was no escape.

A porter hared across the lawn, like a raven flapping in his long black gown, yelling for us to stop. The production team went to him, while I hustled Clive through a 'No Exit' sign to the Backs. Perhaps King's hadn't known what they were taking on when they agreed to let us film there. The crew were shaken, but full of compassion. Having watched Clive through the viewfinder for a few days, they had come to understand something of the trauma he was going through every second of every day. They hadn't known such a torment existed. They were a hundred per cent committed to telling his story right. The cameraman observed with all the skills he had. Focusing on Clive's face, picking up his whisperings, he could register on film the depths of feeling that Clive was unable to articulate.

A good half an hour after the fracas at King's, the sound man was twiddling his knobs, wondering what on earth was wrong with his equipment. Over the sound of Clive and me talking, there was a loud knock-knocking. It was the lapel mike picking up my heart still thumping. This was not turning out to be an easy day.

Back home, Clive watched the LLE sequence on video. He was upset and bewildered to see himself in a scene that had never occurred in a place he had never been. We called a halt, fetched coffee. Five minutes later Clive watched the video again: for him, the first time of viewing. This time he had a totally different reaction. He was tickled, he thought it hilarious to see himself conducting when he had no knowledge of being conscious.

'*Look!*' He pointed to the screen, delighted, intrigued. 'I'm *chatting*!!'

For the purpose of the film, I helped Jonathan Miller quiz Clive, to try to arrive at an understanding of how he saw things. I would never have pursued this line ordinarily, but we were trying to show how much Clive understood, the extent of his memory. Miller persisted in his opinion that Clive had no memory, while Clive fiercely defended his dictum that it was consciousness he lacked. Finally Clive erupted:

'I *wasn't conscious*, I have *no knowledge of it at all*! *Consciousness has to involve ME!!!*'

And here Miller had to concede.

'You . . . you're quite right,' he said humbly.

Without memory, without something inside oneself available to conscious inspection, there is no evidence of consciousness. Unconsciousness then is the only tenable explanation.

The film attempted to capture an idea of Clive's experience of constant awakening, although we knew it would be no more than an inkling, the shift of mindset required to grasp it being perhaps impossible.

Clive's observations about himself were completely valid. He was able to give a lucid eyewitness account from the standpoint of the person with the worst known case of amnesia ever. He was describing his pinprick light-hole of conscious experience; he could explain what happens to a person when time ceases to exist.

To help explain it in the documentary, I used Proust. His eight-volume search for lost time, entering memory through the smell and taste of a madeleine dipped in herb tea, starts with a description of awakening in a strange room, that moment when you open your eyes and cannot for the life of you think where you are. As I read it to Miller, they played time-frame footage they'd shot of Clive in his hospital room from a camera left running behind the one-way mirror hospital staff used to observe him as he was thought to be at risk. The camera shot a frame every so many minutes, which, very much speeded up, showed a jerky representation of morning light dawning in his room through closed curtains, and his actual awakening, his getting up, and making his first entries of the day in his diary on his bed. Awake first time, really awake first time, completely awake first time, superlatively awake first time, first true consciousness . . . Proust wrote:

> . . . when I awoke at midnight, not knowing where I was, I could not be sure at first who I was; I had only the most rudimentary sense of existence, such as may lurk and flicker in the depths of an animal's consciousness; I was more destitute of human qualities than the cave-dweller; but then the memory, not yet of the place in which I was, but of various other places where I had lived, and might now very possibly be, would come like a rope let down from heaven to draw me up out of the abyss of not-being, from which I could never have escaped by myself: in a flash I would traverse and surmount centuries of civilisation, and out of a half-visualised succession of oil-lamps, followed by shirts with turned-down collars, would put together by degrees the component parts of my ego.*

Then the film cut to Clive in our bedroom at home, describing in his own words this abyss of not-being from which he cannot escape. I think it was just him and the cameraman while the rest

*Marcel Proust, *Swann's Way*, Part One of *Remembrance of Things Past* (Chatto & Windus, 1922), p. 4.

of us were in the kitchen. And what Clive said was uncannily close to the Proust. He spoke of awakening in a strange place, how at first 'you are still mentally in your imagination . . . Gradually you open your eyes and they focus on the things around you and they remind you and tell you and it all settles down. And I've been in that before-settling-down all the time.'

So he knew. Clive's insight and his eloquence in describing his perceptions were quite remarkable, given his problems. His memory loss had no effect on his sense of identity or on his human qualities. Clive's 'soul', I told Miller, was intact.

'I haven't lost sight of the Cliveness of Clive,' I said. But I asked, 'I don't know at this stage how to see the next thirty years stretching ahead of us. What will it be? Twenty-four hours after twenty-four hours of perseverating and agony for him . . .' Given that he had the capacity to be a huge human being through his music and through loving me, I wanted to know how to help him. How, I asked Miller, do I make his life worth living?

No answer comes. The film ended there.

*Prisoner of Consciousness* struck a chord with all who saw it. It attracted an extraordinary amount of attention in the press and media. What particularly spoke to people was the way Clive would behave every time he saw me again. As Nancy Banks-Smith wrote in the *Guardian*, 'A sudden, piercing joy transfigured Clive Wearing's face: "Darling," he cried, "oh darling," and, jumping up, held his wife with the shuddering gasps of a man just saved from drowning. We saw the incredulous blaze of joy three times, each time so intense you'd think he would die of it. It was the look of a man who believes his wife dead and sees her alive and smiling.'

The documentary sold to TV stations in twenty-five countries.

It was nominated for a BAFTA and became a teaching video for psychology students. Professors who showed it to every new intake learned it off by heart. It even left a residual impression on Clive. He started to ask, 'They haven't been making films about all this, have they?'

Barbara Wilson and I asked Channel 4 to help us launch a national charity by putting a card up after the broadcast with a PO Box address. We would name our charity The Amnesia Association. I went out one lunch hour to order headed notepaper. I had to choose the colour instantly so I said forest green, the house colour of John Lewis. I knew the Pantone number.

The Amnesia Association was still only nominal until formally incorporated and registered but we had the notepaper, and seeing was believing. We set a date for an inaugural meeting in the autumn of 1986 at Charing Cross Hospital.

Around the time of the broadcast, our story was everywhere. I saw people reading about Clive's situation on the Tube. Barbara and I did many interviews. As we described the appalling lack of suitable facilities in Britain and our intention to press for decent services, all sorts of people got in touch with offers of help. Lowe Howard Spink, the ad agency, offered us a free poster campaign on the London Underground, which went on to win an industry award. Artists were inspired to draw cartoons, which I would later use in *Recall*, the magazine I created for our charity. *Prisoner of Consciousness* inspired over three hundred relatives of people like Clive to write in. Here was a nucleus for the association. We filled the lecture theatre at Charing Cross Hospital at our first gathering. Many had travelled long distances to be there. We had a mission. There was a whole mass of people out there with problems of memory, behaviour and thinking who were not served by health and social services. Even those with relatively minor or moderate brain damage might have bad enough problems to make it impossible to hold down a job or to manage their own affairs and live independently. They might have undergone a shift in personality, and seem changed in outlook, character and mood.

We quickly built up a picture of where specialist services existed nationwide. In very few places, it seemed, did people with acquired brain injury (ABI) fit into a category of care in the NHS. In a very few enterprising places a local authority or health authority would have created a small extra classification designating funding and services to brain injury. But typically, if the brain damage had caused motor or physical problems, the individual would be seen as a physically disabled person, and cared for under that heading. The rest were largely ignored, unless their behaviour or dependency level was so acute as to make it necessary to give them some kind of care, in which case they were dealt with ad hoc. Sometimes brain-injured people would be lumped in with those suffering from dementias such as Alzheimer's or Huntington's Disease, which present an entirely different set of needs and problems; sometimes they ended up in homes for people with learning disabilities or for the elderly, despite being relatively young, and sometimes they were sent home and given very little help or support because the doctors assessing them for benefits had such crude tests that they did not show up even very severe deficits.

We heard of many GPs who had told amnesic people that there was nothing wrong with them. Mothers told me about taking their adult children to the doctor and being told to wait outside, even though their charge had no idea of their reason for being there and would be unable to remember anything the doctor had said when they left the room. What marks out acquired brain injury as different from other disabilities is that very often a person may present absolutely normally. They may look the same, sound the same and, because the memory disorder means they forget how much they're forgetting, they may have scant idea just how disabled they are. When damage is specific to one part of the brain rather than widespread, an amnesic person is likely to have preserved intelligence and skills, with areas of knowledge reasonably intact. It is this mixture of severe disorder and preserved intellectual functioning which makes the condition very hard to grasp. It also means that the needs of the individual are greater, because they don't know what they don't know.

'How are you feeling?' a GP may ask.

'Fine!' may come the response.

'How's your memory?'

'Not too bad,' is a typical amnesic answer. And so it goes.

Families and lives were falling apart because the help that should have been given was not available. Perhaps the ultimate irony was that some of the best work on brain injury and memory had been developed by British psychologists. Their books were on bookshelves in brain injury care facilities worldwide. But they had no rehab facility in their own country.

We registered with the Charity Commissioners and were incorporated as a company. A committee was elected and officers appointed.

One of the biggest causes of brain injury is road accidents, and the biggest group affected is young men. The greatest fear we encountered was that of exhausted, ageing parents who worried what would happen when they died, or when they were no longer fit enough to cope. We began to see that the numbers of people so affected had shot up dramatically as resuscitation techniques and drugs improved. People who before would have died now survived, but with worse brain damage. There was a whole new group of brain injury survivors with more severe problems and no appropriate services to treat or care for them.

Everyone I met, every family who phoned me at the end of their tether, every story I heard, confirmed the need to start The Amnesia Association. With funding from the Department of Health, the Mental Health Foundation and a growing cohort of charities and benefactors, we began to get organized. We employed a part-time secretary to work from home and provide a helpline, we produced leaflets to explain the brain in language that families and a cross section of professionals could easily understand. Our team consisted of neuropsychs, families and legal advisers all working closely together. Our first project was to write a booklet, to be produced by Thames TV's *Help* programme, giving families and lay people the explanations of memory and cognitive deficits they so desperately needed. It made a big difference if people understood the neuro-pathological reasons for particular behaviours. Wives told me that they argued with their brain-injured husbands when they talked nonsense or didn't take in or accept some truth. Once you could show them that the cells or structures necessary to taking in information were simply missing, it helped them see there was no point in arguing. They could find other ways of relating to a husband, accepting who he was now. If they understood what was causing the personality change, it helped them not to take his behaviour personally. When a brain-injured son was behaving aggressively and the parents knew that this stemmed from frontal lobe damage, instead of talking back or getting angry themselves, they could shrug and think, oh, he's being a bit frontal today, and move on.

The vast majority of people who contacted the association

were looking after their brain-injured relative at home following minimal or no rehab, and without any appropriate support. Time and again we would hear from family members who did not know how they could continue with the strain of caring. Despair and thoughts of suicide were topics that came up frequently. Often a man who had been the breadwinner was now brain-injured, but it could work the other way. A wife and mother might be the one needing full-time care from a husband or elderly parent. To be refused benefits on top of all that made an already terrible life quite impossible.

Our Scientific Board of neuropsychiatrists and neuro-psychologists made their priority the provision of workshops and seminars to professionals from the many disciplines who worked with brain injury. With their guidance we went on producing leaflets, advising the NHS and professional institutions and developing better assessment tools. In addition, our experts were a source of advice and information to anyone seeking to know more about amnesia. A network of local groups offered a local focus and a way for families to share and promote their needs in their own communities. Centrally we worked with government and media to lobby for services and care standards. We called the charity AMNASS for short.

I gave up my job at John Lewis in order to be more available to the charity as a non-executive director, and earned money at an arts sponsorship agency two or three days a week.

I decided to sell our flat in Maida Vale. It was too painful to come home to the flat where Clive had lived and wasn't living now. In my fight to stay afloat, I ate too much, worked too hard, and was subject to over-the-top highs of adrenalin as well as terrible lows. But any discomfort I felt was as nothing compared to what Clive went through all the time.

I bought a flat in Crouch End. Clive would have called it out in the sticks. It was further to bring him home at weekends, but he had no idea how long we were in the car. He liked the place and could tell it was home because of his bookcases.

AMNASS soon became too big to operate out of a family's front room. Happily we secured premises at St Charles Hospital in Ladbroke Grove. I often worked there when I wasn't at the office where I was freelancing. We were a last port of call for many families.

If acquired brain injury was not already in anyone's remit, then no one wanted to take it on now. Every so often a report would be published looking at the problem. The authors were in agreement about how severe the situation was in terms of service provision, but there was no funding, no mandate for change. A report by the Social Services Inspectorate was honest enough to say that one reason for not creating brain injury services was it might 'open the floodgates' and be too costly. In the meantime patients like Clive were languishing on expensive and inappropriate hospital wards. They were known in the system as 'bed-blockers'.

Nobody seemed to take into consideration that the new generation of survivors would all be thrust upon the state when their elderly carers died. We judged it to be a time bomb.

Our problem – and one we kept coming back to – was the dearth of statistics on ABI: the way brain injuries were recorded – or not recorded – in hospitals. Records taken referred to the primary reason for admission rather than to secondary damage, even if this turned out to be, as it generally was with any brain injury, the most debilitating feature of outcome. There were many possible causes of brain damage. For example, lack of oxygen, which led to diffuse damage over a wide area, could occur with near-drowning, carbon monoxide poisoning or cardiac arrest. More local and specific damage was caused by aneurysm, cerebral haemorrhage, tumour, and diseases such as meningitis or encephalitis. And then there was the kind of damage caused by chronic alcoholism coupled with a want of thiamine leading to Korsakov's syndrome, the illness that struck Jimmie G (the case Clive read about shortly before his own amnesia). The chief cause of brain injury was, however, head injury, but even these were often multiple injury cases. It was difficult then to go to the government and say we knew the need was big because they only asked us, 'How big?' The Department of Health gave us a sympathetic hearing and talked it over, but although they encouraged us we could get little commitment from them. The sticking point always seemed to be statistics. They needed statistics to justify expenditure but no one seemed prepared to get hospitals to collect them in a different way.

The other thing that taxed us was the fact that paramedic ambulance crews and A&E teams had no set way of gauging whether a patient might be brain-injured. The first hour was crucial in limiting damage and preventing secondary damage, yet hospitals often started treating a fractured jaw while failing to notice rising intra-cranial pressure, brain swelling that would have a far more devastating impact on someone's life than the broken bones. We were looking for the universal adoption of simple systems to ensure that the tell-tale signs of a brain in trouble were picked up straight away.

As for treatment and support following the acute phase in hospital, we had to get health and social services to recognize that people with acquired brain injury had different needs from those who were born with brain defects or those with a dementia. ABI caused selective impairments, leaving people with preserved skills, parts of the pre-injury self intact. People with a dementia such as Alzheimer's will be affected more generally as the disease progresses.

There was another problem. With so few specialist brain injury services around, professionals with expertise were thin on the ground. After all, why train in a specialism for which there were hardly any facilities, a handful of jobs? The cognitive neuro-psychologists or -psychiatrists associated with AMNASS were mainly academics, based in universities or with the Medical Research Council. Patients were referred to them for assessment because there was no one in clinical practice in their region. They had chapter and verse on how brain-injured people were affected, sometimes over long periods when they involved them in studies with long-term follow-up. But although the assessments were sometimes useful in convincing benefits assessors or GPs that an individual was truly incapable of independent living and dependent on high levels of care, many had little access to the help or care that might have made life more bearable or at least safe.

Serious studies on brain injury were being published by august bodies – the Royal College of Physicians, the Royal College of Surgeons, the Welsh Office, the Social Services Inspectorate, the Medical Disability Society. The acute need for rehab and longer-term services was not in doubt. We knew that a million people a year were admitted to UK hospitals with a head injury. We knew memory impairment to be the most common consequence of head injury. As a nascent national charity with only a part-time secretary in post, the best we could hope for was to campaign, draw attention to the problem, provide a teaching resource, a collaborative base for research and an advice and troubleshooting service.

I went to a conference of occupational therapists. Someone

asked a government health minister what the government was doing about brain-injured people with memory problems. He replied that they were funding The Amnesia Association, as if an £8,000 one-off grant would be sufficient for the nation's entire memory-impaired population, as if we were solely responsible. There was a sea of questioners waiting to ask other things but he said he had to leave and disappeared into his big black car.

It was all a bit chicken and egg. No stats, no staff, no places, no system, no clue what to do and everybody passing the buck. We decided we would have to make such a fuss that they would not be able to ignore us, but it would have to be a closely targeted fuss with clear, achievable objectives for the government to take forward.

One of the problems was that there were few precedents for this kind of care in Britain and the authorities would need clinical evidence and examples of best practice to use as models. All our psychologists told me the US was the place to look and spoke of the many kinds of rehab to be found there in a single region.

So it was that in the summer of 1988 I discovered America. With introductions from neuropsych colleagues, I gained entrée to the best units coast to coast, east, west, north and south. I arranged a lecture tour and was offered accommodation in the homes of doctors and psychologists. WNET Channel 13, the public service TV station in New York, had made a series on the brain with the BBC featuring Clive. I was invited to New York for the series launch in the Rainbow Room. I thought I would spend a couple of months gathering data and return with a grasp of America's best-practice models, and then things could get under way in Britain. The AMNASS line-up of expertise was impressive. I would be out there, on the credentials of my colleagues, as an

AMNASS director, giving talks on all sorts of things I had known nothing about until the last few years. I mostly talked about long-term outcome after ABI, about which there had been little research, and the treatment systems that existed in the UK and had so far failed to accommodate brain injury.

The idea of being away for two whole months felt like a much-needed escape. I didn't know whether Clive would miss me, since he missed me all the time anyway. Would my not being there make a difference? I managed to find a care agency that would go into the hospital several times a week to collect his washing and bring it back ironed. It couldn't just be a laundry service because the person would have to be sufficiently trained to encounter Clive.

The day before the grand tour I was dashing about with last minute errands. I happened to be in a taxi somewhere around Edgware Road when I looked out and had a shock. I thought I saw Clive standing in a crowd in the street watching a man selling something. It couldn't be Clive, but it looked just like him.

'Stop the cab please!' I called out. I persuaded the driver to back up to where I had seen him, under a bridge. I had to have been mistaken. But it really was Clive! We were hugging and kissing when the lady by him looked round. It was Alicia, one of his care assistants. They were out for a walk. I had planned to see Clive that evening to say goodbye – or hello, as far as he was concerned, for even when I was turning to go at the end of a visit, he had still only just spotted me that moment. But now I asked Alicia if I could take Clive with me, take him home for tea. She acquiesced, happy for us, and Clive and I hurried off, like a couple eloping, to the waiting taxi. At home, I was full of excitement. Once out of here I would be my own person, with none of the usual daily ties. Sitting across the kitchen table eating his dinner, Clive could have no conception of what I was about to embark on. The big news for him was that he had woken up. He didn't know that it was unusual for him to be at home on a weeknight, because he had no memory of ever being either at home or in hospital. It was a real bonus for me to share this meal with him, then leave him drinking coffee while I rushed about packing. I was going to miss him dreadfully.

My first stop was Canada, where I stayed for a week with an amnesic woman and her family. They had seen *Prisoner of Consciousness* on TV and were struck by the similarities. They wanted me to see how care was organized in Canada. This lady had recovered enough to continue working as a teacher, but nevertheless had a big struggle to get by. Even the bus ride to school was hard work, as she had to follow every street with her finger on the map so she would know which direction she was travelling in and when to get off.

I had never been to America before and landed in Pittsburgh just in time to watch a high-school football match. The area had been sooty and industrial, but had now turned into a clean 'silicon valley'. They seemed to have some kind of brain-injury facility on every street corner. I was staying with two British psychologists and their kids. They introduced me to the whole network of ABI treatment and care.

It seemed to me they had the whole thing sewn up here. First of all, a percentage of all car tax was paid straight into a fund to deal with care provision after road traffic accidents, so there was a constant pot of public money available. Then the insurance companies who paid out in personal injury cases wanted to have confirmation that their bucks were being used effectively. Weekly reports were submitted on patient progress, so that they could see the long-term economic value of effective rehab, with different services picking up the rehab baton at different stages along the path of recovery.

The assessment and treatment of ABI patients was complex, and demanded a good cross-disciplinary team observing and working with patients round the clock, not just in the care setting but also in their normal environment. Where the ability to learn was much reduced by amnesia, it was important to use what learning capacity there was in a strategic way. If you can learn only one thing, the best thing to learn is that when your alarm goes you look at your schedule, fastened to your belt or wheel-chair or handbag, to see what to do next. For people capable of working, there was vocational rehab and supported employment programmes. A job coach would be deployed to work side by side with the brain-injured person every day for up to a year so that an employer could feel confident about taking them back to work after their injury. Even if that person didn't get out of bed one morning, the coach would turn up to work and do the job for them.

In Britain, brain-injured people who had physically recovered would return to work and, without help, would repeatedly fail. They would be unable to hold down a job because there were no experts to help them over the humps, modifying behaviour, adjusting tasks, changing the environment, educating colleagues.

I went on to Atlanta, Georgia, to Cleveland, Ohio, and to Los Angeles, La Jolla and the University of Irvine in California. I went to Boston and New Hampshire and back to New York to visit a programme where patients were called 'students' and I could not distinguish them from the staff. I collected so many books and papers I had to keep shipping them home. It wasn't utopia. There were many people without insurance whose degree of support or abandonment varied according to where they lived. And there were few options for those needing long-term residential care. I spoke to family groups with similar experiences to my own. I learned that living with a person in this much grief is the same in any country.

And I realized that in a place with no developed public health system you were even more likely to be a casualty of circumstances. The penal system there, as in the UK, often neglected to assess suspects or convicts for possible brain injury underlying their apparently criminal behaviour. A brain injury study of prisoners on Texas' 'death row' showed somewhere near 80 per cent of offenders had significant brain damage that might indicate they were not wholly responsible for their behaviour.

I went home with examples I had gathered of good care. The proof that it was effective that would, I hoped, speed up the development of services and the release of funds. Studies looking at far greater numbers than in the UK provided convincing evidence that rehab worked.

Clive was pleased to see me on my return. He hugged me, kissed me, swung me round.

'You're the first person I've seen!' he exclaimed. 'My eyes have just come on. I'm seeing everything perfectly now! It was in black and white a few moments ago. Now everything's in colour. I'm alive!' He kissed me again but immediately started belching and jerking, unable to catch his breath, turning red, his eyes watering.

I asked the staff if they'd seen any difference in him while I had been away. I'd asked the same question in my calls to the ward while I was travelling. Their answers were always the same. He had seemed less agitated, calmer. Perhaps my being there was just too much of a reminder of the way he was, and the life he had lost. Certainly, my presence always brought on his belching seizures, and he was nearly free of them without me.

In the spring of '89 Clive's ward from St Mary's was temporarily transferred to St Charles Hospital, upstairs from where I was working part-time at AMNASS. It would mean I could pop in and see him easily. However, I could also hear him when he was shouting. I would have a distraught family on the phone in one ear, and Clive yelling in the distance in the other. Although he had no memory of St Mary's, moving to St Charles had clearly unsettled him. Through his years there he had acquired a sub-conscious familiarity with St Mary's and now that had gone. Here he was more lost than ever. Even I didn't like the change. I had become used to where we were. His room at St Charles was smaller, but they'd managed to bring his electric keyboard, so he did have something to play. I spent my breaks up there, and took him for walks around the neighbourhood.

One day I brought him down to the office to sit with me, but I couldn't get anything done as he needed to quiz me and demanded all my attention. That had never changed; there was no let-up.

'How long's it been?'

'Four years.'

'For years! Four years?! . . . Is that F-O-R or F-O-$U$-R (ha ha ha ha!)?'

'F-O-$U$-R.'

'What do you think it's like?'

'I don't know, darling.'

'It's been like death. How long?'

'Four years.'

'Four years!! One long night lasting . . . how long?'

'Four years.'

'Four years! Is that F-O-R or F-O-*U*-R (ha ha ha!)?'

'F-O-*U*-R.'

'Good heavens . . . I haven't seen anything until now. My eyes have just come on this moment. I'm seeing everything properly now. In colour. It was in black and white until a moment ago. How long's it been?'

'Four years.'

'Four years??!! I haven't heard anything, smelled anything, felt anything, touched anything, seen anything the whole time. How long?'

'Four years.'

'Four years!!! Is that F-O-R or F-O-*U*-R?'

'. . . F-O-*U*-R.'

'It's been one long night lasting . . .'

'. . . ' I sighed, unable to say it again.

'Four years! I haven't seen anything, heard anything, smelled anything, felt anything the whole time. It's like death! One long night lasting, how long?'

'Four years.'

'Four years! Is that F-O-R or F-O-*U*-R?'

'F-O-*U*-R.'

'Good heavens . . . ! I bet this is very rare. Is it rare?'

'Very rare, darling.'

'I bet it is. You're the first person I've seen. My eyes have come on just a few moments ago. I can see everything properly now! Everything's working normally! How long's it been?'

When the office phone rang, he stopped, stayed quiet, his head bowed, listening but not really following. Whenever he was out of his depth, which was when there was an ordinary conversation, or even when there was any speaking on a radio or television in the room, Clive would sink into this hunched attitude as if he were ashamed. He looked as if he could cry, as if he was being squeezed, making himself smaller so he occupied less space in the room.

Sometimes people came to the office. One man came in with his wife. He was carrying many plastic carrier bags full of paper. He made notes, he explained, so he would remember things. The trouble was, he was surrounded by bags and bags of paper because, basically, he forgot everything. The bags he carried around just contained the things he needed to know all the time. He began pulling out papers and looking at them before stuffing them back roughly. The trouble was, he said, he didn't know what was in the bags and he didn't know where to find what and wasn't sure what it was he needed to remember, and it took so long to keep looking when he couldn't recall what he was looking for. He ran his own business, he told me. But it wasn't going very well, admitted his wife. They had come to see us because he just had these problems remembering things. Nothing serious, of course. It wasn't as if it was anything like the AMNASS people they'd read about, but it was proving troublesome.

'Has your husband ever had a brain injury?' I asked.

'No!' replied the wife.

'So when did it start?'

'Oh, about seven or eight years ago, must be . . .' she said.

'And did anything else happen around that time?'

'No!' she said.

'Nothing,' he said.

'No illness of any kind, a fall, an accident?'

'Well, he did once fall off the roof . . .'

'And when was that?'

'Oh, about, er . . . well, it must be about eight years ago . . .'

And there we had it. We came across case after case of 'minor' brain injury that had occurred as part of a more complex injury and had never been picked up, never diagnosed. People were stoical, took doctors at their word. If nothing showed up on the scan, then there was nothing wrong with them. Forgetfulness, changes in mood, trouble concentrating or sleeping, recurrent headaches, all were put down to the shock of the accident. Then lives would come unravelled, and poor health, unemployment, divorce and depression were the result. But the thing causing the most problems for the rest of these survivors' lives was the loss of memory.

The difference when someone received better diagnosis and treatment for this kind of brain injury was astounding. A young man called Peter was an undergraduate when he suffered a cerebral haemorrhage. It left him with damage to both temporal lobes and a very dense amnesia.

I visited him in his home and he showed me the system he had developed with the help of Barbara Wilson and her team. To my amazement, he was able to live on his own and was attending college to learn a craft that would enable him to earn his own income. He had a highly structured day, a routine that varied only slowly. All around the flat were Post-It notes acting as prompts for each stage of certain activities. A routine was broken down into chunks, and Peter would remove each yellow note the moment he had completed that part of the task, so that he would know whether or not he'd done it. In the mornings he prepared a sandwich for his lunch and put it in the kit bag on the kitchen counter. He had trouble knowing whether he had made the sandwich or not, and had to keep looking in the bag to check. So he added another Post-It note on the bag to be removed when the sandwich was in there.

For Peter to run his life he had needed to learn one procedure that would compensate for his lack of memory – that is, to take the yellow note down the moment he had achieved something, and to put them all up afresh last thing at night ready for the next day. The agenda for his day, including remembering to put up the correct sequence of Post-Its, was programmed into his computer-watch and also appeared on logs and lists pasted in strategic places about the flat. His day literally followed a prescribed map.

Peter talked to me about how he learned cabinet-making. 'If you were to ask me,' he said, 'whether I am able to make a dovetail joint, I couldn't tell you. But if you said to me, "Make a dovetail joint," I can pick up the wood and make one.' He does this because his procedural memory still functions and the craft does not require episodic memory. By making the joint over and over correctly under supervision, he acquires this skill as a conditioning effect, without knowing he has it. And the tutors know not to vary the way they teach him. Procedural memory is all about rehearsing a procedure.

He pointed out a small rack. 'I made that.'

People phoned him, friends from university and school, but he could recall nothing of their conversations afterwards, had no memory of seeing anyone. He showed me a book he kept by the phone. In it he would note down who he telephoned so that he didn't call them twice. In his own way, he had triumphed over his amnesia. He had made a life for himself through having the right help from a team with the right specialist skills when he needed it for as long as he needed it.

His system worked because he had sufficient memory to know

he attended college and to get there independently each day and involve himself in each process. It would not have worked for Clive who had so much less memory that he was not able even to root himself in a single moment, let alone a whole sequence.

We wanted all brain-injured people who could benefit from rehab to have the kind of chances Peter had, and we wanted them to have ongoing support, community, meaning to their lives. AMNASS was looking for a sea change.

To be successful, we would have to involve all the clinical disciplines with a bearing on brain injury and many others whose work impacted on the lives of brain-injured patients' families – personal injury lawyers, insurers, officials in education, social services, employment services and housing associations.

The insurers did not seem keen to do anything differently, and the public sector providers wanted the resources first. I had more joy with personal injury lawyers. They sat alongside me on conference platforms. They were introducing a new kind of structured settlement, the American way of paying out compensation over a lifetime, adjusted to need. They understood the benefits of putting resources into maximizing potential recovery.

Some time into our campaign, Channel 4 repeated *Prisoner of Consciousness* and we held a press conference to review what AMNASS was doing and why. Among the speakers at the Channel 4 studios was the poet Andrew Motion. His new book of poetry, *Natural Causes*, was named for a poem written after seeing the film's first broadcast. I was working in an office across the other side of Bedford Square from his publisher and we arranged to meet one day on a bench under a tree. I asked him if he would read out his poem at the press conference. He did and it bore witness to how hard it is to forget the idea of Clive trapped in his moment.

> . . . the thought of the man
> with no memory came to me – as it had come,
> I should say, hundreds of times before –
> nervously, slithering into my mind
> like a dog on a heavy painful rope,
> yet lazily too, like a dog on a dusty day,
> and stopped there: sinewy, not to be argued with,
> bitter, but somehow banal, dragging behind it
> other thoughts: *Those whom the gods . . .*
> *In the midst of life . . . The Lord taketh away . . .*
> *What do we do to deserve . . .* that sort of thing.

> I've told you already, it's come to me
> hundreds of times, the thought of the stranger
> prowling his tucked-away hospital room

When I read that and other pieces on amnesia, I saw what they saw – the abstract, a fearful thing, just the way Clive and I had seen the case of Jimmie G before Clive's illness. At first sight, when you are looking only at the amnesia, it is scary beyond belief. But I was looking at Clive, and he was living evidence that you could lose almost everything you ever knew *about* yourself and still *be* yourself.

# 9

## DITTOS OF DISCONTENT

DESPITE THE FRANTIC CAMPAIGNING, AND THE MANY PROJECTS THAT seemed to offer hope of a special home opening, somewhere that could look after Clive, that haven would be a long time coming. Meanwhile, Clive continued to write in his diary and say the same thing over and over again every hour of every day, year after year. That kind of constant repetition seemed impossible to listen to for the first year, but the loop tape shortened until he only said three things to me, although he might attempt to round out his conversation with strangers. He continued to live in the same room in the psychiatric wing of St Mary's, Paddington. Five years on, a student psychologist took an interest in him and began to record the number of times he repeated monologues, the number of times he went into belching fits. Clive had lived in one room for five years and yet it was still completely unfamiliar. One day in 1990 the trainee psychologist recorded and transcribed a conversation with Clive. It shows Clive at his expansive best. He appreciated this young man taking an intelligent interest and was as eloquent as he was able to be. When the same psychologist recorded Clive's

5.26pm · · · · I DO LIVE!!!!

7.46am   I WAKE FOR THE FIRST ~~Conscious~~ TIME

7.47am   THIS ILLNESS HAS BEEN LIKE DEATH TILL NOW ALL SENSES WORK

— " —   FIRST THOUGHT: I LOVE DARLING DEBORAH FOR EVER∞ OUR FATHE

7.51am   FIRST CONCIOUSE STROLL

8.07am   I AM ~~TOTALLY~~ ~~PERFECTLY~~ AWAKE. 1st Time DK B'FA

8.31am   NOW I AM ~~REALLY~~ COMPLETELY AWAKE (1st Time) PATIENCE

8.38am   TIME TO SEE RELAXING TV.

9.06am   NOW I AM ~~PERFECTLY, OVERWHELMINGLY~~ AWAKE (1st Time) 1st STROLL

9.34am   NOW I AM ~~SUPERLATIVELY,~~ ~~ACTUALLY~~ AWAKE (1st Time) LOO CALLS

· · ·   NOW I AM MAGNIFICENTLY, ~~PERFECTLY~~ AWAKE (1st Time) Aft (1st STROLL

9.54am   I AM COMPLETELY AWAKE WITH 1st CUP OF COFFEE. PATIENCE

· · ·   NOW I AM ~~TOTALLY,~~ ~~MAGNIFICENTLY~~ AWAKE (1st Time) · · ·

10.38am   TIME FOR FIRST STROLL + ? TV.

11.01am   I AM ~~REALLY~~ SUPERLATIVELY, PERFECTLY AWAKE (1st Time). PATIENC

11.03am   FIRST THOUGHT — I LOVE DARLING DEBORAH FOR ETERNITY (1st Time)

11.15am   FIRST ~~CONCIOUSE~~ WALK

11.26am   NOW I AM PERFECTLY, COMPLETELY AWAKE (1st Time). ~~CONCIOUSE~~ WA

11.37am   I RETURN AND AWAITING 1st COFFEE, PATIENTLY, AND THINKING OF DEBRA

11.45am   1st CUP OF COFFEE ARRIVES — I LIVE FULLY AWAKE. IT TASTES SUPERLATIV

12.31pm   AFTER LUNCH I AM ~~REALLY~~ ~~PERFECTLY~~ AWAKE (1st Time). PATIENCE

12.54pm   TIME FOR ~~1st~~ ~~CONCIOUSE~~ WALK

1.30pm   I AM REALLY SUPERLATIVELY, COMPLETELY AWAKE (1st Time) · · ·

4.05pm   I RETURN AFTER DRINKING ? TEA. (PATIENCE begins to be learnt) + SEE

4.24pm   I PATIENTLY WAIT FOR MY DARLING DEBORAH, WHOM I'VE NOT SEEN YET

5.26pm   DINNER IS OVER — I AM ~~TOTALLY~~ ALMOST AWAKE NOW (1st Time) ~~Not Befo~~

5.26pm   HURRAH X ♀ ⚭ ♂ = I DO LIVE   (FIRST TIME KNOW

5.32pm   ~~FIRST~~ ~~CONCIOUSE~~ STROLL — I AM ~~TOTALLY~~ AWAKE ~~(1st Time)~~ NOT BEFO

5.37pm   I SEE AND PLAY PATIENCE (FIRST TIME REALLY AWAKE) NOT BEFORE

5.48pm   FIRST CONCIOUSE ~~STROLL~~ MOMENT 5.58am I RETURN FROM 1st MEDICINE

5.59pm   PATIENCE AS I WAIT FOR DEBORAH TO APPEAR · · · 1st STROLL TO

6.39pm   NOW I AM TOTALLY AWAKE (FIRST TIME FOR ? 3/4 YEARS?)

7.09pm   ALL PREVIOUS CLAIMS ARE RUBBISH. DARLING'S ARRIVED.

Deborah worked in Southampton today + arrived v tired
as she worked last night until 2am + got up at 7 ~~am~~ yawn...
we watched the Same Bend film + I ate a hamburger (yumyum)
I adore you with all my heart — Big Hugs! DXXXXX

9.22pm   MY DARLING LEAVES — I HOPE TO SEE YOU TOMORROW DARLING.

9.39pm   I WAKE UP FOR THE VERY FIRST TIME. 1st STROLL

9.50pm   TOTALLY AWAKE — PATIENCE. 10.04pm. FIRST CONCIOUSE MEDICINE 10.07pm TIME FOR BED conversation with me that same month, the range of what he said reduced considerably. With me, Clive could be himself and only needed to say what was uppermost in his mind.

Clive at this stage used to mix in a little confabulation. Since he could assume that his awakening from coma had not been at that very moment, he would deduce he had been capable of some thinking previously, despite being without any actual memory of it.

CW: How long's it been? Any idea?

PSYCH: I think it's been about five years.

CW: Can you imagine one night five years long? No dreaming, no waking up, no touch, no taste, no smell, no sight, no sound, no hearing, nothing at all? It's like being dead. I came to the conclusion that I was dead. The only explanation, occasional thought, I thought about three times for about a minute each, that's all.

PSYCH: What did you think?

CW: First question – am I alive or dead? The fact that occasionally I could think, at that time, occasional things within a period of about three minutes I was slightly awake – very distant – I came to the conclusion I was probably alive. That's as far as I could see. No other information at all – coming from any of the senses at all – no touch, no taste, no sight, no sound, no smell, nothing. Suddenly I can see. It's all happened since I sat down here – so this drink is obviously the world's best! Cheers to you! [Laughs – they clink mugs.] You put gin in as usual, did you? [Laughs.] It's amazing, I thought I was dead. The only explanation, occasional thought, that's all I've had.

PSYCH: The occasional thought . . .

CW: About once in about three or four months I think without any . . . that's all. Unconscious the whole time, I don't know a thing about getting dressed for example – it's totally unknown to me. Any eating I've done is completely unknown. That's the first taste I've had, the drink just now. I've never seen a doctor of any kind. How long's it been? Any idea?

Psych: It's been about five years.

CW: Can you imagine one night five years long with no dreams? No evidence at all that I was alive – in fact, I came to the conclusion that I was dead. Occasional thought, about once in six months – that's all, for about thirty seconds, that's all I've had – and I've never seen a doctor of any kind or a nurse. I've never seen my room yet either. My eyesight has started since I've come to this room now. It's all in colour and I can also taste, this is the first drink I've tasted, first drink of any kind. You are the first person I've seen so you are obviously the best person in the universe. [Laughs.] You should be knighted, I think.

Psych: You're terribly glad to see somebody.

CW: Well of course. There's no evidence at all that I was alive, very little thought, so little that I can almost remember it now, it lasted about . . . altogether about twenty seconds – that's all. There's been no thought for the whole of the rest of it: blank. The brain has not been active in anything at all, and I've no idea what's been wrong, no idea. I presume it's a rarity and nobody knows what to do with it. That's my impression. Occasional thought, that's all I've had. I thought for about three times, for about five seconds each, that is all. Snaps off, blank.

Psych: Snaps off, just like that?

CW: Yes. None of the senses worked, no sight, no sound, no taste, no touch, no smell, nothing. I was very very optimistic to feel that I was alive – there was no evidence at all that I was. Occasionally I thought that I was dead, but then I thought that because I can think, I must be alive. Thinking processes lasted about five seconds and I had three of them, that's all – blank. Since I've been sitting down here, my eyesight's been coming back, it's all in colour. I hear also for the first time. Taste, that's the first taste I've had. And I've no idea where I've come from. What year are we in now, hm?

Psych: 1990.

CW: So it's been about seven years. Can you imagine one night seven years long with no dreaming? Can you imagine it?

Psych: That's a very long time.

CW: Yeah. I presume in a hundred years' time it'll be common unless something is done about it, because if you look back one hundred years and see what was rare then, it's a great surprise, it's a great surprise isn't it. Things like cancer, virtually unknown a hundred years ago – because of good treatment it grew and grew and grew – and that's likely to be . . . in a hundred years' time, something that we can't treat now will become common in a hundred years' time. I think it's very unlikely that we shall always be able to solve all the problems, highly unlikely, and what we can't solve will grow and grow and grow eventually over the years . . .

Psych: Until it demands a solution.

CW: Yes. What year are we in now?

Psych: 1990.

CW: So it's been five years, hasn't it? Can you imagine one night five years long with no dreaming?

Psych: That's a long night.

CW: Since I've been sitting here my eyesight's come back. It's all in colour too. I can also hear for the first time. I don't remember coming through that door. I don't know where my room is. I don't know this room. I presume it's rare what I've had, is it?

PSYCH: You presume that it's rare. You feel that you've had an illness.

CW: Well yes, there's no evidence at all that I was alive. If none of your senses work, what right to conclude that you're alive? Now I can see that I am . . .

That monologue was going on pretty much all the time, who-ever he was with. It just got shorter with me.

Here Clive speaks to the trainee psychologist about running hospitals when he was a student at Cambridge. This is what is known as a confabulation. I was told that when an amnesic person is unable to furnish much real information about his life, his unconscious will often unknowingly supply something made up. Some amnesics confabulate new things each time, but with Clive the same few fixed confabulations tended to surface again and again. My theory on this one is that Clive vaguely remembered working in a hotel in the vacation while a student at Cambridge. The words hotel and hospital are semantically close. Clive has by now developed a sense of being in hospital but the memory trace is so shallow that he has to assume the memory must be twenty or thirty years old. Hence he must have been in hospitals when he was at Cambridge. A reasonable construct to put on the small crumbs of information available to him.

CW: Suddenly I can see; since I've come to this room, I don't remember before – very vaguely very distantly – I've met you before, very very distant black and white. Suddenly my eyesight has come back, it's all in colour, I can also hear now properly for the first time. I came to the conclusion I was dead.

PSYCH: You thought you were dead.

CW: Yes, the occasional thought, that's all I've had, lasting about ten seconds each time; there were about three or four of them.

Psych: Ten seconds each time.

CW: There was no evidence at all that I was alive. No difference between day and night, all exactly the same – no taste, no touch, no sight, no sound, no smell, nothing at all, none of the senses work. So you are the leader of the world, sir, head of the United Nations and the British Empire; you should have a crown on. [Laughs.]

Psych: I think you're very glad to meet me, since I'm the first person you've seen.

CW: Yes, you are. Since I've come to this room, I don't know where I've come from. I don't know where my room is, I came to the conclusion I was dead. What's it like to be dead? Does anybody know? Exactly, nobody knows.

Psych: Nobody knows.

CW: No. If none of your senses work, what's the difference . . . It's exactly like being dead, no difference between day and night, all exactly the same; no evidence at all that I was alive, and no thinking processes till now. It's happened since I've come to this room. I don't know where I've come from. I've got no idea. So you are a genius, sir, you should be knighted [laughs] with a cane or without. I used as a child to think it very strange that the words 'knight' and 'night' sounded exactly the same but had two different spellings and meaning rather different things. Very strange language at certain times, English.

Psych: Very strange language.

CW: Any other foreign language would pronounce the 'k' somehow, 'K'night'.

Psych: K'night.

CW: What year are we in now?

PSYCH: We're in 1990.

CW: So it's been six years, hasn't it?

PSYCH: Six years.

CW: Can you imagine one night six years long?

PSYCH: It's very difficult.

CW: No dreams, no breakfast, no meal, no nothing at all, none of the senses worked at all the whole time. I thought I was dead. The occasional thought, that's all I've had, lasting about ten–fifteen seconds, that's all I've had. The only evidence at all that I was in any sense possibly alive. That was all I had. I've never seen a doctor yet of any kind.

PSYCH: You haven't seen a doctor.

CW: No, this is my first taste. [Drinking coffee.]

PSYCH: This is your first taste.

CW: My eyesight is working again. It's amazing – I thought I was dead. Occasional thought – that's all I've had. Probably once, once a month I've thought for about ten seconds, that's all. It's very very difficult to measure things like that when it happens so rarely as that, because all the systems of timing completely disappeared, no difference between day and night, all exactly the same. There's no going to sleep and waking up, nothing of that kind at all.

PSYCH: So there's no time for you, in a sense.

CW: No method of measuring time because there's no difference at all between day and night, all exactly the same, blank. I've never seen a doctor of any kind.

PSYCH: You haven't seen a doctor of any kind.

CW: I know nothing about this hospital at all. I used to know a fair amount about them. I always used to be rather busy with them, in the summer when you were away on holiday. I ran them for the entire country for about twenty-five years.

PSYCH: You ran . . . ?

CW: Hospitals.

PSYCH: You ran hospitals for the entire country?

CW: Yes, for about twenty-five years.

PSYCH: For about twenty-five years.

CW: While you were all away on holiday in the summer. That was my summer holiday, doing your job. A very very good thing to do, very very important – and you need to get the best possible people you can lay your hands on to do it. So I used to get university students from Oxford and Cambridge mostly, and other universities sometimes in England, sometimes in more dis-connected areas away from there. But that was something which had to be done and always all the time, planning ahead, so that you plan about six months ahead, so you knew exactly what's going to happen, and trying to put them into teams together so that they could look after people's lives.

PSYCH: That's a lot of responsibility.

CW: Yes, it is. It's very very difficult because there were no doctors available at all.

PSYCH: No doctors . . .

CW: No, nobody at all. You have to do everything yourself. Therefore you manage to. How you tend to do it is to mix up the sciences and the arts together in order to . . . have a balance of one sort of sanity with another kind of sanity. It seems very important. The scientists must be there – they've got to be there, otherwise there's chaos within the artists. The artists are very busy in a sense with people – they're much more sensitive and much more reflect-ing . . . so a mixture of the two is really quite good; you get that in universities anyway so that's quite good. But that's what I used to do – balance it all out – I did it all over the country for about thirty years . . .

PSYCH: That's a long time.

CW: Yes, that's my summer holiday.

PSYCH: That's your summer holiday.

CW: Cheers to you. [Drinks some coffee.] I started when I was at Cambridge. It seemed to be such an extraordinarily important thing to be done properly because otherwise people would die, and the mixture you get in universities is very useful – a mixture of arts and sciences, you know, because you can balance the resources to the requirements of people, and so I used to put them together in teams, mixtures of the two worlds. I did that for about twenty-five years.

PSYCH: How old were you then?

CW: About thirty-five. I started when I was at Cambridge, doing it there.

By now I had become fascinated with the human brain. I often went with committee colleagues to conferences and thought seriously about taking a degree in cognitive neuro-psychology. I looked at syllabuses for various universities, but realized that to study the parts I wanted, I would also have to get enthusiastic about a wide range of topics that interested me not at all – statistics and the eating habits of domestic fowl, for example. I dropped the idea. Anyway, I could not see my future working with patients. It would be too hard. I couldn't cope with Clive, let alone others.

In fact, when I left the charity in 1990, having decided it ought to be able to fly on its own, I resolved to leave the world of brain injury altogether. I had just one engagement left in my diary, to speak at a conference run by a company called AMI that was already offering the kind of care we had been lobbying for. At dinner after my talk they asked me, would I come and work for them. No way, I thought. I had a holiday booked to visit Clive's family in New Zealand after Christmas. I planned to come back and carry on in arts PR. 'But it's only October,' said one of the directors. 'How about you come and work for us until you go? Put together a feasibility study on how we can help regions develop brain injury services.' It was only for a couple of months. Then I could take off into the sunshine and not look back. OK, I told her, I'll do it.

Apart from the weeks in New Zealand, I stayed three years. At first my office was in London but then the brain injury division moved its headquarters to Northamptonshire. Since I wasn't prepared to move house, it meant driving seventy miles to work each day up the M1.

The office was housed in a rehab unit. I'd taken Clive there for an assessment once. Patients stayed up to eighteen months and had severe problems. Staff and patients took meals together and I also saw residents as I went about the house. There were some remarkable transformations, and others who did not seem to improve. But as I got to know the residents, attending a weekly ward round, I could often see the subtle changes that signified progress. There was a man who screamed and shouted but never spoke. One day a therapist reported with great excitement that this man had shouted a swear word. 'It's language!' they said. 'He has language!'

I learned a great deal from that team. I learned even more from the residents they were helping. At first they might seem strange, frightening to be around. These were broken men and women, smashed up in a car crash or some other mishap, and yet deep down they were still themselves. I will never forget the devastation among the staff the day they first realized that one man who had no speech actually did have insight. To be locked into such a broken mind and body, and yet to be aware, must have been torment in the extreme.

I started early and worked late, sometimes driving back in the early hours. And all that time, if there were fog anywhere, it was always on that stretch of the M1. Often on that journey I could barely see.

I spent a lot of time in my car, a capsule speeding through space up and down the motorway, speakers at full blast to drown out thought. The Pet Shop Boys, the mystery of the Cocteau Twins on foggy mornings, the Eurythmics, Earth, Wind and Fire. If an idea about work occurred, I'd grab the dictaphone and dictate a couple of key words as an aide-memoire, although as often as not, when I listened to the recording afterwards I couldn't work out what I'd been talking about.

With 140 miles to drive each day I wanted to get them over with, so I'd put my foot down. The roads were empty at two or three in the morning. I don't know why the work took so long. At least there was no one waiting up for me. I couldn't have done it if Clive were at home – but then I was only in this work because he wasn't.

'FISHFACE!!!' I'd see my fist lam into the car door. One minute nothing, tootling along, and then some painful thought I could not bear, and a shout would burst through as if to drown the thought, pulverize it – ridiculous words that left the dashboard ringing. 'FISHFACE!!!!' I drew sidelong stares from faces in wing mirrors, regards from behind passing glass. In the rear-view my face was calm, calm . . . The shout was a surprise like a fish leaping, breaking the surface, disappearing instantly, but you knew it was lurking there, ravenous, and would jump out again, just when you least expected it.

Engrossed in the music, or in combat with needling thoughts, I would not see that the cars ahead had slowed. I'd have to slam on the brakes. Then my face would be white for a while.

Sometimes on the way home from work dawn broke over the motorway and spread first light all over the horizon. My days ran into each other. I was grateful for sleep, sorry when the alarm clock meant I had to face another day. Days kept coming with solid regularity. They wouldn't leave me alone. I couldn't seem to match my days to everyone else's. They'd go home when I felt I was just getting somewhere. They'd arrive for work and think I was early, when all I was was late, still immersed in yesterday, so I'd keep on working and leave when they left at five, and someone would say, 'Going on time today, Deb? Feeling all right?' And then it was good to get home to my bed and I'd read a page and fall asleep.

The anger broke out at home as well as in the car. My fist shot out and slugged walls, furniture, doors, unpremeditated, like a physical reflex. Screams came, but I couldn't release them because of the neighbours so I'd scream without sound, just a rush of air. I'd look in the mirror to see the scream. I'd flush red, eyes watering, mouth a great dark cavern, stretching sinews, shaking as the scream pushed through. Silent screams are the only kind permitted in a flat. Afterwards I'd check my smile, and make as if I were having a conversation to see if I could look normal again immediately. I wasn't fooling anyone. It was all there in my eyes: despair, a terrified tilt to the eyebrows I could never quite disguise. I wore dark glasses whenever I could. Fortunately deep black Ray-Bans were high fashion then.

I could not modify the facts of my existence. I loved Clive, he loved me. I couldn't live with him, I couldn't live without him. He was barely living, but with no end in sight. A normal lifespan stretched ahead of him.

3.04pm  FIRST STROLL DARLING – PLEASE ARRIVE

3.07pm  FIRST STROLL DARLING – PLEASE COME AT THE SPEED OF LIGHT.

3.11pm  PATIENCE WAITS FOR YOU DARLING. I'M AWAKE

3.12pm  FIRST DEAL DARLING. PLEASE COME!

3.14pm  AWAKE FIRST TIME

3.15pm  FIRST REAL AWAKENESS DARLING. FIRST CARDS SEEN. PATIENCE.

3.19pm  GAME OVER UNRESOLVED DARLING.

3.20pm  FIRST THOUGHT IS OF YOU DARLING

3.39pm  FIRST STROLL DARLING

3.42pm  FIRST STROLL DARLING. AWAKE FIRST TIME

3.45pm  FIRST STROLL DARLING. REALLY AWAKE FIRST TIME

He started using a lot of ditto marks.

Awake first time.
Really ditto ditto ditto.
Completely ditto ditto ditto.
Superlatively ditto ditto ditto.

To make sure the wrong times were properly crossed out and the new times clearly marked he pressed harder and harder with the pen until the pages had rounded dents in them on every line, burnished.

His handwriting was interrupted by mine so he would know I had visited him. 'DARLING!!!!!' His delight knew no bounds.

On Clive's part, he was so habituated to our dialogue that, though he had no knowledge of it, he abbreviated his questions more and more. And though he had no feeling of knowing the answers, if asked to guess, he would usually say them correctly.

But I'd long since passed saturation point with his questions. I couldn't seem to hear which question he was asking any more. My brain was unable to produce a sensible answer, or I'd fish out the next answer but one, and get them all out of sequence. I knew I was off kilter but was past dealing with it.

I was like a musical box winding down, getting slower and slower, off key, the tune breaking up, whereas Clive rapped out his questions more and more urgently. Nevertheless, he was patient for my sake. If I slipped up, he tended not to notice but to plough on as if I'd given the correct answer, prompting me in his own way.

'How long?'

'Er . . . How long?'

'Yes, how long's it been?'

'Er . . . how long, how long . . .'

'Come on, tell me, how long have I been ill?' Then quietly, 'Forgive me . . .'

'Er . . . they miss you . . .'

'How long?'

'Miss you, they miss you . . .' I knew that wasn't quite right but could not shake the correct answer out of my head. I wrenched my mind to understand the question. 'Er . . . er, seven years.'

'SEVEN YEARS???? Seven? Is it?'

'Er . . . or eight.'

'EIGHT years! Well, what d'you think it's like, one long night lasting eight years? I haven't seen anything, felt anything, smelled anything, heard anything, tasted anything. It's been like death. What's it like to be dead? Answer: nobody knows . . . What's the BBC say about all this?'

'Yes . . .'

'They *miss* me?'

'They miss you . . .'

'Do they?'

'Yes.'

'They've not been making films about this, have they?'

Silence.

'*Have* they? . . .'

'Er, they miss you . . .'

'Really?'

'Yes.'

'Well I never . . . How long's it been now?'

'Um, eight . . .'

'Eight?'

'Years.'

'How many?'

'Er, I think eight.'

'Well I never . . . Eight years . . . How's our flat doing?'

'They miss you . . .'

'Has it gone up in value?'

'. . . doubled . . .'

'I *thought* we got a bargain! How long's it been now? . . . Darling . . .' [Blowing me kisses to encourage me to answer.] 'How long?'

'Guess . . .'

'I don't *know*! How *long*?' [Kisses.]

A great struggle to understand the question and untangle an answer from my brain . . .

'Er, yes . . .'

'Come on, darling! *How long?*'

'Yes . . . eight . . .'

'Eight years! Well I never . . . Well, my eyes have come on. I can see properly for the first time. I can see you, darling! Everything's working normally!'

'Good . . .'

There seemed no way out, no way down. What was I supposed to do? How could I live this way? My life was fiction. It couldn't be real. Doing any ordinary kitchen chore, doing anything routine, seemed to make no sense. Pretending to be cheerful on the phone to others cost effort and was meaningless. There was no point to anything except the work, making the country shell out for decent aftercare for brain injury, lifting the heads of families worn down by the sorrow of it. Apart from that, what was there to do but scream and scream and run about the streets tearing your clothes. These are the things felt under the surface of an ordinary-seeming exterior.

I used to imagine taking Clive away. I imagined taking him to the seaside for oysters and champagne. Then I thought we'd walk out in our best clothes and walk into the sea and keep walking. I would explain to him what we were escaping from and then just slip in and let the sea take us together. Only snag was that, inevitably, Clive would rescue me. He'd forget what I'd just said and save my life, bring me back to shore. And he was stronger than I was, so he'd win. And he'd be right. And I would thank him. And we'd go in and dry off and sleep and have breakfast and then I'd take him back to the hospital.

*

Thinking of Clive and the hundreds of brain-injured people and their families I had met was what kept everyone going in that line of work. Seeing the results of good rehab was a great reward. But the job and journey were strenuous. When I made it home at night, I would go to the gym, or to see Clive. When I told him how far I was driving to work each day he said it was too far. I watched TV later than I should. I needed time alone, to wind down. Going to bed late was often my only way to achieve that, but it increased my exhaustion.

When I went to bed at night it was not neurological literature I dreamed of but the other kind. Poetry woke me up. I wet my sheets with black ink as I repeatedly fell asleep with a pen in my hand. Images and phrases pushed their way out of me all night and then it would be time for the alarm to ring. I couldn't stop writing. One of these days I was going to have to give up sleep or give up work.

A new residential unit for people with ABI finally opened that was just right for Clive. In fact the consultant neuro-psychologist there told me it was designed with Clive in mind. Nevertheless it still took nine months to secure his funding to go there. A general election was announced. I wrote to our MP, expressing my intention to cause a stink in the press if Clive were denied the only place that had been offered to him in seven years. How could it make sense to leave him in a costly and inappropriate bed in an acute ward in the middle of London? They said yes within three days of my letter. I wondered afterwards what would have happened if it hadn't been election time.

I took Clive home for a last weekend before accompanying him down to his new home in the country in April '92. It was terribly sad for me to have Clive leave London – it was like a real split.

Clive didn't know any different of course. And after most of six and a half years in the same room on the same ward Clive did not recognize it at all. The staff who had been there longest said they were going to miss him and made their goodbyes. 'Hello!' Clive greeted them all with a small bow. 'You're the first people I've seen!' he said as we went out of the door for the last time.

Now that he was so far away, I would not be able to visit him so frequently. I had been used to popping in to see him on my way to and from places. Nearly all roads had led to or through Paddington. My car knew its own way to St Mary's. This felt like a giant move, signifying a new acceptance of the permanence of Clive's condition. And yet Clive was never not with me. He was still writing me into every line of his diary.

'Please come, darling, please arrive at the speed of light! Awake first time, first thought is of you, darling. Please arrive! Now really awake.'

His new country seat was lovely – a beautiful house for a small group of residents in the grounds of a big rehab centre. The manager was a nice man, about Clive's age. I drove away with Clive and his new careworker waving goodbye to me in the rear-view mirror. I struggled not to cry at the wheel. When I passed a funny chef sign that Clive had made a joke of on the way down, I did break into tears.

The next time I visited, Clive's hair had been cut differently and he looked happy, a lot calmer. He had been taken off most of his drugs. His life consisted of walks around the village and in the home's pleasant gardens. They had a putting lawn and masses of rhododendrons. They told me Clive did not have fits any more (other than during my visits). The food was good and freshly prepared. Clive looked more content on it. His life was significantly more comfortable. Now he was in a lovely house, spacious and airy, and there would never be more than half a dozen other residents. The house manager had the support of a full brain injury team over at the main hospital.

Back in London, with Clive gone from the city, I was no longer bobbing in and out of St Mary's. And with this mission accomplished and Clive settled into a unit that offered him a safe and comfortable home for life, I could begin to plan my own extrication from the brain injury world.

I was by now stuck into an international brain injury project that would take me to 1 April '93. I would see it through, but I planned to leave the very next day. Ever since a visit to New York in January '91 I had longed to live there. I loved the aesthetics.

I knew I would not be able to stay in England and not visit Clive. Visiting him still caused him to fit, and made me crumple up inside. What was to hinder me from moving to New York, and living there for good? I knew Green Cards were tough to come by but I believed that if I wanted to do something enough, no obstacle would be insuperable. And I wanted to get out of England very much indeed. I thought leaving the land would perhaps be a way of leaving all the pain.

I'd been twenty-seven when Clive got ill. I was now turning thirty-five. I read articles about fertility declining and wondered would I ever have a family. 'How's your love life?' people would ask, as soon as they decently could. I could hear the question bursting to come out. It was all some wanted to know. Doctors, people in general, talked as if I were bereaved, as if it were unhealthy to cling on to Clive.

I did my best to live a life, to break free from grief. Sure, I was attracted to various men at various times, but I knew I had never stopped loving Clive. How could I marry another? I would never be able to say 'forsaking all others'. And if I could not commit wholly to a man, what would be the point of committing at all?

If I happened to mention a man's name, any man, even the most unlikely, people would prick up their ears and ask, 'Is he married? What's he like?' I guess they'd seen me a long time sad.

What I wanted was to go home, but where was home now?

The best times these last years were when I'd gone to America – sitting by a spring in bear country, a stroll in the Tucson desert, wandering the streets of New York. I would go there and stay there.

I couldn't help Clive, and was fed up being without him.

The International Brain Injury Forum was to be held in Oxford. I wanted it to have the best possible impact.

'Go for it!' said the Americans on the steering group. So I did. The forum had government funding and sponsors. Speakers included Princess Anne and Jim Brady, the White House press secretary brain-injured when he took a bullet aimed at President Reagan. It was the first time he and his family had left the US since the shooting in '81. The last-night dinner would be served at Blenheim Palace complete with a string quartet. The programme ensured a comprehensive debate with scientists and clinicians, single cell people and neural network people, rehab and vocational support specialists, government officials, drug companies, insurers, re-insurers, lawyers and staff from long-term living centres. Key among speakers and discussants were brain-injured people and their families from all over Europe and the US, who made it to Oxford in spite of all their difficulties. There was even a motor insurance expert from Australia. We appointed cross-disciplinary panels to comment on every speaker. We appointed *rapporteurs* to capture the debate.

We were pushing for a breakthrough in advancing care systems for brain-injured people. Mixing brain-injured delegates and family members with the many professional and clinical disciplines put everyone on their mettle. We set goals to ensure we got somewhere by the end of the four and a half days.

The work felt like a kind of reflex, something I had to do as the only right response to what had happened. I was trying to grab back missing parts, like Jacqueline Kennedy in her pillbox hat, clambering over the expanse of moving limo to pick up the piece of her husband's head that had been shot away. She said, 'I have his brains in my hand.'

She held that most private of all her husband's parts wetting her white cotton glove until someone took it from her at the hospital. The weight of it will not have left the cup of her hand as long as she lived. People say they always remember what they were doing the day Kennedy was shot. Now I think of that pink suit stretched across the sun-drenched car because I know what she's doing. I was there.

When the lights went down over the audience thirty seconds before 9 a.m. on Monday 29 March 1993, I waited on the rostrum, wristwatch ticking towards the hour, cue cards ranged. At nine the platform filled with light, and I told them it was eight years to the minute since I ran after a stretcher carrying Clive through the doors of Casualty. I spoke of why we were there and what we needed them to do. I saw my pink-suited arm reaching into the dark.

Over five hundred people debated through to practical solutions. Another couple of hundred from brain injury support groups turned up for the last day. Afterwards they gave me roses, red ones. I forgot them under a chair. It was April Fool's Day. I prepared to give my old life the slip.

I was so keen to get over to the States that I didn't wait to put my flat on the market. I decided to take a couple of months out there, some breathing space, and then come back and sort out other details.

With no income, and pre flat-sale, I sold my piano, a Broadwood my great-aunt had left me. I had taken all Clive's multiple sets of music to the Royal College of Music library and had given away many of his books, such as the complete bound volumes of Schütz, to musicians who could use them. It was a time of emptying out.

Going through our books one day I noticed a library label on a slim volume of Petrarch lyric poetry. I opened it to see that it had been due back at the BBC reference library on 4 April 1985, six days after Clive was admitted to hospital. There is only the one date stamp. Clive must have been the first to borrow it. They probably acquired it at his request. The pages of the first half where he'd read it were loose. The pages of the second half were stiff, undisturbed, virgin. What poem had he read last? What was on his mind when he began to slip into oblivion? The book fell wide at Poem No. 40: 'If love or death does not cut short the new cloth that now I prepare to weave . . .'

He read that in his last days before losing the thread himself. Did he have any sense in the depth of his soul that these words were prophetic?

I closed the book and prepared to close our marriage. I initiated divorce. I closed the flat and took a plane to Washington DC. I had booked myself in for a weekend writing course at Johns Hopkins University in Baltimore. I had no plan beyond that weekend. I only knew that I would stay out there until it was time to come back and sell the flat, sell everything, in order to have no strings. Forever was how long I had in mind to stay away. Forever away seemed to me the only plan I needed as my plane flew out across the sea.

I holed up in a motel opposite the campus where there was free coffee in the lobby and a 7/11 across the street plus a diner with meatloaf. I showed up for the course, which was run by a science-fiction writer. Sci-fi was not my scene but it was the only writing course I could find that weekend anywhere in the USA and I didn't care what it was about as long as it provided a place to kick off from. And it provided more. The teacher was about to go travelling and wanted to sublet his room in Manhattan. That was to become my home for much of the next couple of years.

I spent that summer on a writing residency at an artists' colony in Vermont, consisting of fifty visual artists and three writers. I wandered in and out of people's studios watching their work take off on the walls. I worked eight hours a week in the vegetable garden. One of my duties was to squash cucumber beetles to protect the crop. This was not my favourite. After dinner on 4 July – Independence Day – I gave my first public poetry reading and then there were fireworks and line-dancing in the streets. I had on a mango-coloured Mexican-fringe skirt I had bought in a second-hand shop especially for the occasion. I was full of joy that evening. I wondered about living right here. I could even learn to squash cucumber beetles.

In Vermont I made friends with Rubin, a sculptor. He lived in a log cabin in the woods near the Canadian border. We met again afterwards in New York and said goodbye under the clock at Grand Central Station. He cried. I imagined teaming up with him and when I got back to England at the end of the summer I looked for letters from him in his big round hand. But when he came to visit we both realized that the love had been make-believe. Whoever we were looking for, it wasn't each other. In a while, I thought, I might go ahead and live alone in a log cabin in the woods too, a place cut off and quiet and dark. But for now, it was New York I wanted, with its lights and 1930s fire escapes and toasted bagels for breakfast. The sci-fi writer's room was waiting for me, while he was off travelling in Asia. All I needed to do was sell my flat, throw a farewell party and go.

People asked me, are you sure? Why not rent your flat so you have somewhere to come back to? But I was determined to exit. I had no visa to work in the States, but I didn't care. The money from the sale of the flat would keep me for a time. I just wanted to immerse myself quickly elsewhere. I'd deal with the practical aspects like earning money when I had to. For now, I wanted out, and I wanted time off.

At my leaving do, there were so many chicken legs baking, the oven caught fire. There were flames leaping up the kitchen wall. The soot came off with a little Flash. I didn't really say goodbye to Clive, but quite a few hellos and then he was seized with belching. I left quietly and then he was all right, at peace again once I was out of the room. I knew he knew I loved him totally, forever, and vice versa. Anything less than that is not love, not in my book, not in his.

On the very eve of my departure, when I was sitting amid boxes all packed up for the removal men arriving in the morning, the phone rang. It was gone eleven. A man's voice I did not quite recognize greeted me. I thought it was someone having a joke.

'It's Jim,' he said.

'Jim?'

'From the garden centre.'

'Oh, hi! Good heavens, it's a bit late . . .'

'Yeah, sorry, an' I 'ad to get drunk to get the courage to phone yer.'

'Oh . . . I'm leaving tomorrow.'

'Yeah, I know . . . You see, the thing is . . . I really love yer! And I wanted to tell yer.'

'Oh. Well . . .'

'I'm sorry . . . I hope yer don't mind me sayin' it.'

'No! I mean, thanks, but no, Jim. I'm sorry, it's late and the removal van arrives first thing. You're a nice man, but I'm away tomorrow and that's it. I won't be coming back.'

I liked him. He had sold me many different kinds of lavender and a number of small green shrubs but I'd never been home long enough to look after them, even to water them. Everything died.

# PART III

## THE SPEED OF LIGHT

# 10

## GETTING AWAY

*Clive's diary, January 1994*

| | |
|---|---|
| 7.04pm AWAKE FIRST TIME | FIRST THOUGHT: PLEASE COME DARLING! |
| 7.19pm REALLY " " " | FIRST THOUGHT: PLEASE COME DARLING! |
| 7.21pm TOTALLY " " " | FIRST THOUGHT: PLEASE COME DARLING! |
| 7.30pm COMPLETELY " " " | FIRST THOUGHT: PLEASE FLY HERE D—- AT THE SPEED OF LIGHT |
| 7.33pm SUPERBLY " " " | FIRST CONSCIOUS STROLL. PLEASE FLY HERE DARLING |
| 7.35pm SUPERLATIVELY " " " | FIRST THOUGHT: PLEASE COME D——-! |
| 7.50pm AMAZINGLY " " " | FIRST THOUGHT: PLEASE COME D——-! |
| 7.55pm PROPERLY " " " | FIRST THOUGHT: PLEASE COME D——-! |

| | |
|---|---|
| 8.08pm REALLY " " " | FIRST THOUGHT: PLEASE COME D———-! |
| 8.21pm MAGNIFICENTLY " " "FIRST THOUGHT: PLEASE COME D———-! |
| 8.23pm TRULY AWAKE FIRST TIME | FIRST THOUGHT: PLEASE COME D———-! |
| 8.28pm ABSOLUTELY " " " | FIRST THOUGHT: PLEASE COME D———-! |
| 8.34pm ACTUALLY " " " | FIRST THOUGHT: PLEASE COME D———-! |
| 8.56pm ENTIRELY " " " | FIRST THOUGHT: PLEASE COME D———-! |
| 9.00pm TOTALLY " " " | FIRST THOUGHT: PLEASE COME D———-! |
| 9.04pm COMPLETELY " " " | FIRST THOUGHT: PLEASE COME D———-! |

In moving to New York I thought I was removing myself from Clive but the never-ending rhythm of his never-ending night still beat in me. I could feel him calling from between the lines in his diary. But at least I was no longer surrounded by all of his things, his books with his carefully handwritten notes in the margin, so many boxes of his unpublished work. There was some relief in consigning it all to crates in storage in a warehouse off York Road and in libraries in London and Cambridge. I could postpone thinking about it. His papers and research notes had all this time been spilling around my feet, like chickens needing feeding. *He's not here! He's not coming home!* I had given a certain amount of his work away to colleagues because I wanted the music to be out there, performed, not wasted, but mostly they didn't like to take it.

In New York, I started again with a blank sheet. It was sink or swim – give in, give up, lie down and wait till one of us was dead

– or run for my life and keep on going, *la la la la la*, I'm not listening, *la la la, live! live!* until I couldn't hear his unremitting lostness any more. No amount of non-stop work or mind-blamming pop music could drown it. My husband and I were closer than twins, but I reckoned I had a duty to both of us to try at least to save myself. As my plane came in to land at JFK one Thursday afternoon in January '94, my will to live was strong.

I slept on a futon mattress on the floor of a big room hung with Indian silks. The sci-fi writer would be in Asia till spring. The apartment was airy and spacious with Afghan rugs on woodblock floors and every so often snowdrifts against gaps in the wall around the air-conditioning unit. I found a kind of peace here. It felt like home. For one thing, I could get *chrein*, horseradish and beetroot sauce, essential with matzo kleis soup; I could order a bagel with lox and a *schmear* in any deli and get one. People laughed when I was being funny. In England they laughed when I was being serious.

I had the place to myself most of the time as my flatmate Carl was almost never home. He was either at work as a psychiatric social worker or at the gym. The one time he was at home was if there was tennis on the telly. Every morning I awoke at seven to the sound of the front door on its squeaky hinge slamming shut as Carl set off for Staten Island. He put on his shoes in the lift so that his footsteps up and down the corridor didn't wake me any earlier. Some mornings when I woke I didn't know for some seconds where I was and had to wrestle with my memory until a clue broke through.

Being in America was a huge relief. One day my world was Crouch End, where rows of dull brick houses crowded out sunset; the next I was on my thirty-sixth-floor balcony in TriBeCa, with all of Manhattan before me and sunshine glittering on the Hudson River. In the last minutes of a fine day there would be liquid gold poured out on the faces of the buildings and I'd race down in the lift and out, as the sun sank behind tower blocks across the fire-flecked river.

TriBeCa, short for triangle below Canal Street, in downtown Manhattan, became the art area when SoHo got expensive; then TriBeCa got expensive and the artists started moving their studios off the island. Still, quite a few remained, wandering around in paint-spattered jeans. On Canal in Chinatown I loved to go to a department store on five floors, Pearl Paint, selling nothing but art materials.

In this strange city where I'd come to get away, lots of people seemed to know me. 'Hey, Deborah!' I heard from across the street, in cafés, on the subway. People I'd met in Vermont turned out to live here. My friends Jane and Charlie introduced me to interesting new sides of life, people with names I recognized, rock musicians, sculptors. The mailman would see me at breakfast in some café and park his trolley outside while he brought my mail to the table. People in stores and the doormen in my building said hi. Carl would ask about my week. I'd ask about his. On a Saturday morning one of us would go down to the farmers' market outside our building and buy mahi mahi or bluefish or tuna from the fishman who sold it off the back of his truck. We'd souse it in soy sauce and eat it as sushi for breakfast. I met ladies in the laundry room. They knew my washing by the inkstains on my sheets and they'd fold it for me while I was in the apartment. We chatted over our detergent and quarters. They told me their life stories. The Twin Towers filled my kitchen window and helicopters buzzed around them like bluebottles, showing sight-seers the Battery City sights, Ellis Island, the Statue of Liberty and Governor's Island, bought from the native inhabitants for a handful of nails. They must have been really keen on nails. Around the cobblestone corner I could stop in the doorway of the police-horse stables and smell fresh dung, hear hooves clipping stone, or see the fire engines at bay across the road in Varrick Street.

In no time at all I had community. This was my neighbourhood.

I would go out on my balcony in all weathers, first thing in the morning, last thing at night, and many times in between. It was like standing in the sky. Around me, the glittering river, eight blocks south, the Twin Towers like a giant rudder to the island, the Brooklyn Bridge opposite on the east shore, the Woolworth Building, the Chrysler Building, the Empire State that changed colour with the season's neon and, in the distance, a flat green that was Central Park. I had Manhattan. Manhattan had me.

I was here on a visitor's visa with a six-month limit. I could not work, but then I didn't want to. I wanted rest, time, rescue. I would just pop home for a visit every six months until I was ready to commission an attorney to get me a Green Card, but I wasn't going to think about that for a while. I felt confident I'd get one – American professors from my brain-injury days said they'd vouch for me.

I would be thirty-seven in May. If I wanted a husband in time for kids I'd have to get a move on. But first things first – I would enrol in some classes, concentrate on forgetting, stay home to watch *Columbo*, spend hours in art museums, go to poetry, movies, the theatre, and walk and walk, stare at the river, take coffee in the park and sit and find out what on earth I was now.

I had a call not long after my arrival from Jon, an actor I'd made friends with when he'd worked in England whom I'd not seen in a while. He said he was in New York, but his voice snagged as if he were speaking long distance.

'I'm right on your doorstep,' he said. 'We're at Chanterelle's.'

'Who's Chanterelle?' I asked.

'It's the name of the restaurant.'

I'd been settling down for the night to read a text I had to finish before class the following evening, a book called *The End of the World* by Ron Rubewitz. I had left it till the last minute.

'I have to read a whole book by six o'clock tomorrow,' I said.

'There's plenty of time!' he said. 'We're having a party. Come on! It'll be fun. One night only – I have to fly home in the morning. Look, we're ordering dinner – what'll you have? How 'bout the soft-shelled crab? They got snails. Here's the deal . . . come right on over, dinner's on me, grab the crab, go go go, get your *escargots* . . .'

I started to say I had on an old grey cardigan with holes, but I could hear him trying a few times to slot in another quarter.

'Aw . . . ! Come as you are. Ask for the Ted Bloomberg party.'

'What?'

At that point the phone went dead.

I had last seen Jon when someone took our photo at the Globe Theatre in London when he was over here filming. I had this picture of the pair of us looking innocent and incredibly young, my curls squished against his baseball cap. That was over a year ago. Since then he'd phoned every so often out of the blue, and I'd had the odd wistful letter signed J squiggle. He addressed me as Debra. Just 'cause the H fell out of your name, I wrote back, don't think you can take liberties with mine. The H is the most important letter.

Inside the restaurant a man looking like a waiter floated

towards me, his face waxy over a cream shirt. It was Jon. Had he changed so much or was it only that I'd never seen him in winter or in formal garb? We hugged. A woman was watching, someone I knew from the movies. I was glad I'd changed.

'Who's Ted?' I asked as Jon led me to the table.

'Ted's dead.'

I wondered if I'd heard correctly.

'What? Since tonight?'

'It's his funeral party,' he said. His voice sounded kind of concertina'd. He had a way of speaking that sounded like he was sucking the words back as soon as he'd spoken them.

'Wait a minute . . .' I yanked him by the back of his shirt to stop. 'You're kidding me, no? What am I walking into?'

He held out his hand for mine. I withheld it.

'Are you crazy?' I whispered above the hubbub.

'It's not the funeral,' he said. 'It's dinner!'

'Well, who's here?'

'Just a bunch o' people!'

'His *family*?'

'We're all his friends . . . Come on, come an' meet 'em! I told 'em about you. Let's go.'

A table-full was looking at us. We advanced.

Jon made the introductions. The man to my right turned out to be the only son of the one who had died. I wondered how he felt about sharing his father's funeral meal with a complete stranger. He poured wine.

'And this,' said Jon, gesturing to a man with a ginger beard, 'is my good friend Ronnie.' The man stood up and shook me firmly by the hand, grinning. His glasses were off-centre.

'Ronnie Rubewitz,' he said. Something about that name seemed familiar.

'Rubewitz?' I mouthed. He's nodding. 'As in *The End of the World?*'

'That's me,' he said.

'No jokes . . .' I stared at him, put down my glass. 'Mr Rubewitz! You know what? I almost didn't make it tonight because I *have* to read *The End of the World* by six o'clock tomorrow.'

Instead of letting go of my hand, he wrung it in both his.

'Wow!' he said. 'Listen, everyone, this woman *HAS* to read my book by six o'clock tomorrow. Isn't that great? She *HAS* to.'

'Yes,' I said. 'It's compulsory at NYU extramural.'

'I'm compulsory, d'you hear that? Com-puls-or-y at NYU, whaddaya say!'

The happy writer led me to the next table to regale more of the party with the news, holding my arm up like in a boxing ring. I hoped maybe he could fill me in on salient details to save time the next day.

'No, no, you *have* to read me – ' he seemed to enjoy this sentence – '*have* to read me!'

For a funeral party, it was pretty jolly. Jon and Ron took it in turns to tell jokes. Jon leaned his arm along the back of my chair and trailed his fingers on my shoulder. Later he moved his chair right next to mine and his arm encircled my waist. When the restaurant closed, four of us took a cab uptown to a café that stayed open all night – Jon, Ron, myself and the unfortunate Bloomberg *fils*, Gerry. Jon's arm around my waist felt stabilizing. There is something lopsided in going about the world on your own when the inside of you thinks it's in a marriage but there's no actual husband present. I liked sitting close with Jon at this ritual farewell to someone I'd never met. I realized that though most ceremonial events since Clive's illness, and particularly weddings, had been an ordeal for me, funerals were not half so bad. I could do funerals.

The waiter reached between us for empty bottles, which he waved in time to the Cuban music.

Gerry seemed in good shape, considering, and ordered us special liqueurs, which arrived on a tray over the waiter's leaning torso as he bent further and further backwards in limbo. Nothing spilled.

In between jokes we said small things about our lives. I heard Ron say, with an exasperated edge to his voice, 'Jon, why don't you just settle down with Marsha.'

I was about to say my name wasn't Marsha when it occurred to me he wasn't talking about me. So who was Marsha?

It was nearly 5 a.m. I got up to go. I had a book to read and my face muscles were tired from laughing. Jon came with me into the street to wait for a cab while the others settled up. As soon as we were alone on the pavement he asked to come home with me.

'I'll call you,' I said.

'But I'm not done talking. I got so much I wanna tell you . . .'

'It's late,' I said. 'Tell me on the phone.' Cabs came and went.

'No, don't take it, wait. I'll be back home tomorrow, tonight. I don't want this to stop . . .'

'It won't evaporate,' I said. I was an expert on love *in absentia*.

I could see the other two standing inside the café. Ronnie peered out of the dim interior, as though watching out for a kid brother he knew was making an ape of himself.

Finally I walked out into the street in front of a cab and got in. The others came out and waved. Jon stood in the road and watched until I turned down Seventh Avenue.

After that it was just me and the city for a while. I lived in the Metropolitan Museum with disembodied marble limbs and gold-leaf tombs. I peered at alabaster from ancient Mesopotamia and paintings on plaster and words on walls. On Saturday afternoons I would go from gallery to gallery in SoHo to see the week's new shows over glasses of chilled white wine. Clive and I used to go to galleries together. I missed him alongside of me, but I could see through his eyes.

There were certain poetry cafés where I hung out, a small dark-red velvet space with candles called Hell's Kitchen after the neighbourhood of the same name, the Drawing Centre on Worcester, the Ear Inn on Spring, St Mark's on Second Avenue, the Nuyorican and various spoken-word clubs on the Lower East Side where I could catch the latest bands and poets. New York's poetry calendar for the month could have fitted London's poetry calendar for the next ten years on to its pages and still had room for advertising.

I regularly stood out on my balcony to phone Clive. First I'd ask the staff how he was because he wouldn't know himself. One day they told me his shoes were worn through and a nail was sticking into his foot so he was in sandals now though it was February. I felt as though I were the only person in the world able to purchase a pair of shoes for Clive because only I knew which ones were comfortable for his slim size seven and a halfs. And, rather than pass on the knowledge and enable anyone else to buy them, I called up John Lewis Oxford Street with my credit card and arranged for them to mail the right shoes to Clive later that day.

I called the keyworker back to let her know.

'Mr Wearing's standing right here.' She passed the phone to Clive. He was usually by the phone when I called. Perhaps he stayed in the lobby waiting for me all the time.

'Hello, darling!' He sounded ecstatic.

'Mmm, hello!'

'Keep talking!' he said. 'Your voice gives me ecstasy. X to C, *ha ha*!'

'I love you!'

'Mmmm, I don't love me, I much prefer you! I'm not good enough for you. Ladies are better than men!'

'You're the best man in the world!'

'Keep talking!' he said. 'Your voice gives me ecs-ta-sy. X to C, *ha ha*! Isn't that a funny word? X to C, third letter from the end of the alphabet, third letter from the beginning, like the Trinity.'

'Mmm. Do you know that I love you?'

'I can tell from the sound of your voice!'

'Are your feet hurting?'

'My feet? No, they're fine . . . Oh, wait a minute, there's a little tickle there just on the, what do you call it . . . ?'

'Sole?'

'Yes, that's right . . . *ahh*! When I put pressure on it, oohh, it's quite sharp, on the left, er . . . foot.'

'Are you wearing shoes?'

'Er, sort of . . .'

'What, ordinary lace-ups?'

'You know, with the, er . . . toes, the toes showing.'

'Sandals. But it's still sore?'

'Yes, like a knife, ooh, that hurts!'

'Well, don't press on it.'

'All right. I'll stand on one leg and talk to you!'

'Darling!'

'I don't mind! I'd stand here on one leg for twenty-four hours if I could talk to you . . . although it might be a bit expensive on the phone bill!'

'I don't care – you're the best man in the world. Remember, I love you,' I said.

'I can't forget you for a moment,' he said. 'We're not two people but one. You're in my right ear!'

'Well, put me on your left foot – I'm sending some kisses . . . stand by! *xxxxxx*.'

Some time into my stay in America, the quality of our conversations had started almost imperceptibly to change. It was partly a function of our communicating on the phone, I think. There were fewer distractions. Just my voice in his ear. He felt safe in his place and under no pressure to be anything more than he was. My presence made him worry about what he had lost, what he could not be. My absence was never truly absence. It made no difference to Clive where I was – down the road, on the other side of the world – I was always with him because he loved me and he was awake now, completely awake for the first time, so everything was different. Whatever I was doing was fine by him, he understood I had things to do, work, studies . . . 'I understand, darling,' he'd say. 'But please fly here at the speed of light.'

'Guess where I am!' I'd say.

'I don't know, love . . . home?'

'Guess.'

'London?'

'New York!'

'New York? Terribly noisy place New York, I remember no one could sleep there.' It was true that he had been to New York to make a recording a couple of years before his illness, and he had come back complaining he hadn't had a wink of sleep. He couldn't have remembered the incident itself, but it had made a general impression on him. And he was right, the noise was incessant. But I liked it. To me it was life – sirens whining, chirruping and shrieking at all hours. The noise came right up in a funnel between tall buildings and what with the police and fire houses right below, there was no lack of activity. I never thought much about what the sounds implied or where these vehicles were headed. I took for granted the mêlée of city chaos and thrived on the busyness. In fact there was something about the very cacophony, in particular the sirens, that made me feel right at home. The background din signified life on the edge. It was a highly suitable soundtrack for where I was then. The sci-fi writer would return six weeks before I was due in Europe for a family holiday so I moved to an apartment in the Singer Building on Broadway and Spring, sharing with a painter who kept a stuffed bobcat outside my door. I might come out of my room to put the kettle on and find a naked man standing conspicuous in the light of the big arched window, surrounded by students painting, talking to each other about the frocks at the Oscars, boyfriends, rent, as if the model were a still life. Just before my return to Europe I had an invitation to spend some days in New Haven chez Chuck, a man friend I'd met in the head injury days. It seemed like good timing so I put things in storage and took off. Chuck was Chippewa, the only Native American of my acquaintance. Accepting his invitation would be a symbol, I thought, a ritual welcome from someone who had a right to be there. I wanted to make more of a connection with the US, to feel I wasn't just skittering about on life's surface.

Chuck told me my Christmas card was one of only two on his mantelpiece. The other, he said, was from his parents. He told me this in April.

I took the Amtrak. The horn sounded husky as we rounded a bend and the guard passed me a blanket. I felt as though I were on the Chattanooga Choo-choo. Nothin' could be finer, sittin' in the diner than to eat your ham and eggs in Caro-*li*-na.

*

Chuck met me at the station and as soon as we'd dumped my bags he offered to show me round his neighbourhood and take me for 'a cup of tea' – he pronounced it with exaggerated Englishness – in his favourite bookstore.

Walking towards the local Safeway we saw an argument taking place between two men, one with his back to the main entrance, the other standing on the kerb. They were shouting. They sounded pretty mean. As we approached, the one to our right with his back to the store reached into a holdall he was carrying and pulled out a gun. We could not have been more than five yards from them. I looked at Chuck to see what to do. He'd fought in 'Nam, he was Chippewa, this was his country, he'd know. There was a small muscle movement in his cheek, a gritting of the jaw, but no other detectable reaction. He continued right on walking towards the two men without looking at them or at me, without varying his step in any way. I did the same although my head went cold and the blood sang in my ears. We kept on walking until we were clear. The men were still shouting. I turned to see one still waving his gun, the other, his arms out defensively, his tone conciliatory.

'Don't look back,' said Chuck.

'What happened? Why didn't you stop? Why didn't we cross to the other side?' I seemed to have run out of breath and my heart was beating its way out of my ribcage now that the danger was past. Chuck kept on walking, looking straight ahead.

'If we'd 'a' stopped or crossed the street or turned back,' said Chuck, 'they'd 'a' seen us. It's important to keep on going – that way they may not notice you. Don't change a thing, keep on walking.'

A man was approaching and I instinctively made way for him to pass. Chuck did not.

'Keep your place on the sidewalk, Deborah,' he said. 'Let the

other people move. That way you have the power.' He talked
without looking at me, nor did he look about him, though he
seemed more aware of what was happening around us than I was.
He suddenly put his arm out to bar me from walking into a
roller-blader speeding round the corner towards us. The roller-
blader swerved on past. He wore headphones.

'And never,' he said, 'never walk around with those on your
ears. The muggers will know you are not aware and they will
come up and git you.'

Nobody was going to come up and get Chuck. His job was
protecting native landrights. I could see he'd be a stickler. He'd
have indigenous populations all over the globe keeping their place
on the sidewalk.

He put his arm around me in the bookstore and looked straight
at me for the first time since I'd got there. He smiled, his face
suddenly soft. He enjoyed talking about books and shared with
me his family's story, and spoke about Native American history.

He said little about his own history and he turned down the
volume on the answerphone so that I wouldn't hear messages
from a woman called Susie. We'd got on very well as part of a
crowd but had little to say to each other after one meal.

I walked about New Haven. A mother with two small kids in
the back wound down her window at traffic lights and told me I
shouldn't be where I was, offered me a ride to the mall. I said
thanks but no. 'Get off the streets, lady,' a policeman told me one
bright afternoon when I was admiring chokecherry on a gracious
boulevard.

Chuck was silent, preoccupied, and didn't come home till late. I
told him I was checking into a hotel.

'Don't leave,' he said. 'I'm sorry . . . it's just real bad at work.
Please don't leave . . .' He seemed genuinely sad, in trouble, but

though he made some small efforts he was still mostly silent. Hotels in safe districts were pricey and my plane ticket was the fixed kind with no change permitted.

Maybe sleeping with someone outside marriage was against his religion, like being photographed. But then one day I found a photo of Chuck and a ring of people with what looked like the Mayor. Chuck was looking at the others and laughing. Perhaps he did it for the team. Perhaps he thought it was all right as long as you didn't look at the lens. I wonder if he regretted that moment afterwards, if he was angry at himself. Maybe he believed that when the shutter opened, some of his own inner light leaked out into the camera.

Maybe it was me. When I slept with a man it was as if a piece of me came away. Afterwards all I really wanted was to go home. I felt I was emptying.

Before leaving New Haven, I called Clive from the middle of town.

'When are you coming to see me?' he asked.

'Soon,' I said.

'Dawn?' he asked.

'Soon as I can,' I said.

'Come at the speed of light!'

'I'm in America,' I said.

'Really?' he said. 'New York's an awfully noisy place. Terrible racket, day and night!'

'New Haven's no haven either.'

'I see . . . Tell me, *xxxx*, how long have I been ill?'

And there we were, back to our place in the conversation, the territory we occupied together, the one place we knew where we were. Stasis.

I wanted refuge but, as ever, came up against the blank wall that there was nowhere to go but this conversation. I told him I would spend the summer in Europe – I'd see him before I decided where else to go.

'Stay here with me!'

'In your room?'

'I've never seen my room . . .'

'I could hide under your bed for the summer and you could bring me bread rolls from the dinner table.'

'I'm sure they wouldn't mind!'

'I'll be back to the US in the fall to keep on studying.'

He noticed my Yankee vocabulary. '*Fall*,' he said, 'is *autumn*. You know what autumn means?'

'Tell me,' I said. He had started to invent bizarre word derivations which stayed the same, another of his fixed confabulations. He'd say it once and repeat it verbatim ever after. For no reason I could deduce, he came out with this at any mention of the word 'autumn'.

'Autumn's from the ancient Greek,' he said, 'for *an-te am-ne-sia*,' pronouncing the words a syllable at a time.

'Ante amnesia?'

'Yes,' he said. 'Before (from the Latin) amnesia (from the Greek). Didn't you know?'

The fall is autumn, autumn is before amnesia. He still had the mind of a crossword expert. And from among the broken recesses of Clive's brain, he was pulling out clues to help me understand the essence of where we were; he was letting me know we were in winter. Now was the winter of our discontent – our life minus content. Our life. But even in the dittos of our dittos, we were in there. It was winter frozen over, but we were in there, and we knew that we knew that we knew.

# 11

## ANOTHER COUNTRY

*Clive's diary, 1994:*

| | |
|---|---|
| 4.30pm AWAKE FIRST TIME | FIRST THOUGHT: PLEASE FLY HERE DARLING! |
| 4.19pm REALLY " " " | FIRST THOUGHT: PLEASE FLY HERE DARLING! |
| 4.21pm TOTALLY " " " | FIRST THOUGHT: PLEASE FLY HERE DARLING! |
| 4.30pm COMPLETELY " " " | FIRST THOUGHT: PLEASE FLY HERE D——— AT THE SPEED OF LIGHT |
| 4.33pm TRULY " " " | FIRST CONSCIOUS STROLL. PLEASE FLY HERE DARLING |
| 4.35pm SUPERLATIVELY " " " | FIRST THOUGHT: PLEASE FLY HERE D———! |
| 4.50pm AMAZINGLY " " " | FIRST THOUGHT: PLEASE FLY HERE D———! |
| 4.59pm PROPERLY " " " | FIRST THOUGHT: PLEASE FLY HERE D———! |

| | |
|---|---|
| 5.08pm TRULY " " " | FIRST THOUGHT: PLEASE FLY HERE D——-! |
| 5.11pm COMPLETELY " " " | FIRST THOUGHT: PLEASE FLY HERE D——-! |
| 5.14pm ABSOLUTELY " " " | LOO CALLS: FIRST STROLL |
| 5.23pm ACTUALLY " " " | FIRST THOUGHT: PLEASE FLY HERE D——-! |
| 5.28pm ENTIRELY " " " | FIRST THOUGHT: PLEASE FLY HERE D——-! |
| 6.50pm TOTALLY AWAKE FIRST TIME | FIRST GAME PATIENCE: PLEASE FLY HERE D——-! |
| 7.02pm REALLY " " " | GAME UNRESOLVED: PLEASE FLY HERE D——-! |
| 7.07pm PERFECTLY " " " | PATIENCE NEEDED: PLEASE FLY HERE DARLING! |

Clive never knew we were divorced because he was incapable of knowing anything. I discussed with his family and with his consultant whether we should seek to involve him, but agreed it would only upset him at the time, and he would remember none of it afterwards anyway. Legally he could not give informed consent, so his son acted for him. Everyone understood that the divorce was partly one of expedience, since I would not be in the UK to look out for Clive, and partly an action to help me move on to a life beyond Clive. But I would remain joint next of kin with his son because I wanted to continue to be involved in taking decisions about Clive, even from the USA, to continue to be his advocate. His family supported me in that.

Nine years into the amnesia, there was some difference in our reunions. For the first few years Clive had always found them intensely emotional, bringing on either grief, high-note joy or furious anger. Now, when I came back from America, it was my turn to feel intensely emotional. I was longing to see him. When I put my head round his door, his face registered a rush of delight and surprise as if he were about to dash to me as usual and lift me up and swing me round, but then he checked himself. He stood where he was, diffident. He knew enough about himself to realize that although it might seem like months or years of absence to him, I might only have been to the bathroom.

Once I arrived and was shocked to see a front tooth missing. His big grin showed a large dark gap. It was a sign that time was moving on even if Clive wasn't in it. With each visit I noticed more teeth missing, and he was continually puzzled as he didn't remember losing any of them. He'd woken up just a moment ago and found himself with far fewer teeth in his head than before his illness. The dentist told me it was on account of the drugs, which had a drying effect on the mouth. He fitted bridges while there were teeth to attach them to, and Clive's careworkers stepped up his mouthwash regime, but the decay continued. 'Oh dear,' Clive used to say, feeling the gaps with his tongue, 'Anno Domini!'

He seemed to be learning, through a kind of interior rehabilitation. He was developing a growing sense that he had asked and heard these questions and answers of awakening before. Without conscious memory of ever asking and hearing, he had, after nine years, got used to the experience of first awakening. Though his stump of memory never allowed progression from first moment to sustained time, his acute intelligence, applied to the shallow traces of implicit learning he had, let him understand something of his situation, enough to help him relate to others and engage in activities without constantly shouting to be let out of his amnesia. As I observed these and other subtle changes in Clive since my absence overseas, I could not suppress a flash of hope. What else might he accomplish?

The staff had learned that when Clive was seized with fitting, the offer of a cup of coffee was usually enough to bring him straight out of it. So when we were a few moments into our reunion hug and Clive jerked backwards, convulsed, his key-worker was ready.

'Mr Wearing! Shall we make Deborah a cup of coffee?'

Clive was immediately calm and smiling. 'Oooh, what a good idea!' he said. 'And – ' here he looked reticent – 'could I possibly have one too?'

'Of course you can!'

'Would that be possible?'

'Certainly, Mr Wearing!' The staff had picked up that it was important to address Clive by his formal name because they would always be strangers to him. Being called by your first name by a total stranger can be unsettling, so using 'Mr Wearing' made Clive more comfortable. He seemed to accept them calling me Deborah, because he assumed I knew them even if he didn't. If I ever asked his opinion on anything, he'd reply, 'You know everything that's going on here, darling! You decide! I trust you!'

Clive had the biggest room in the place as he spent most of his time there, unable to socialize with the others. Since he could not remember the sentence before the one he was in, following a conversation was beyond him. And, of course, to Clive, every person apart from close family or old friends was never anything other than a complete stranger, however many times he saw them. Nobody in the place looked familiar to him from one year to the next. Conversation was only possible one-to-one with a person expert enough in Clive's way of perceiving things to avoid up-setting him and keep to neutral subjects, cueing him into the areas he knew. When talking to staff, he liked to hold forth about

Erdington, Birmingham, where he was born, and comment on the relative size of Birmingham and Aston and how Aston used to be the superior town until the industrial revolution. And how Birmingham was a more sensible location for the capital of England, being in the middle. Anyone would think he liked the place, and perhaps he did at heart but, before he was ill, he'd always say how pleased he had been to leave and go to Cambridge.

From Clive's point of view, he was conscious now for the first time in many years. He could not follow television or newspapers or books. He was not going to sit down and chat with a roomful of strangers. Staff had to have training to chat to him. Agency staff quickly came unstuck. Unless one is skilled and savvy about amnesia, it is really difficult to have a dialogue without ever asking a question or assuming some knowledge, even when such a slip could elicit a most terrifying eruption. There was nothing Clive was able to do other than household tasks, play the piano or go for walks with the staff. These activities relied only on procedural memory, not explicit episodic memory, and, with these, he did not need to remember what led up to the current moment in order to understand and continue with what he was doing.

Clive's room had a sign on the door, 'CLIVE WEARING'S ROOM'. Other notices pointed to THE BATHROOM, THE KITCHEN, THE LIVING ROOM, so that Clive could move about the house. He was allowed a cigarette after meals and would go outside to the front step to smoke. He knew to do that and was always accompanied until he stubbed out the end and came back inside. In his room he had his upright piano and his own furniture – our wedding-present white sofa and a nice cherrywood Shaker chest of drawers and matching coffee table. There were brass label holders on the front of every drawer so that he could locate socks, pants, pyjamas, thin jumpers and thick.

My letters and postcards and Christmas and birthday cards going back years were all where he had left them on the table by the window, some still in the envelopes, yellowing with age. In the drawer of his bedside table were more letters and all his Christmas cards, many from other patients and their families and from the staff. It was touching that individual care assistants had sent cards, knowing patients did not receive many from the outside world. And how dreadful to be brain-injured and have less than a handful of cards on the sill at Christmas. Even if residents couldn't identify all the senders, at least they could look at the array and see that some people still cared about them.

As Clive sat by me on our sofa playing a hand of patience his eye caught a birthday card I'd sent him two years before that was still on his bedside cabinet, and he reached out for it.

'Mmm, "with all my love forever kiss kiss kiss . . . to the power infinity".' He laughed. 'I like that! Kisses to last forever and a day, mmm.' I nuzzled his cheek with my nose and he put the card back and shuffled and dealt.

'Do you feel my kisses even when I'm not here?' I could ask him abstract questions like this, even though he wasn't able to answer specific questions.

'Ooooh yes! You're always here, darling! You're with me all the time, all the time!'

'That's right! And do you know how much I love you?'

'I can hear it in your voice.'

'But do you know it all the time, when I'm not here, even when you're asleep?'

'I know we're one person, not two. You're the *raison d'être* for my heartbeat and my brain.'

'Ï lo-vé yo-uu!' We had used to pronounce it in a kind of old English with all the syllables distinct. He'd not forgotten that.

'Ï lo-vé yo-uu!'

Every so often Clive picked up his mug, saw only the dregs, but made motions of drinking the last drop to save the embarrassment of putting it down again. I should have taken it away, but although at the start of the visit I had been fresh, chatty and full of ideas about what we'd do together that day, I soon ran out of steam. I had thought being away in America would have raised my coping threshold, but we quickly slumped back into the old dialogue. I tried to break out of the loop-tape monotony and divert his angry outbursts or fitting by telling him I loved him, but the amnesia seemed to engulf us both.

In the evening, we sat with other residents in the lounge after supper. I sat in a wingback armchair holding hands with Clive in the armchair next to mine. He was enduring the news with odd comments. I wondered if he would storm out of the room blazing, or switch off from the voice of the newsreader and fall asleep. I didn't want to leave but wasn't sure how much longer I could take it. The longer I was with him, the less competent I became, sinking into an amnesic quicksand. I knew I had to get up and get out while I still could. It would take the rest of the evening to re-gravitate into the world of timeflow. To be with Clive I had to step inside his perspective. When I came out I wasn't sure I was safe to drive.

One of the few mercies of amnesia was that Clive was spared some of the effects of repetition. He did nevertheless speak his questions faster and faster, increasingly abbreviating them, and the look around his eyes was sometimes dull, for in his heart he knew this was not the first time of asking, for the muscles of his mouth had formed these words ten thousand thousand times before. He did know at some level that he was repeating himself because he detected how hard it was for me to keep responding to the same questions. He never had any conscious knowledge of asking any of them before, and yet he apologized for asking them and would occasionally say, 'Sorry, darling . . . if I've asked this before, I've no knowledge of it.' While I struggled to respond with the right words in the right order, Clive would sit, head bowed, eyes lowered, as if he were ashamed. Sometimes he blew little kisses to encourage me, for the answers were imperative. He had to hear them. He had to know what was going on, and he could not wait. This was urgent.

'How long? . . . Darling? . . . *xxx* . . . Come on, darling, tell me . . . how long have I been ill?'

'Er . . . sorry, darling . . . Er . . . let me see now . . . er . . . nine . . .'

'*Nine years!!!* Good heavens! Nine years . . . I haven't heard anything, seen anything, felt anything, smelled anything, touched anything. It's been one long night lasting . . . how long?'

'Er . . . er . . . um . . . how long, er, nine years . . .'

I developed a neuro-psychological hypothesis of my own. If you have the same conversation, answering the same few repeated questions from the same person every time you have contact for a considerable number of years, your mind ceases to be able to take in and process those questions or to produce the appropriate response. Maybe uttering the same dialogue over and over all that time could even have had its own physiological effect, making changes in my thinking, tramlines along which our dialogue flowed and from which we could not deviate. Somehow I was unable to be spontaneous.

When learning takes place, that is, when a piece of information is registered through the senses, encoded and stored as memory, we know that a physiological change does occur. I had a professor explain the chemistry of it to me once, sitting in a pool bar in California. He described the process, known as 'long-term potentiation', where the brain undergoes plastic changes at a sub-cell level. It's all to do with electrical charges, neurons, magnesium, calcium, and the dendritic 'spines' or protrusions on the branches of axons. He explained the principles with a puddle of beer on the table, some salt (for the magnesium), a couple of knives (dendrites) and beer mats (for something called NMDA receptors).

'NMDA?' I asked him.

'N-Methyl-D-Aspartate.'

'OK . . .'

He called to the waitress, 'Miss! Miss! We need another couple o' beer mats over here! . . . Great! OK, now here comes the calcium!' (appropriately the end of a sachet of longlife milk). He made it all seem so easy to understand that I was ready to enrol in a Masters Neuroscience degree then and there. But reading the papers about precisely how chemicals inhibited the pre- or post-synaptic potential and about how electrical charges excited neurons in various channels, I realized I would have needed a degree before the degree, just to get the hang of the principles (and vocabulary) of physics.

So the scientists did know that learning went with some organic change, but had not yet found what they termed 'the engram', a more precise trace of where memory is 'housed' in the brain. Psychologists and physiologists (and those combining both disciplines, neuro-psychologists) had searched for years to know where and how the images and sequences retained in the mind's eye or other kinds of memory are stored. They know that different cell areas or neuronal circuits are involved in particular categories of memory because they can see what malfunctions after those regions of the brain are damaged. The densely amnesic person with damage to the hippocampus and little capacity to take in and lay down new information or retrieve episodic information nevertheless is able to call on a number of different kinds of long-term memory that operate within different neuronal circuits.

Scientists have endeavoured to crack the code of what happens where by comparing impaired function against areas of cell damage, and noting whether lesions are discrete, that is, well defined, or diffuse, where cells have atrophied over a wider, more general area.

One of the scientists who taught me a lot used to say, 'Well, if our brains were simple enough for us to understand, then we'd be too simple to be able to.'

I wonder what a close examination of my brain at the time would have shown, whether they could have identified which cells were employed in conversations with Clive. Maybe the dendrites of our endless repetition got so thick, I could no longer see the wood for the trees.

As for my heart, I was a bundle of walking dichotomies – in love with a husband I was divorcing and could not live with. Wanting to be alone yet fearing to be. Wanting to love again and unable to. Not wanting to go through life without having kids, yet not wanting kids with anyone but Clive. I couldn't stand England but wasn't allowed to stay in the US.

Back in Europe I thought I should tarry. I knew it was best to avoid New York in August, but I didn't want to remain in England. Where was I to go?

For no particular reason I went to Greece. It was not England but nearer than New York. It was neither East nor West. I had a friend there who knew of a house near hers to rent. I could take it for three months and put off the final move across the Atlantic.

*

I rented a house in Limni on the isle of Evia. Evia was a headland of the mainland until an earthquake snapped it off, and now it hangs by a causeway at Chalkis where two seas meet. The tides flow in two directions at once. The current changes up to fourteen times a day. Aristotle nearly drowned trying to understand those currents. The locals thought he was attempting suicide but I believe he could not fathom the patterns simply by looking so he leaped in to feel the tug and counter-tug of tides on his body.

I first saw the sea from the bus driving down into Limni. The water was gleaming, glassy blue. I was renting a two-storey white-washed house with yellow shutters and bare wooden floors, withdrawn from the other houses. It faced the sea, half hidden behind a plane tree. Out back, stone steps led from the kitchen door down to a high-walled courtyard. Steep cobbled alleys, scarcely more than gullies, led up the hill to the road out of town.

In my courtyard grew a vine. When I arrived in June, pale and blinking, it was covered with a thin canopy of leaves shielding grapes no bigger than peas.

Topping my green metal gate was a brush of jasmine. The tangled mass caught on the metal as I went in or out, and sprinkled me with dried leaf fragments, twigs and ants. The clang of gate hitting post echoed to the top of the hill and made people look down. The whole valley knew when I came in and when I went out.

I leaned a ladder on the wall and took shears to the dead wood, hacking back to the green. Brush tumbled round my feet, piling up. Soon new growth came, the leaves bright green, and a mass of tiny white petals, and corkscrew tendrils winding around and around. Each time I opened the courtyard gate a flowerfall of soft white blossom pattered on my face and over my shoulders. Petals in my hair felt like a wedding. I was always looking for signs in those days. My hair grew fast too, spiralling towards the sun.

The Limni day started with shouting, the call of the donkey man around six, leading his donkey through the cobbled streets and waking the town with guttural cries: '*Piperiés, melitsánes, angoúri, domátes!*' – peppers, aubergines, cucumbers, tomatoes!' Then the neighbours started up. I was conspicuous for being alone, to myself as well as to them. Being stuck in this big empty house in a place where few spoke English now seemed to me a bit of a mistake. I had wanted to be free from people, but the solitude only intensified my difficulty in being in the world. I did have my friend around the other side of the bay. She and her parents invited me for dinner at their house and to a taverna a number of times and took me about the island every so often, but by and large I was keen to stay home and work. The Limniots got used to me. I shopped sometimes, swam each afternoon. But in the evenings, the townsfolk strolled on the promenade in families, crowds or couples. I was the only one alone.

In the mornings I read in the cellar, where it was dusty and cluttered but cool. There were logs, swollen driftwood and battered furniture stacked to the ceiling, rusty trunks and broken things – electric fans, a barrel of wine, tables, empty jars, a split-open plaster cast on chicken wire. Through the low, barred arch window I could see people's feet and hear their voices talking under the plane tree. Little children liked to crouch by the window and peer in.

I was expecting my boxes to arrive on the bus from Athens. At eleven each morning I went out to look. The driver sounded the horn when he rounded the clifftop road – the signal for people to leave their houses. We waited on the sea front. After the

horn would come shouting when the bus got lodged between a
wall and a parked car outside the baker's – a fugal mounting
of sound as shopkeepers came out one by one as far as the
corner; finally the police would join in from an upstairs window
at their station on the T-junction, bellowing instructions through
mouthfuls of elevenses, *tiropità* (cheese pie) in hand, until the bus
scraped through.

After a week with no boxes, the driver knew to signal '*NO!*' to
me before he had even applied the brakes. I called the despatch
docks in Athens and London repeatedly. I knew my bill-of-lading
number off by heart.

Finally I gave up looking and then the boxes arrived. The local
taxi driver rescued them from the side of the road where they had
sat without theft or injury for some hours. They were warm from
the sun when he brought them round. I got out all the neuroscience books, opened them and closed them again. This wasn't
what I needed.

Dinner alone in my high-walled courtyard was a sorry affair.
All around me was the clatter of dishes and families chatting,
playing the guitar, laughing, yelling at each other. The sound of
crockery at open windows had made me sad for years. I opened
tins mostly. Stuffed vineleaves, *dolmades*, with feta cheese and
tomatoes was my staple. Local ewe's milk yoghurt with honey
usually cheered me somewhat. Why on earth was I here?

I could not find quiet in my soul. I decided to send for help. I
bought a fistful of faded 1950s postcards from the corner shop and
wrote them to friends.

'Sun, sea and wine fresh from the barrel,' I promised. 'Long
Greek dinners in my grape-slung courtyard and a shooting
gallery of stars over the sea. Bring suntan lotion. Bring Earl Grey

tea, loose leaf. There are geckoes in my china cupboard. Please come.'

I wrote the same thing to everybody, improving on the sentences card by card, working out better where to fit the words, the addresses. I sent it to names from my filofax AB to XYZ, in England and in the US. The men I wrote to seemed to me to have little in common. One friend had pointed out that men I thought attractive all bore a resemblance to Clive.

'You're looking for Clive,' she said.

I don't know.

I am not sure I expected anyone to arrive, but one day a telegram, a flimsy envelope, was pushed under the side door I never used. It contained a slip of white paper edged with blue, faded as if the previous telegram had been sent a long time before. Inside were these words in faint print: 'ARRIVING LIMNI STOP – PLEASE CALL STOP – JON STOP.'

I saw Jon again, receding through the rear window of a New York taxi. The flimsy paper was still in my hand when I walked out to the taverna to use the telephone. The slow American ringing tone made me think of an imaginary apartment and Jon starting at the sound. High on the wall I saw myself in a mirror above a row of Metaxa bottles.

Jon sounded tinny, like a person winded.

'Got your card,' he said.

'Got your telegram,' I said.

'I got time to kill,' he said.

'Sounds dangerous,' I said.

There was a pause and then a sound like dragging on a cigarette followed by a sigh.

'You wanna see me?' He made it sound like he was shy.

'If you'd like to kill your time here, I can accommodate you.'

'OK, I'll be right over. I'll let you know my flight details.' I started to tell him about Limni, the fishermen mending nets on the beach in the afternoons, seeing a funeral procession with a man in his best suit on a bed of white chrysanthemums, the chopping of vegetables on balconies, the townsfolk carrying their trays of stuffed peppers up to the baker's to use his oven, and fresh yoghurt with honey . . .

'You should write a piece for the *Limni Gazette*,' he told me.

I laughed.

'What will you do now?' he asked.

'I'll take a swim.'

'Take one for me,' he said. 'A long cool swim.'

I did not take long cool swims. I dabbled in the shallows. I never went out of my depth.

I stood up, catching the octopus rod hanging by the phone. Brown tentacles slid against my calves and on to the floor.

The owner's wife helped me right the thing. She was kind and laughing. 'No damage done,' she said. The pink suckered ridges looked unearthly. On the way back to the house I hit a sudden stench of drains on the corner.

Why had I invited this man?

At the edge of the sea I dropped my sarong and weighted it with a large pebble. Blue and orange silk billowed out. This swim marked the spot. I am here. Jon's arrival gave me a co-ordinate. You need two references to plot a point. That was my trouble in life. Without Clive I had no point. Jon arriving seemed to amount to more, a convergence, a starting point maybe. I'd show willing. I'd take a long cool swim because he'd asked me to.

The stones were hot and sharp. I walked into the water, leaned into the pale gleaming surface and broke it. I swam, striking out at right angles from the shore. I gave myself entirely to the water, in no hurry to surface from each long slow breaststroke. I watched small shoals of brown fish darting in and out of the rocks; my arms made patterns on the seabed, dappled with ripples.

Towropes snaked out to fishing boats. I swam in a straight line out from the shore, my body making a punctuation mark on the waves. I wanted to pitch myself into the deep, a gesture of trust that it would hold me. Swimming in the salt sea felt like purification.

There was music in my head, Smetana's *Vltava*. Aged eleven in Junior 4, we were mermaids in Aertex shirts putting a drama to the music. It now played wide and watery and full of hope. I was level with the first boat. The shore noises were muffled by wind and water. I heard the continual slap of water on wood, flags flapping, pulleys clanking. White hulls reflected the glinting ripples. If I can swim level with this boat, I thought, I can swim level with the next. A regular swell lifted me up and dropped me down, cresting foam. I matched my stroke to the rhythm of the waves, to the tune of the violins.

Maybe all of life broke down to this stroke, this stroke. Being present only in this stroke made progress possible. If you stopped to think of the whole distance, you would sink. I was emptying, swimming on and on, *Vltava* playing full force. I reached the moment where the bottom of the orchestra falls away, leaving a flurry of violins winding over stones before the next triumphal surge. There was a small white building to my left on a promontory around the bay. I was beginning to tire but would get level with that. I wanted to be sure I'd swum far enough to be free, cut off from everything that bound me.

The rollicking cadenza gathered pace, and I was satisfied I was on a latitude with where I wanted to be. I rose on the swell and saw the house, triumphant. I could turn back now.

I let down my legs to swivel round. The water was icy here, and black. It must be deep. I turned back to face the shore and that's when I realized. The music cut out and I was fighting water. The shore was a pale strip of sand in the distance, edged with a thin black line. It looked like land the way you see it from a ship, only no ship, just a wide expanse of sea from here to there. I flailed, sank, gasped and took in water, fighting to stay in control. The sea was freezing, opaque. I wondered about the weight of water under me and would I be visible from the sky. I knew I was in danger without articulating that thought; I could be at the point of death, of nothing or infinity. I returned to myself in a moment of steel clarity. Don't look at the beach. Float. Swim, breathe. Did the last stroke, can do the next. And then I was swimming again, heart batting, but swimming like before. Arms, arms, watching the small piece of water in front of my face.

I don't know how long it took. Progress was slow. There might have been a current dragging me out. I kicked harder. At some point I could make out that the black line at the water's edge was a row of motionless people, like Giacomettis, looking out to sea. If I stuck an arm straight up, like a drowning person, I wondered would anyone come, would they think it worth the trouble? If I signalled now, would they get to me in time? But I needed the arm to swim. Everything that floats free, the sea casts up to the shore. Littoral litter. Ha ha. *Vltava*. Safe like in Junior 4 when the teacher told you what to do. I was maybe this tired because of being this scared.

As I got closer the figures relaxed, shrugged, began to move. A ball was thrown, people returned to rush mats and windbreaks, beach noises started up. I didn't want to face them yet so when I was in my depth again I stood, hauled myself up the shingle and sat on a rock with my back to the beach, trying to suppress the loud noise I was making, gasping for breath. I heard muttering. My Greek was rudimentary, but the meaning was plain enough. 'Silly cow,' they were saying. 'Silly English cow. Could have got herself drowned.' I leaned back on my elbows, facing the horizon, my chest heaving. I did feel transformed. I had come through like an initiate. I'd survived.

The night before Jon arrived was festival night. Limni was full of entertainment. We had fireworks on the sea – men out in rowing boats, a firework on the end of a rope that they twirled in the air so all we could see was the fire going round and round in the dark and occasionally a dim shadow of a man in the middle silhouetted against the light of a fishing boat. I felt the festival was for me. My divorce had come through on 5 August. White jasmine petals had been falling on my hair several times a day. I had purchased a simple fitted white dress, sleeveless, grosgrain to the knee and a slash of white organza around the hem. The shop had it altered to fit at the factory but when I collected it that day it had not fitted at all: it bulged where I didn't and was too tight where I did. I had thought the dress would feel like a symbol, that I was clean and new, ready to be a bride again. I thought if Jon was coming all the way to Limni then he must love me. I was expecting something akin to marriage, as long as it did not require forsaking Clive.

Jon appeared in the arrivals hall, familiar in old fatigues and lilac tanktop, a baseball cap low over his eyes. He grinned. He had a way of walking that looked like he wanted to be invisible, a result of dodging sniper fire maybe, or acquired before that.

While he rested for a day in Athens he talked to me of splitting up from his girlfriend Marsha earlier that year, and how any civilian life seemed to him mimsy after his war. The war was still in him. I don't think he could hear very well over the sound of it.

Jon could not believe the view as our ferry followed the coastline to Limni and we peeked out over the rim of the boat at wooded thickets, small campsites with washing lines, green marble cliffs. Sunlight glittered on azure sea and dazzled us. He didn't say much, only gripped the rail at chin height and kept raising his body up and down off the ground, biceps bulging.

We landed in Limni around five and walked along the promenade to 'my' house. I opened the gate to show him my vine. Petals fell as usual. Jon brushed them off. He looked out of place, hunched as if he expected the sky to fall in at any moment.

'I'm just a little dazed by all this,' he said. 'It's, like, too much.' He sloped up the courtyard steps, tapping out a cigarette from the pack in his pocket. He sat down on the top step and sucked on a ciggie while I collected a tray of drinks.

The grapes above our heads were fat now, purple, great juicy bunches, hanging heavy under a thickness of leaf shade.

'We can't pick those,' I said. 'They were sprayed with sulphur. I think they said not to eat them.'

'OK,' he said. I don't think he would have thought of picking them anyway. Jon mostly ate restaurant food.

He walked around rubbing his eyes, blinking. We went to the beach. Jon was puckish in faded jeans and white sneakers that seemed not quite to touch the ground when he walked. When he played other people on stage he seemed to have more power, a different presence. Left to himself it was as if he wasn't quite sure who to be.

\*

Over dinner in the courtyard Jon told me more about his struggle since Marsha left. Scenes of his life as a foot soldier in Vietnam were returning to his mind again and again as if it were yesterday. He kept his shrink's number on a scrap of paper on the door of his refrigerator. Now the shrink was on vacation and he didn't think he could stay in his empty condo knowing he could not call him. That was what had made him come here. So, he needed looking after. It had taken him a long time to pack, the yellow pills in and out of the bag. They were supposed to help him forget the war.

What he'd decided for this trip, if it was all the same to me, was to start telling the truth. As if to prove it, he began to tell me truths, waiting to see my reactions.

He had not, he informed me, brought the 'Lord Grey tea' as per my request because he had not made it to the shops. All right then, he had not known if he would really come until he got on the plane, so there was no time to shop. I wondered if he called Earl Grey Lord Grey deliberately. Or maybe he just never went supermarket shopping.

Then there was the tape of love songs he'd given me earlier.

'If you want to know the truth,' he said, 'I made them for Marsha.' Then he thought for a moment. 'No, I didn't,' he said. 'I made them for me.'

He told me about the night chills when he saw scenes from the war play over and over on his kitchen wall and all he could do was eat Sara Lee's packet cakes to numb the pain, or cling to his kitchen counter and wait for the nightmare to end. He ate to stay awake because he was afraid of what he might do in his sleep. Sharing a bed with Marsha had proved impossible. He could not sleep with another person there. He had ended up most nights on the sofa with a big history book. He pumped iron in the gym to work off the cakes and help tire himself, to stand some chance of sleeping. Sometimes he woke in his apartment and didn't know where he was. He would see familiar items like the Dustbuster and the pile of newspapers by the stove so he could check the date, 'And I do see there's other news now . . . But it don't mean nothin'. 1994 is just numbers. I wanna . . . jump off . . . jump right off, like we used to jump outa the choppers into the mud, and you knew where you were then. Now I walk out for a pack of Marlboros and I am still in a paddy field looking for cover.'

As he talked, Jon paced up and down, his head bowed, unseeing. When he'd done he stopped, stretched out on my bench and looked up at the starry sky.

'My,' he said, 'I never saw so many stars! Look! Look, there's a shooter! Amazing!' He sat up, excited. 'Let's go to the roof. The sky's bigger there . . .' He should have been tired but he seemed hyper and happy.

We lay on the still-warm stone and took in the sky, pointing to the pictures, the bear, the plough, the dogstar. The scents of bougainvillea and jasmine were overwhelming. I lit candles and we drank wine and he relaxed, forgot about the war and told me he'd never seen anywhere as lovely as this place. He let out a big sigh.

'I left home yesterday, I don't know when, and now where am I? I've come up from the deep so fast I could get the bends . . . Is this real? I can't stay here. This time next week I'll be back in the gates of hell. I oughta go and live somewhere where nobody knows me, somewhere hot like Guatemala . . .'

I told him about the festival and the fishermen, and the beehives at Prokopi, where I'd take him if he wanted a sortie.

'You are making my head spin,' said Jon, 'I can't take all this paradise. Where am I?' He lay back and closed his eyes, crossed his arms over his eyelids and talked some more about Marsha.

'I'm gonna get nailed.'

'What for?'

'For telling the all-out this-is-the-truth-of-me truth. I'm gonna get nailed, I know it.'

He took some pills before we went to bed. They made him sleepy. As he drifted off he said, 'Are we in Guatemala yet? Do you know me?'

That night he called out 'Marsha' in his sleep. Later I heard squeaking from inside his mouth: he was grinding his teeth – a side effect of medication perhaps, or an attempt to keep the fibrillating memories from pressing a scream from his mouth.

He spent his days talking about the war, about how it was to see his best friend blown up a few steps in front of him and come down in pieces in the jungle. To go from killing in the bush to a suburbia full of neat lawns and miniature shrubs was impossible. He could not pick up where he'd left off. Now he saw life through the killing scenes ever running through his mind; he saw every-thing through steaming red blood. The dailiness of life, the chit-chat, were so much double Dutch. I saw how it was for him. It was kind of like that for me. Jon couldn't see beyond the horror of 'Nam. I couldn't see beyond the loss of my husband.

As we lay together in the night, Jon asked over and over, did I love him, did I really love him, how much, could he trust me, could he rely on me not to leave. I took these questions to mean that he must really love me. He said he was telling me things he'd told no one else. I was lingering still in the illusion that we were kindred spirits, that I understood him, and he me. Then I noticed I had barely told him anything at all about my life since his arrival.

We spent our days talking, reading, sitting in restaurants by the edge of the sea. At night he seemed to go into a kind of panic. Once he woke and found me not in the room. I was feeling sick and had gone to another bedroom.

'Where were you?'

'Right here. I feel sick.'

'I woke up and you weren't there!'

'I'm nauseous.'

'I thought you'd gone.'

'Gone where?'

'Don't ever do that again.'

He scared me.

We hadn't finished breakfast when the taxi arrived to drive us the few hours to Athens airport. We'd arrived by water but departed by road. I hoped to show him the beehives from the car window but he slept the whole way. He embraced me at the customs point, held me close and whispered, 'Thanks for everything, Debbie,' though that is not my name and nobody calls me that. Then he walked through the glass doors and did not look back but lifted his hand, the way you do to the driver behind you for letting you in. And then he was gone. I had to chew gum a lot of the way home to try to keep from crying but I cried anyway, all the way back on the bus and the whole ferry trip, looking out to sea.

Back at the house our breakfast things were where we'd left them. I picked up his coffee cup. It smelled sickly of sugar. He'd be almost home, a world away, before I had had a chance to wash up. Other lives moved ahead at speed while mine was held snagged.

Jon's song tape was still in the machine. Without him it sounded full of pathos. I was a storm of emotions.

I turned off Jon's music mid-croon, and sat down on my

kitchen steps. Summer was almost gone. So what had happened here? The grapes had grown fat, turned purple, dusky black, luscious, dripping heavy overhead. I left them to dry and shrivel and drop off in evening breezes. That night they fell in the one big storm in that long Greek summer. The rain smashed the grapes and pounded them into the flagstones. I swept up, but they stained the stone. They stained the stone until after I was gone.

Clive took me in his arms, squeezing the breath out of me.

'*Darling!*' He lifted me in the air and swung me round, then hugged me again. 'Something's happened,' he said in my ear, in some distress. 'I'm conscious! Everything's normal suddenly, just before you came in . . .' He held me at arm's length and looked at me. 'In fact I don't remember you coming in, it's since you've been standing here . . . My eyes have come on suddenly. Everything's working normally. I can *see* you! I've never been conscious before about two minutes ago. I haven't seen anything, heard anything, smelled anything, touched anything. It's like being dead! What's it like being dead? Answer: nobody knows. How long's it been?'

'It's wonderful looking at you,' I said. 'You are gorgeous!'

'*You* are . . .'

'No, *you* are . . .'

'Oh no . . . I don't like me. *La-dies are better than men,*' he sang. 'Where are your wings? You're an angel. My word, you're look-ing . . . so . . .'

'Brown?'

'Yes, that's it.'

'Tanned.'

'Yes! I don't think I've ever seen you this colour before . . . Have you been somewhere exotic?'

'Greece.'

'Greece! Is that G-R-double E? Or G-R-E-A-S-E?'

'Double E, Greece the country.'

'Oh really? Have I been there? I don't think I've been there.'

'Not yet.'

'Well, I'm awake now, everything's different.'

'Good.'

'I'm seeing everything for the first time. How long's it been?'

'A while, a while . . . But I love you.'

'Oooh, I can see that by your eyes, and by your smile. It speaks volumes.'

'I'll call you from London.'

'All right, love, or is it all left?'

''Bye, darling.'

We hugged each other tightly while the careworker keyed in a security code and undid locks, bolts and chains on the door.

'Bye bye, darling, bye bye, *bye bye* . . .' he whispered.


When I heard my old room in TriBeCa was free since the sci-fi writer had married and was moving to the country, I booked a flight to JFK. It felt like home. Poetry at the Y, sushi on Saturdays, walks on the esplanade and salt beef on Second Avenue. I wasn't sure how to live, or what should be my future now. Inside, I felt I was supposed to be married and bringing up children; people are made to love and be loved. I had a heart full of love and nowhere to put it.

Jon called me one day out of the blue. He invited me on a trip to the rich green forests of Connecticut. Looking back, perhaps we both wanted someone just to buffer us from being alone. Keeping each other company a couple of days, we could kid ourselves we had a life the way others had lives, with love and companionship and choosing things in shops together. Since Clive went away I had grown more and more isolated. I guess New York was a good place to live because I could be alone and it didn't matter. You could go out on your own to the theatre or a movie or eat in a restaurant and no one thought anything of it, whereas in England a lone woman doing these things can be the focus of attention.

So at first it felt like something to have another person in the vicinity, someone to make-believe like we were a couple; and it was a treat to get out, right out in New England and bat along straight roads cut clear through the trees. Having a man alongside, a man in the guise of the one who loved and was loved, helped me see there might be some point, a reason for being there.

The forest was beautiful, lush green, high on either side of us. We spoke a kind of improvisation, and whenever I looked at him there was a flicker at his jawbone as he reset his face, flinty, towards the road ahead.

'Connecticut,' I said, copying his squeezed-out accent. 'Why is the second C silent?'

'Connect-I-cut.' He spoke it in exaggerated British with spit on the Cs and the Ts. I looked off into the deep green rushing past.

'I guess it's Pequot,' he said, 'the language of the Pequot. This is their land.' A rabbit bounded out of the woods and right into the road in front of us. Jon half braked but did not swerve, though there was no other traffic on the road. I looked behind. The rabbit was flying back to where she came from, terrified but alive.

Where are the Pequot now? I wondered.

'Couple miles ahead there's a casino. They own it. We took their land and they got gambling licences, gives them a chance to make a killing this way rather than through real estate.'

The casino was an enormous purple edifice with angles jutting into the sky, an assault after all the soft green leaf.

'Let's go play craps,' said Jon. I'd never been inside a casino so I was curious. As we drew up a young boy ran round to open the door for me. Jon gave him the car keys and some dollar bills and the boy drove away.

'You sure he's a valet?' I asked.

'Come on,' said Jon. 'Let's go and play.'

It was like stepping into some other dimension, the building opening up even bigger inside than it had appeared outside, as if we'd stepped through the looking glass. We wandered through room after room 'to get a feel of the games', said Jon.

We stopped at a table where there was some space but people on three sides. The wheel spinning was kind of mesmerizing.

'This one's hot,' he said. 'It's waxy. Let's play.' We went to the cashier's window and he bought a lot of chips.

'How many you gonna buy?' he asked me.

I hadn't wanted to buy any, but I took out my credit card and blued more than was sensible. I kept putting my chips on the one number, 33. When I'd trebled the stake, I was going to cash in the chips and keep the profit. I knew that if I stayed at the table I would lose the lot.

'Aw, honey,' he said, 'stay and play.'

I don't know why, it makes little sense to me now, but I wanted to please him.

Hostesses in pretend squaw outfits kept coming by with trays of free drinks, Coke or 7-Up. Jon had been losing since we arrived but he seemed to be enjoying himself. I spread my chips on a bunch of numbers. It all went.

I told Jon I was all done. He wanted me to buy more stake chips.

'Steak and chips,' I said, 'now you're talking!'

He asked if I would wait an hour as he didn't want to leave the table yet. He thought his turn to win might be right around the corner. He suggested I go and get dolled up in the beauty parlour.

'Take my card,' he said. 'It has points on it so you get stuff here for free.'

'You been here before?'

'Some,' he said.

I didn't recognize myself in this season's earth tones with splashes of magenta and ruby nails. I looked weird. The women around me wore a lot of make-up, clothes with big patterns on, bags with chains and high-heeled shoes. This face didn't suit me. In the ladies' room I soaped it off and daubed on my usual colour lipstick.

Jon was not where I had left him. I wandered up and down but he seemed to have vanished. Clive would never have done that. Clive would have waited. Clive would not have brought me here. What was I doing?

I traipsed through a few rooms. The building was kind of disorienting. The outside world was screened off so you could see nothing, not the weather, not day or night. Instead of proper windows, there were dark glass walls like one-way mirrors. The gaming rooms were enormous and bright with gleaming chrome and brass. A sea of slot machines had an endless cacophony – snatches of signature tune, dings and thuds and clunking as they punched the money out. They seemed designed as a come-on to the lonely, restless, blinking and winking, as if they promised entertainment, company, the possibility of winnings if you stayed around long enough, like bribery for loyalty. The world might let you down, but we're here for you. And men and women leaned on machines, staring intently into their twitching faces. Come on, pull my handle, you could hit the jackpot, this could be your lucky day. Chance is a fine thing. And somewhere across the room at another machine, the sound of chunk, chunk, chunk and tinkling as golden tokens tumble from a height like pennies from heaven. It could be you, says the hush that comes after. It could be you.

It would be easy to get lost here in time and space, forget where you were going and who you'd come in with. Maybe Jon didn't want to be found.

In the end I saw the familiar baseball cap. He was perched on a stool at a different kind of table. I went up behind him, put my hand on his back. He turned and grinned at me, his eyes all over the place, not quite meeting mine.

'Wow,' he said. 'You look peachy.'

'Really?'

'Absolutely.'

'What you playing?'

'Craps. You wanna play?'

'If you give me some of your chips.'

He stood behind me and explained the principles while I rolled dice. He whispered in my hair, his arm around my waist, as though he were revealing the mysteries of existence. I kept getting double sixes and winning an extra throw.

'Good job! *Way* ta *go!*'

I shivered. The air conditioning cut right through my blouse, so I reached for his jacket on the stool.

'No way!' he said. 'Not while you're throwing doubles, you're hot.'

'I'm frozen.'

'But you're on a roll,' he whispered. 'Don't do anything different!' I thought of Jon aged nineteen, an eternity of nights in the jungle, waiting for his life to go *blam*, up into the air, blown to small pieces, or to get hit by a bullet and die with his face in the mud. Why this one or that one gets killed and he gets saved. What did they do different? What were the deciding factors? He'd met *mama sans* in burnt-out villages speaking of the fall of chance, of fate dealing terrible blows. I knew that at the back of his mind the whole time were questions, why was he here twenty-five years on, and how was it, whatever he did, he could not escape the memory of one year, one place. He carried Vietnam on the inside, over-shadowing all the rest of his life. And when I tried to get closer, I fetched up there too, up to my neck in the swamp. Crapshooting was 'R&R', rest and relaxation, at their US base between missions. They came back, grinning at being alive, and partied on beer and dope and girls and craps until it was time to head back into the jungle.

'Let's go get some beers,' I said, shoving my plastic winnings into my handbag.

'OK,' he said.

'And dinner.'

'Sure,' he said.

The restaurant was vast. Jon had so many points on his advantage card, we could have ordered vintage champagne every night for a week, but stuck to beer and steak sandwiches. Here he went into a soliloquy about Marsha, trying to put his finger on what went wrong with them. It was shocking to have her name dragged up when my reason for being there was to see if anything at all might be right about us. After Marsha left, he'd gone into overdrive trying to get her back, sent gifts, letters, made a tape of 'their' songs and put it through her new letterbox, the one she shared with her new man in another part of town. 'Too little too late,' she'd told him on his answerphone before he was home. 'You don't know what you've got till it's gone,' I said. He was making patterns with packets of sugar in a dish and staring, miserable, across the rivers that separated him from a time back then when it had all been hunky-dory with Marsha. Only, from what he'd said before, it was never hunky-dory but did at least have slivers of hope, moments of tranquillity. I decided to stop responding and see, would he notice. After a good twenty minutes, I felt him look at me. He asked me what was wrong.

'I just thought I'd stay *shtum*.'

'What's up?'

'Seems to me Marsha's your other half, whether she likes it or not.'

He looked across at me and did what he always did when I made him nervous, picked up his pack of Marlboros from the table and shook out a cigarette.

'I made her unhappy. I don't know why.'

'If you love someone, if you really love each other, the love continues across every boundary, come what may, and then nothing can keep you apart, nothing, not even physical absence, no-thing.' I could have gone into my own soliloquy and there we'd have been, him with his loss and me with mine, our separate sorrows not connecting.

He started to cry. The tears ran from his eyes and he wiped them away with a crimson paper napkin. It was like someone had switched on the taps: his eyes brimmed over, soaked his eyelashes, rivulets running down his face. I went to the waiter trolley and brought back a fistful of napkins. He went on crying and mopping, and when the waiter came he spoke through the tears to ask for another coffee. I asked for the bill. He took his plastic points card out of his wallet and threw it down.

They were putting out croissants as if it were breakfast. We could not be sure what time of day or night it was because of the eternal bright light and hubbub. We were stuck in one long day all the time.

'Shall we go now?' I said.

'Not yet . . .' he said.

'Do you want me to go? I'm not sure why I'm here. You could drop me at a station.'

He shook out a cigarette.

'Let's at least stick our heads outside, find out what day we're in, or if it's still night. I need to get some fresh air. You OK, Jon?' I put my hand on his on the table. 'I'm sorry you're this sad. I don't know what to do about it. I'm not sure . . .'

He said nothing. I'd have done a lot if it could have helped him out of where he was. But I knew I wasn't making any difference. I would have hung on in much longer, but it was plain he didn't want me.

It was daytime outside and Jon drove me to a bus station where I could pick up a connection to New York. He stopped the car outside and took out my bag. Suddenly he hugged me. I thought it was sweet to hug me for no reason – until, instead of stooping to pick up my bag and coming to see me on to the bus, he got back into his car and drove away, leaving me and my bag on the pavement. I saw the side of his face behind glass, then the shape of his baseball cap not looking back as he fled into the forest.

There was a hunch to his shoulders. He might have come back from 'Nam with all his limbs but I sensed a deep shame at being alive. The memory of that time was raw and he could not see past it. Being an actor provided regular chances to hide in another man's story. Between shows, as himself, it was as though he were wriggling to slip his skin. I stared into the trees where he'd vanished, but the day was dazzling. I turned to look for the Greyhound.

\*

I had Thanksgiving dinner with seven different kinds of cranberry sauce, champagne at the Lincoln Center, breakfast in Little Italy and lunch in Chinatown.

I was here to have time to think. Writing poetry was my way of thinking deeply about something. What I understood least was love. I had huge to-die-for love with the man doctors said could never be my husband again. I had to work out what that meant.

Night-time was best for the workings out. Sometimes I might spend days and nights hardly ever coming out of my room. Carl would scratch on the door to signal he'd left refreshments outside. I'd open the door and find a cup of coffee with a saucer over the rim to keep it hot, or maybe a cheese sandwich which I'd squirrel back into my room and eat while I kept going. The strange small products, or the labour itself, gave me some temporary shelter.

They were all a kind of lament. I had gone to the ends of the earth to try to make a new life but the grief was as potent as ever – I felt as though I were pulling it around after me like a bag of artefacts, mementos, the scars of other relationships, dichotomies, mysteries, things I could do nothing about but could not leave behind. I had Clive's voice and the voices and faces of tens of thousands of amnesic people, real, read about and imagined, the weight of them dragging behind me. And the fetid helplessness of all their families. It was quite a bagful, not something I could give to the international shipping and storage. So I tried laying out the items in my writing, transmogrified through fictional or other characters. I thought I could bury them that way piece by piece.

I wrote about people who had lost their heads. Cheerful stuff. I studied the letters of Sir Walter and Lady Elizabeth Ralegh. He wrote to his wife from the Tower two letters fourteen years apart saying 'my braynes are broken' – a turn of phrase of the time, but poignant to me. He wrote the first after the death of their son Watt, the second on the eve of his own execution. Lady Elizabeth kept her husband's head in a red leather bag, dragging it around with her for sixteen years until her own death.

I wrote of an old woman with a sweater over her head. Her husband died in his armchair while she was in the kitchen preparing lunch and after she'd finished deciding he must be dead, the lid of the saucepan was rattling and she wondered what now should she do with the potatoes. And when they'd buried him and come back to the house for cold cuts, she sat in the blue armchair in his dent, and her daughter asked if she would take the sweater from off her head, but it was comforting to have the wool caught over her face, so she stayed where she was in the dark of it.

I was interested for a while in the Greek saint Nektarios, who was associated with miracles of the brain. I didn't know if miracles still or ever happened, but I was interested that his name meant like nectar, and my name is Hebrew for bee.

I was like a detective, pouncing on clues, without the first idea of what I was looking for, yet determined to make a thorough job of it. In addition to the poetry, I took classes in acting, painting, dance, tarot cards and native American shamanism. I went to writing groups, poetry slams, art happenings and contemporary dance – Meredith Monk at St Mark's, John Cage in the open air with impromptu helicopters overhead. I did a yoga class but they made me stand on my head in the first lesson and my subway tokens fell out of my jeans pocket. I went to a lot of lectures. When the Gate Theater did Beckett I saw at least a dozen plays. Winnie in *Happy Days* buried up to her waist was the image I was drawn to. After the interval, when the house lights went so slowly down and the stage lights came so slowly up, suddenly people saw

Winnie behind a gauze curtain buried up to her neck, where she'd been all this time we'd been chatting, and a gasp tore through the theatre. After that I wrote to offer myself as a sweeper-upper to the Gate Theater but I don't think they took me seriously. I took myself way too seriously.

I stood one day in the aisles of Ralph's Discount selecting another hair conditioner – none of them worked like the one I used in England – and I saw that some time soon I would have to face a day of reckoning, and add up the cost of all this – but for now, I felt I needed to spend the bricks and mortar money on learning how to think, on discovering how to live the life I had.

My friends Jane and Charlie had lived in Time Square. Charlie filmed and Jane painted. In *Doing Time on Time Square*, which Charlie shot from their bedroom window over the course of a year, a bent old woman in a headscarf and long coat walks past on the opposite side of the street. She is dragging behind her what looks at first like an animal of some kind on a lead, but it is a plastic bread crate on a rope. She walks across the frame from right to left. Later she appears again going the other way. She holds the rope at her shoulder and the bread crate drags along behind her. Jane painted the same image in oils. Ladies and gentlemen, I was that woman . . . well, no, not really . . . but she looked like I felt, dragging around my sick grief and nowhere to put it.

I did skits on the bread-crate lady in a couple of one-woman shows where I was spouting my writing to see if I could get rid of it that way. There was one show I did as Lady Elizabeth wearing a dress full of peacock feathers – only I didn't get time to make the costume until the morning of the show, when I was also rehearsing with Russ, the euphonium player acting as the ghost of Sir Walter, and simultaneously conditioning my hair. A friend helped me staple feathers to elastic and then on to my dress while singing Monteverdi. She asked if there was any particular reason why I'd stuck my head in a bucket of slime that morning. I washed the stuff off and struggled to Union Square with my props on the subway – the most precious being a giant eye painted by Jane on Astroturf and worth thousands of dollars. Carl had hold of my peacock on wheels, commissioned from a local carpenter – the Lady Elizabeth equivalent of a bread crate – and the euphonium player's children carried my costume and my script. Since there was no time to learn lines I was going to read it and drop the pages as I was done with them and then sweep them all up with a broom at the end. Their mother, Andrea, who was reading her own poems in the first half, produced a bottle of Wild Turkey, a potent bourbon, in the dressing room. I said I'd have it later, but as I stretched the elastic waist to get the dress over my head, all the staples with which I'd so carefully attached my peacock feathers popped, and the feathers, instead of lying flat to my skirt and trailing on the floor, stuck out around me in a rather undignified way. I took a nip of the Wild Turkey to lubricate my by now frozen throat.

Things might have been all right if the harpsichord hadn't got caught up in midtown traffic but it was carried into the hall with moments to spare, so I had no idea that it was a quarter tone flatter than the euphonium until I struck up the opening chords of the Monteverdi. My hands fell from the keyboard in horror and I had to sing the rest of it, including bits of accompaniment, to La. The worst, though, was when I was dragging my peacock box across the stage at a particularly sorrowful and serious moment. I was bowed with the weight of it, the rope cutting into

my shoulder, and right in the middle of the stage when . . . the
castors got stuck. I tugged, yanked on it a few times, then dragged
it noisily across the rest of the floor, yelling to be heard over the
din. Another poet was videoing all this, but later she wouldn't
show it to me. She said anyway she couldn't see my face because
there was always a piece of paper in front of it, and so she had
thrown the tape away.

At around this time I decided I should get a job. I found an
immigration lawyer in New Jersey who had never lost a case. She
was going to build her application for my Green Card on my
career in brain injury. It didn't mean, she said, that I'd actually
have to work in brain injury again, just that it was a domain
where I had skills and experience that the American immigration
office would count as worthy. I would have liked to add Mrs
Custard, a character in long coat, headscarf and fluffy slippers, to
my CV. She had a rapid-fire monologue on the neuro-anatomy of
memory that took my breath away, but I could see she wouldn't
cut any ice with the authorities.

My immigration lawyer said I didn't have to go back to Britain
when my visa was up this time. She could get me a temporary
permit, even a work permit. The Green Card would follow and
then I could make my life here in New York, for good.

I phoned Clive. Our telephone conversations had been improving by leaps and bounds. Lately I'd taken to taping them.

'Marvellous invention the telephone, isn't it,' he would tell me
often. 'Comes from the Greek *tele* – from a distance – and *phone*,
to call. Isn't it amazing our voices can travel to New Zealand in a
split second, faster than the speed of light?'

I had to agree with him. Most of our contact these days
was on the telephone. He wondered at the miles of cable strung

along streets or slung under seas. There were birds sitting on our words.

Clive was still repetitive in that he had set themes – electricity, the telephone, the Tube, the creative arts, space flight, stars and planets, politics.

'Is the House of Commons fifty:fifty now, ladies and men? . . . Is it better than it was? Oh good!' And he would go on to protest at the inequity of opportunities for women to play their part in governing the country.

He might go round and round these themes a few times each phone call and stick to them for years, but it was still an improvement on his narrower repertoire of the first ten years.

I had got into the habit of constantly recapping on what we were saying to help Clive keep track. Now, when I did that, Clive might wonder why I was repeating myself. Apart from a certain vagueness in the way he expressed things – it's difficult to be incisive if you cannot clearly remember the subject or how the conversation came up – and his tendency to confabulate, he could, to someone listening to him for the first time, sound amazingly normal, somewhat eccentric instead of obviously brain-damaged.

I thought perhaps I would go home and check if he was really better in person, or only on the telephone. I needed to earn some money and I might pick up something short-term in England rather than bother with the temporary US permit. After all, I would be living the rest of my life in America; I might as well make the most of my freedom. Soon enough I'd be back in a full-time job here, where employers give you only a fortnight's leave a year. I rang Clive.

'I'll be home on Tuesday.'

'Oh goodo! I never think of anyone else . . . You're so superlative!'

'You are!'

'Ah . . . I've never seen any human being yet except a nurse who just came in and went straight out again. Yours is the first voice I've heard.'

'I love your voice, darling . . .'

'You're so superlative . . . When are you coming?'

'Next week!'

'Ooh goodo! You are the most perfect lady!'

'So I'll see you soon!'

'You're here all the time! I don't do anything else but think of you . . .'

'Ah . . . sweetheart!'

'Look after your wings!'

'I'll see you next week, darling . . .'

'Hurrah! I never do anything else but think of you.'

'Ditto ditto.'

'Lovely word, "ditto". Look after your wings.'

'And you yours!'

'Fly here at the speed of light.'

We usually spoke for twenty or thirty minutes. Ringing off was hard. There was nothing like his voice.

# 12

## GETTING DARK

THE VOLUMES OF CLIVE'S DIARY WERE STACKING UP. IN SOME PERIODS the paper was pockmarked, curling, shiny with graphite. It was like holding a fossil. Line upon line, year upon year, a compression of single moment on single moment. He had the bones of life but not the content. The writing had become a cacophony of numbers, of a.m.'s and p.m.'s, time obliterating time, no room for words any more, save two key phrases at the top of each page for the hoped-for reader to see.

REAL LIFE RESTARTS
PLEASE COME, DARLING

I like it that even in his desperation, he never forgets the comma. Down the left-hand margin and the right-hand margin and scattered over the page there are ticks next to a time to verify that it is valid, each one crossed through afterwards to signify it is not valid. The ticks and crosses themselves grow wilder as each day passes. What was a neat parade of ticks in January showed more of a wrist movement by March and stretched to half a page wide by July. It was as if, shut in this crippled moment for eleven years, the anguish had increased with every new day, every new turn of the page. No matter how frantically he scrabbled to get out of there, he always arrived back in the same place. '7.39pm' in page-high figures over a mess of other figures, and '4.52pm' like a cry to the universe. 'I'm awake now! NOW! Now is the first awakening! Reality! I DO live. Awake first time!!' And the subtext – were he able to acknowledge his authorship of all previous entries – might have been, 'So how come I'm here in this first awakening, where I've been a trillion times before?' One can infer from the darkening mass of diary entries that, in the deep place, this is the question screaming out through every line of every page.

The words from his mouth, same on same, were hard as old bone. The patterns of darkness in his head had become the tableaux of psychology textbooks. But in all the papers about him I never saw mention of the blue of his eyes, or the sweetness of his laugh, or the extraordinary gentleness of his heart, towards me and towards patients in worse situations even than he was. His teeth continued to decay and fall out but he still had the best of smiles. There was no man like him.

Time turned to sand in my mouth. I made it back to London. I had put off initiating the Green Card process, put off committing to a life in America. I stalled returning until my money had dwindled, forcing me to make some changes, even if I deferred a final decision. Because of Clive's background of struggling as a freelance musician, he was always asking, 'Are we in the red or the black?' 'You're in the black,' I'd say because he was. My pockets, however, were emptying fast.

*

5.58am ✓ ✗    6.18am ✗

5.58a ROADLIFE RESTART

PLEASE COME, DARLING

WHITE CURTAINS!

✗ 6.18am ✓    6.18a ✗

✗ 6.18am

6.48am

July
Wk M T W T F S S
28         1 2 3 4 5 6
28  7 8 9 10 11 12 13
14 15 16 17 18 19 20
30 21 22 23 24 25 26 27
31 28 29 30 31

6.58e ✗ 6.58am    6.58am

✗ 8.48am    8.48am ✓    SIREN

8.59am ✗ 8.59am    8.59am ✗

8.59am 8.59am

9.24am ✗

9.24am    9.24am    9.24am

10.28am ✗    = SIREN    10.28am ✗

10.45am    10.45a    10.45c ✗

11.38am    8.48

11.46am

1.13    1.17p

1.46 1.46p

1.48    N46p

2.45pm

4.46    4.46pm    4.46    1ST

5.40    5.40    5.40    9.8

5.40am    5.40am    6.18

5.42p

6.18    1ST PATIENCES

6.18    6.18    6.18    7.08    7.58

8.08p    8.08

I lived in Nottingham for a while from 1997 to 1998. I'd got a job with Headway, the brain injury association with which AMNASS had merged some years earlier. It made little difference if I was calling Clive from Nottingham or from America. I heard the staff relaying that I was on the phone, and his joyful and triumphant laugh getting louder as he rushed to speak with me.

'Where's the phone?' I could hear him looking about for it.

'Just there, Mr Wearing.'

'Oh yes . . .' They still had to tell him every time. 'Hello?' he asked, shy, checking it was the right person.

'Hello!' I said.

'*Darling!*' he hailed me, jubilant. It was marvellous that he knew my voice straight away from just one word.

'Guess where I am,' I asked Clive.

'New York?' he asked.

'No, Nottingham.'

'Oh! Not Nottingham! Do they make knots in Nottingham?'

'They make lace.'

'Oh, *do* they?'

I heard the 'not Nottingham, knots in Nottingham' quip every phone call, until I gave up asking if he knew where I was. It didn't matter.

Clive and the other residents moved to a new house. Clive, of course, had no knowledge of having moved at all. It was news to him.

'I'm conscious for the first time . . . about thirty seconds ago just before I got the message to come to the telephone; the first person I've spoken to consciously is you . . . I've never seen a doctor yet! I know nothing about this case. They presumably know all about it, do they? The doctors and nurses?'

I said that they did.

'I've just become conscious – it's all happened since coming into this room . . . since picking up the phone – I don't know how I got it in my hand . . . It's all happened since then.'

'What was it like before?'

'Nothing. No dreams, no thoughts, nothing at all. No dreams, no difference between day and night – no sight no sound no smell no taste no touch no thoughts no consciousness of any kind, no evidence at all that I was alive – and no ability to think I was dead!'

'I know, darling. . .'

'I've never seen a doctor yet, ever since it started. I've had no thoughts, no dreams, nothing . . . it's been like being dead.'

'But not now . . .'

'*Now* . . . I can think for the first time – I've had no thoughts, no dreams, no ability to think I was dead.'

'And now?'

'Different! It's happened since we've been speaking on the phone. I have no knowledge of picking it up. I'm holding it to my right ear.'

'I like your right ear! I'm pretty fond of your left ear too!'

'It's funny how left and right have two spellings for each.'

'Two spellings for each?'

'Yes: L-E-A-F-T and L-E-F-T . . .'

'L-E-A-F-T?'

'As in leaft behind.'

'Must be an old English spelling . . .'

'It's the correct spelling – leave, leaft.'

'Well, that's how they should spell it . . . So . . .'

'Marvellous, the English language . . .'

'I enjoy it – I'm doing some writing.'

'Very demanding, isn't it, writing? It's very rare to get a fertile writer, very rare indeed . . .'

'Yes?'

'English is the best language in the world.'

'Why?'

'Because the nouns are not he, she or it. It's a very, very good idea to have all objects neutral, not masculine or feminine. The English language is the only one actually where all nouns are neutral full stop.'

'I suppose there's no reason for a table to be feminine . . .'

'Exactly.'

'Do you know where I am?'

'I suppose you're in Yankland, are you?'

'No, Nottingham.'

'Not Nottingham! Do they make knots in Nottingham?'

'They make lace.'

'Oh, *do* they?'

'You're perfect!'

'You're perfect!'

My task at Headway was to help set up a coalition of all the organizations associated with ABI in the UK: the UK ABI Forum, or UKABIF. Together we would support the all-party parliamentary group on ABI.

In this work I learned a lot more about what motivates politicians, how change comes about. We got involved in ethical issues like the BMA consultation on life support. I discovered that doctors withdraw feeding from people in long-term coma and let them starve to death. Some assumed people with severe disability would not want to be resuscitated. I didn't feel comfortable with what the doctors were saying.

We took part in the Mental Health Act scoping study. Back in 1993, Ted Kennedy had introduced his long-awaited Head Trauma Bill to the US Congress. But England decided to try to stretch the Mental Health Act to take in ABI. It felt like a darning job. The state still did not seem to accept the steps needed to protect this vulnerable group. Yet their vulnerabilities were acknowledged by coroners when amnesic patients wandered out of an unsecured environment and died of exposure. I heard of several deaths – an unlocked door, an unguarded moment. An amnesic person is helpless. Once they are out of care how can they ask for help or tell of their distress, or know what to do next? If they are unseen it is easy to come to grief, die of starvation, thirst, exposure or other misadventure. Such things do happen.

Clive didn't know where he was. When pressed, he revealed he thought it was a general hospital. One day on the phone he was telling me to fly there at the speed of light and to arrive however late. I asked if he thought there'd be anyone to let me in.

'Yes, there will,' he tells me.

'What,' I ask him, 'are they on duty through the night?'

'Yes, they've got to have someone here, more than one, I think, because the operations might suddenly be needed in the middle of the night.'

'What might be needed?'

'M-m-m-major operations – there's no accounting when major things might suddenly develop and have to be treated instantly or the person will die, all that sort of thing goes on so they have to have experts on duty twenty-four hours a day, you know, two different lots of people every twelve hours.'

'I'll have to creep past them!'

'Yes!' He laughed.

'They'll think I'm a nurse!'

But we would have the same conversation in a supermarket or a restaurant. At that time he just assumed he was always in the hospital, whatever it looked like.

Although Clive learned little about his immediate environment, he did learn certain striking facts about the world. He learned, for example, about the reunification of Germany and every so often would ask, 'They haven't reunified Germany, have they?' Framing it as a question was the nearest thing he could get to exhibiting knowledge because he knew his knowledge was too unreliable to trust.

He got used to the fact of decimal currency even though his retrograde amnesia stretched back in some aspects to before '71.

Other facts about the changing world startled him.

'I'm off to Paris tonight,' I told him one day.

'Aha!'

'Guess how I'm getting there . . .'

'Flying by helicopter!'

'No.'

'No? Jet aircraft!'

'No.'

'Swimming!'

'No.'

'Motor car!'

'No.'

'Well, what then?'

'There's a new way . . .'

'Oh, I see . . . Tube?'

'Yes!'

'Huh? Is there a Tube under the Channel?'

'There is!' I laughed.

'Good heavens, no, *really*!!!! I thought it was a *joke*!' He roared with laughter.

'No,' I insisted, 'there is a tunnel under the Channel.'

'Good heavens!' He sounded really stunned. 'That's a major undertaking, isn't it!! Changes so many things suddenly!'

'Yes, I'm going by train.'

'Good lord! How marvellous!'

'Takes three hours from Waterloo station . . .'

'To Paris?'

'To Paris!' I answered, stunned myself that he should have remembered the destination all that time.

'Good heavens above!!!' He laughed. 'It's *wonderful*!!! – it must make such a difference to Europe, doesn't it?'

It was nice to hear him so engaged by a conversation, spontaneous, eager to find out what had been happening.

I left Headway when my contract was up and decided to work freelance, writing and editing specialist publications. I specialized in disability. I had still been toying with the idea of a return to New York, but now I decided I wanted to remain in the same country as Clive and my family. I let the lawyer and the Green Card go. But I still had to make some kind of life for myself, and I had absolutely no notion of how to go about it.

I stayed with friends in a rambling stone house in the heart of the Somerset countryside. I imagined finding a small place to live nestling in a coombe, far from people and hubbub. I could be a freelance editor anywhere with a laptop and a phone line. Lindsay and Phoebe lent me a car, so that I could drive about and find somewhere to live. On one of my reconnaissance outings, I called Clive from a payphone.

'I thought I could get a little place in the country,' I told him, 'though it might be awkward at first as I've no car of my own.'

'I don't think that's a good idea,' he said, with an authority that astonished me. 'You'll be too isolated. Tell me,' he said, 'what city are you near?'

'Bath,' I said.

'Bath Abbey – that's a wonderful building!' said Clive. 'It was the last great English cathedral before the Reformation, built around 1500.'

'Really, darling?'

'Yes!'

I took the receiver away from my ear and looked at it. I wondered if I was hearing things. He sounded so authoritative.

'Do you remember the building at all?' I asked him.

'Of course – marvellous example of the English Perpendicular style . . .'

'Really?' I was amazed that Clive should speak of a place in such precise terms, as if he really did remember it.

'Yes,' said Clive, 'haven't you seen it?'

'No, well, not since I was sixteen and I'm not sure I went inside.'

'Oh, you must go inside. It has the most wonderful fan vault-ing.'

'Does it?' I was agape by now.

'Oh yes, absolutely spectacular. I love that building.'

I was convinced.

'And you remember being there?'

'I know it very well, I've often been there.'

I believed him. His former mother-in-law lived not too far away, so he would have spent time here in the past.

Since I was half an hour from Bath, I decided to go and have a look. I didn't expect the detail to be accurate: he had to have been confabulating some of it, but I was curious. He had sounded so sure.

I didn't know as much about architecture as Clive did so I asked the guide if I was looking at the English Perpendicular style. She confirmed that I was. She thought it might well be the last great English cathedral built before the Reformation. The fan vaulting was spectacular.

Clive had advised me not to live out in the sticks, but I thought prices in the city of Bath were bound to be out of my reach. Coming out of the abbey I saw an estate agent immediately to the left. I went in and asked about renting a flat in the city. The woman I asked had a piece of paper in her hand with writing on it in blue biro.

'This one's just come in,' she said, reading the scrap of paper. It was twenty minutes' walk from where we were standing and the rent was affordable. She took me to see it straight away and it was perfect, a one-bed flat in a Georgian terrace. I took it.

I called Clive again and told him about my visit to Bath Abbey. I was beginning to try to talk to him more normally, though it was hard to break the habit of fourteen years of amnesia when I would just drift along as a supporter to his monologue, interjecting loving asides to his flow.

I was so excited about Clive remembering the history of the abbey, I became unusually loquacious, eager to know what else he remembered. I described my visit to him.

'So the man at the door asked me, do you live in Bath, so I said no – and he said, oh well perhaps we'll stretch a point anyway . . . So that was really nice. So I went in and there I am in the crypt of Bath Abbey . . . I went through an archway and saw preserved several pillar tops from the Norman part of the building which . . .'

'Aaaah . . .'

'Which went on beyond the east end . . .'

'Yes . . .'

'Really as long as the abbey is now!'

'Yes . . .' Clive blew me little kisses down the phone.

I started describing the tops of the pillars, and Clive chimed in.

'Yes, yes, that has happened quite a lot, yes, sort of linked to the geometric . . . the vaulting was so heavy . . . they had to put sort of that special connection with the side.' Clive was speaking quickly and quietly, musing to himself. I couldn't make out all of it.

'Special connection with?'

'With the side walls.'

'With the side walls,' I repeated.

'Yes – the arches go across, transferring the weight from . . . from the roof on to the walls. That holds them up.'

# 13

## THE POWER OF LOVE

CLIVE'S PROGRESS WAS REMARKABLE. FROM BEING WITHDRAWN AND morose in his room, he was now garrulous and outgoing. He could talk the hind legs off a donkey. There were certain themes he stuck to, and some of what he said was rather odd, but he had come a long way from the years of the endless same few questions. Now he would string all his subjects together in a row and the other person simply needed to nod or mumble agreement.

'How's Parliament doing now? Is it fifty:fifty yet? As many ladies as men?

'Isn't electricity a marvellous invention? Think of all those miles of cable going all over the world! It takes just a split second for sound to travel from New Zealand. It's faster than the speed of light.

'Do you know where the word New Zealand comes from? It's neu-zee-land because it was settled by the Dutch.

'Wasn't Queen Victoria a marvellous queen? It was she who invented the bath. They didn't have baths before her, you know.'

'Didn't they?'

'No! They must have been very smelly! And it was under her rule that men started shaving. They had beards until then.'

'Really?'

'Oh yes, didn't you know? Men started shaving under Victoria because they admired her so much they all wanted to look like her.

'Queen Victoria was such a marvellous queen, Britain was the centre of the empire then. She came to Birmingham. Birmingham should have been the capital of England because it's right in the middle. But Birmingham wasn't a city until Queen Victoria brought in the railways. Aston was there and Birmingham was just a tiny village. But the railways opened it up and it grew in the industrial revolution. And now it's one of the biggest cities in England and Aston is the tiny place. Euch! Birmingham. They speak like this – *Beumingham* . . . They had to speak with their mouths closed because the air was so dirty they had to keep out the soot so they spoke out of the sides of their mouths and tried not to open them. *Beumingham* . . . It's 'orrible . . . *Beumingham!* Euch!'

At the start of a conversation he would run through a few of his favourite topics. It was his way of talking to me, offering me these comments as the only communication he had at his disposal. On days when he was in particularly good spirits, he might run through all his topics at once. Then I knew he was happy. If he was unhappy he would revert to the desperate old questions – 'What's it like to have one long night lasting . . . how long?' Now that it had been fourteen years, nobody liked to tell him how long. 'It's like being dead!' The staff had come to call these his 'deads' and they would count them and enter them in their records as a measure of how he was doing.

*

'Have they found life on the planet Mars yet?'

'No, darling, but they think there might have been water . . .'

'Really? Isn't it amazing that the sun goes on burning? Where does it get all the fuel? It doesn't get any smaller. And it doesn't move. We move round the sun. How can it keep on burning for millions of years? And the earth stays the same temperature. It's so finely balanced.'

'They say it's getting warmer now, love. They call it global warming.'

'No! Why's that?'

'Because of the pollution. We've been emitting gases into the atmosphere. And puncturing the ozone layer.'

'OH NO!!! That could be disastrous!'

'People are already getting more cancers.'

'Oh, aren't people stupid! Do you know the average IQ is only 100? That's terribly low, isn't it? One hundred. It's no wonder the world's in such a mess.'

'Cleverness isn't everything . . .'

'Well, no . . .'

'It's better to be good-hearted than clever.'

'Yes, you've got a point.'

'And you don't have to be clever to be wise.'

'No, that's true.'

Clive's scripts were repeated with great frequency, sometimes three or four times in one phone call. He stuck to subjects he felt he knew something about, where he would be on safe ground, even if here and there something apocryphal crept in. To Clive, it was all knowledge, and pointing out any different reality risked upsetting him. These small areas of repartee acted as stepping stones on which he could move through the present. They enabled him to engage with others. The staff were amazingly patient with him, and if the endless repetition of these topics irritated them they were gracious and kind enough not to show it.

Just as I was on the point of moving to Bath, I had another extraordinary conversation with Clive, linked to our discussion of Bath Abbey. It was the first statement of a confabulation which he was to continue.

'Fascinating thing,' Clive told me, 'how when you finished doing the vaulting the last man died . . .'

'What?'

'They had no method of getting him down.'

'The man died?'

'Making the last bricks on the . . . on the vaulting . . .'

'At Bath?'

'Yes, at any church in the country – it's a suicidal thing to finish off the walls because there's no way of getting them back . . . to earth. It's extraordinary, I, I can't remember how it works; that's something I found absolutely shattering when I first discovered it . . .'

'Whoever put the last bricks in . . .' I wanted him to elaborate.

'Yes, he, he couldn't . . . survive, there was no way for him to get out . . .'

'Oh, my!'

'. . . it's extraordinary!'

'Out of the crypt? Or of the actual . . .'

'. . . of the big building . . .'

'Of the building?'

'Yes.'

'Didn't they have scaffolding or something?' I decided to test him by reminding him of the reality. I knew Michelangelo had had some kind of cradle when he worked on the Sistine Chapel, although he died afterwards from the strain of being up there so long. I did wonder if, as with some of Clive's other slightly bizarre confabulations, this might in some way be based on truth.

'No, no, there was no scaffolding in those days – it hadn't been invented so they just got up there.'

'Really?'

'And they, they, as it were, had a little, effort of, of, of worshipping God by, by, by . . . self-suicide as it were – it's very strange like that – it's not been broadcast very often, not been allowed out . . .'

'Oh no . . . !'

'It's secret, yes – I, I can't remember the details of it but I was astonished when I discovered that.'

'What an act of worship!' I felt I had to sound as if I accepted what he was telling me.

'Yes . . . and to God, yes. They'd not got scaffolding in those days.'

'Uh-uh . . .'

'And it was a serious problem and how to do things, finish, without that, they didn't know, they couldn't work it out – absolutely amazing that!' Clive was lost in wonder at what he was telling me.

'Good heavens – so somebody designing fan vaulting or any arches there in a cathedral was, was, was consigning someone . . .'

'Mmmmm,' he assented firmly.

'. . . someone to death?' I challenged him.

'Yes, that was quite a dedication in a way – I can't remember how that came to me – I remember working it out in all sorts of ways from various sorts of information which came, you knew what was meant by it.'

Clive remembered the process of research and discovery even if he didn't remember what it was exactly he used to research.

'What about the roof?' I asked.

'I don't know – I don't know whether or not they had them in the Middle Ages, I can't remember – a roof's a very modern idea.'

'Oh.'

'Mmm.'

'They must have had roofs 'cause they painted frescos on the walls and—'

'—on the walls, yes,' Clive interrupted, 'but not on the roof buildings.'

'They would have had to protect the inside from the weather so they must have had a roof.' I wondered if my reasoning would collapse his theory.

'Yes – it might have been just hay or something, we just don't know . . .'

'Odd . . .'

'There are no pictures, you know, presuming to be a photograph or photographic in the way they are painted – to tell you the truth about them – we never had anything from the Middle Ages at all.'

'Oh.'

'There's no . . .'

'Yes, but they painted frescos of buildings.'

'. . . no but not on paper, you can't get any sort of detail on paper.'

'Oh.' Clive said everything with such authority in his BBC voice, I couldn't argue.

'Yes, the only method they had of passing anything on was basically to carve it in the stones on the wall.'

'They painted it,' I tried.

'Yes, they painted it.'

'And on wood in the, er, altarpieces?'

'Yes, yes, exactly, but they didn't live very long, the wooden ones, they rotted away.'

'Yes . . . but we've got a few left, haven't we, from the Middle Ages?'

'Yes, yes,' he conceded.

'Especially German ones we've got . . .' Clive and I had spent time in German museums looking at a lot of thirteenth- and fourteenth-century altarpieces.

'Mmmm.'

'They're beautiful!' I said.

'Yes, exactly, yes . . .'

'Mm. Not so many in this country, of course, because they all got smashed up by Cromwell's men.' I wasn't sure he'd remember.

'Yes, right, yes.'

'By the Puritans and so on after . . .'

'. . . the reformation, yes.' He did remember.

'It's Shrove Tuesday tomorrow – you might get pancakes.'

'Then it's Lent.'

'Yes . . .'

'Who lent it?' He laughed.

Clive was, granted, still perhaps the worst case of amnesia in the world, but there was no doubt he was learning new things and the difference it made to his quality of life to be able to converse more easily was significant.

As for me, I had come to Bath because nobody knew me there.

I thought it best to live in my city version of an isolated log cabin and manage as well as I could. I had found no remedy for my pain. Neither Greece nor New York were far enough away. Nowhere was. If I could just eke out a living on freelance work from home I would be spared having to show my face at an office every day. It took too much energy to be constantly brave. I had an open wound. I figured I would just have to find a way to live round it. I could manage to appear happy and engage with people as long as I saw them only for short periods. Being with anyone a whole day or weekend was too much. I had to ensure I had plenty of opportunities to retreat into solitude and recover from the effort of pretending to be all right.

Weeks after arriving in Bath, my flat was still a mess of self-assembly bookcases not assembled and many boxes of books half unpacked all over the floor.

One evening, 10 March 1999, I sat in my bedroom, elbows on an old trestle table, wondering what on earth to do next and how I would live and what was I doing here in the first place. All my wanderings had got me nowhere. Relationships with other men had hurt me. I was no further forward in understanding anything. I didn't want to be here. Didn't want to be anywhere. There was nothing I wanted to do and no one I felt up to being with. How could I go on having empty conversations with people, just going through the motions of being alive? They'd ring and tell me their news. I had no news. I was here. That was all. There had to be more to life.

There weren't many people I wanted to be straight with, but I could be straight with my friend Ruth. I dialled her number. She listened. My voice came out flat. I didn't have to pretend with her. What was the point in anything? I looked about me at the disarray of the move. I had to go on bothering for other people's sakes, but it was such hard work. I said it all and Ruth was quiet.

Then she said, 'You poor old bean.'

'Ruth?' I said.

'What, Mrs?'

'Would you pray for me?' I wasn't expecting to hear myself say that. Ruth was a Christian, the only one I knew. She talked about God as if she knew him, as if he were a personal friend. And the relationship seemed to be two-way. She was always telling me about things he'd done at her request. Perhaps she could ask him to do something for me.

'OK,' she said. I thought she would pray later, but off she went there and then, whispering to God.

I still sat slumped, my elbows on the splintery trestle table. I wasn't really expecting anything to come of it. But as the prayer rolled out of her in a whisper, I immediately felt something happening. It was like a force coming down the phone and into me. I dared not move a muscle. This force was tangible and pouring into me and filling me up. I had believed in the supernatural, but only in a remote way. This was physical, something real and powerful. I closed my eyes. After a while, the prayer subsided. I opened my eyes. The room looked different. It seemed to be much lighter, and to be shining, golden, like the landscape after rain in an evening sun. I was stunned, speechless.

'Wow . . .' I said. 'What was that?'

'Well, I don't know about you,' said Ruth, 'but I had a lovely feeling of the Holy Spirit.'

'It was like a force, and like honey!'

Then off she went again in a soft flow of prayer. This time the power I'd felt before, from the phone, was pouring into me from above my head and filling me right up, like strength coming in, building me up.

Afterwards everything was different. It was like waking up new, alive. Until then I had felt like a blob, as though I did not quite occupy space in the room. Now I felt of substance, as if I had been put back together again. And I felt so clean, as if I'd been washed on the inside, and clear, no longer confused. I had no more knowledge about what I would do, but I felt peace.

Having encountered God, Maker of All Things, in my bedroom, and knowing more clearly than I'd ever known anything that he was the Messiah, I felt rather as if I had seen a UFO – that I should report it to someone official. Whom could I tell? The police? The council? Someone had to know. I looked out of the window and saw a church tower. Perhaps a vicar would be a good place to start. I'd found out that God was real. I wasn't sure if the Church knew that.

When I got there next day, the door was open, and a ploughman's lunch was in full swing. I wandered past the assembled company down the nave and sank tearfully to my knees, thanking God for what he had done for me. When I was done thanking him and was heading back past the ploughman's, a lady caught up with me, welcomed me and gave me a yellow card to fill out. She turned out to be the oldest member of the church, baptized there over eighty years before, and I was the youngest, at about five minutes. I would be baptized and confirmed in that church.

I wasn't alone after that. When I went home or went out I never had that cold sense of being abandoned. I found myself smiling a lot and when we sang in church I was so moved I'd cry for no reason. I shed rivers of tears but they were good tears and each time it was like someone kissing me better, washing the sadness out of me. The great gaping wound I had carried with me all these years was disappearing. Falling in love with Clive had brought me some sense of completion. Now I felt a closeness and a love I hadn't known was possible.

I began to see deep changes in Clive too, as I started praying for him. The first thing that happened was that he got a new keyworker. She was not only a competent pianist who could play duets with him and even compose music, she was also an astronomer and could talk knowledgeably to Clive about one of his favourite subjects of conversation. Under her management, Clive came on in leaps and bounds.

When it was coming up to the millennium, Clive seemed to know the date. He'd go up to the staff and ask, 'It isn't the millennium, is it?'

They looked around to see if he'd picked up signs in a newspaper but he genuinely seemed to remember. We celebrated millennium new year at his place, watching TV. The following year, Clive was so much better, I took him to a hotel for Christmas, with a friend acting as care assistant in a neighbouring room. We sat through a five-course meal in the busy hotel restaurant with Bing Crosby playing loudly on the tannoy. Clive would not have endured that noise before his illness, and yet now he was sitting there singing along! Our friend videoed the meal. I was so astounded at Clive's intelligent conversation, I kept repeating everything he was saying to make sure the camera was capturing it. It gives the impression that I am the one with the memory problem.

By 2002 I was stronger and happier than I had ever been. Life was good. Clive seemed so much better in mood and in what he was able to do. He could stay in the living room of the home, whereas before he had usually retreated to his room. He could bear conversation. He watched TV and seemed to follow it better, even to enjoy it. The staff kept commenting on it. Before, he could only cope with one-on-one company. Now he was able to cope better being in a group. When I phoned I'd hear he was enjoying the cricket or a James Bond film. The staff started taking him to the pub, or even to the cinema.

One of his old care assistants who hadn't seen Clive in more than a year came to visit. They spent some time together and she could not get over the change in him. They told me she cried to see him so much improved after being stuck for so long.

I knew what was what now. I knew what was important. I was beginning to know how to live. One day I rang Clive and asked him how he'd feel about renewing our marriage vows. 'What a lovely idea,' he said.

And so, on Easter Sunday 2002, Clive and I dressed up to the nines. Clive's son Anthony came with his wife and two kids, and so did Clive's care assistant, Laura. We had not made our marriage vows in church first time round so this would be much more powerful.

Clive was able to participate completely, remembering the Lord's prayer and saying all that he wanted to say. The best bit was when we knelt down and our joined hands were wrapped in a golden sash. It went beyond a physical joining. It felt like we were touching something of eternity.

Afterwards the tea room served us large slices of Victoria sponge and Clive, although he had no memory of what had taken place, was delighted, laughing and quipping and eating everything put in front of him. Back at Clive's home, they had made up a bed for me in his room, strewn our bed with red rose petals and balloons, with a bottle of champagne and two glasses, like a fairy tale. The decorations made me sad. It's still sad, that he's like he is and that, apart from the heart-to-heart love, we have nothing resembling a regular marriage. Even spending the night together in the same room doesn't work, as he wakes up constantly, several times an hour, wondering who the shape in the next bed can be.

I left next day and we continued with our apart-together lives, speaking on the phone every few days, visits every so often.

'I love your face!' he says to me on the phone. 'It's breath-taking!'

'Can you see my face?' I ask.

'Oh yes!' he says. 'It's always there!'

That's new. He could never say what I looked like, unless he was actually looking at me. He didn't know my name either, not that it mattered to me. He knew me, name or no. But one day someone asked him to say his full name and he said, 'Clive David Deborah Wearing. Funny name that. I don't know why my parents called me that.'

I told him once about the other men and he was all love, all understanding.

'You must have gone through a terrible time with me like this!' he said. 'You must have been absolutely desperate!'

'Do you forgive me, love?'

'Of *course* I do, my darling! I love you!! I'm just sorry you've been through it. I wish I could have been more help to you.'

'You are the best husband in the world!'

'I don't like me; I prefer you!'

*

And he is the best man in the world, and still the most handsome I have ever seen, even if he has lost most of his teeth. We couldn't love each other any more than we do now.

And I don't have to worry about him any more because I can ask God to keep him safe and trust that he will.

And I don't have to worry about my life any more because ditto.

God is with me all the time, he'll never let me go.

'Electricity is the best invention there's ever been. And the Tube. Has it been copied now? Isn't space travel wonderful! You don't need the engine running in space. You go up and you don't need the engine – you keep going because once you get up speed there is no air to stop them moving. Air is the most important thing on earth. Oxygen the most important element, for breathing and for water, $H_2O$. Fascinating, the English language. Very sensible to get rid of sex attached to nouns. Wasn't Victoria a marvellous queen – so many inventions under her: the railway, the seaside holiday, baths, electricity. Isn't the telephone a wonderful invention? I can hear your voice in my right ear! And the voice can travel around the world in a split second, faster than the speed of light . . .'

Clive still writes his diary. The entries have barely changed, but the handwriting is calmer now. And his disposition is a lot happier. He knows he is in his place and I am out in the world.

'When are you coming?' is his regular refrain. But if I hesitate at all he reassures me that he is all right and he understands I have to do what I have to do.

'Get here at dawn,' he says anyway. 'Get here at the speed of light.'

And one day I do arrive at dawn, at the best of times. I drive through the near-empty roads hoping to be there when he wakes. But when they open the front door, he is there, already awake, and I am the first person he has seen and he clasps me to him and sings a high G and waltzes me into the living room.

'My eyes have just come on,' he says. 'I can see everything normally for the first time.'

'And I'm here!' I say.

He hugs me again and he does not subside into belching but only holds me at arm's length and smiles.

Later, when he makes me coffee, he knows where the cups are and the fridge where the milk is kept. I take him for a drive and as we draw near to the house on the way back, he must recognize the place, for he unclasps his seat belt and offers to get out and open the gate. When I leave that night my car doesn't start and I have to come in and call the breakdown service. We make a drink in the kitchen. Seven minutes after the last mention of my car Clive says, 'Well, at least it means you can stay a bit longer!' Perhaps he had been rehearsing the event in his mind through those minutes. When the garage has repaired the fault and the engine is running I come back in to get my things. Clive is ready to say goodbye and not hello.

'Remember I love you,' I say.

'I can never forget you for a moment,' he says. 'We're not two people but one. You're the *raison d'être* for my heartbeat, darling. I love you for e-ter-ni-ty.'

I drive through the night and when I reach home several hours later I call him. I want to tell him I've arrived safely but he's forgotten I was there.

'When are you coming?' he says. 'Please come at the speed of light!'

'I just got home from you,' I say.

'Oh really? Well, come at dawn then . . .'

| | |
|---|---|
| 9.46pm AWAKE FIRST TIME | FIRST THOUGHT IS OF YOU DARLING |
| 10.16pm REALLY AWAKE FIRST TIME | PLEASE FLY HERE DARLING |
| 10.20pm I *DO* LIVE! | |